THREE BELLS OF CIVILIZATION
The Life of an Italian Hill Town

THREE BELLS
OF
CIVILIZATION

The Life of an Italian Hill Town

———◆———

SYDEL SILVERMAN

COLUMBIA UNIVERSITY PRESS

NEW YORK

The Andrew W. Mellon Foundation, through a special grant,
has assisted the Press in publishing this volume.

Library of Congress Cataloging in Publication Data

Silverman, Sydel
   Three bells of civilization.
   Bibliography: p.
   Includes index.
   1. Montecastello di Vibio, Italy—Social life and
customs. 2. Montecastello di Vibio, Italy—
Civilization. I. Title.
DG975.M6736S55   301.35′1′0945651   75-12851
ISBN 0-231-03804-6 (*cloth*)
ISBN 0-231-08365-3 (*paperback*)

For Eve and Julie

Preface

THE LITTLE TOWN of Montecastello di Vibio stands upon a hilltop overlooking the valley of the Tiber, nearly at the geographical center of Italy. As its name suggests it looks like a castle, completely encircled by walls; above the turrets and rooftops rises the civic tower, with its characteristic three bells. Like hundreds of other towns that dot the Central Italian landscape, Montecastello surveys its rural territory, seeming to proclaim: "Here an urban tradition is preserved." This book asks why so small a *paese*—with a town population of only about 350—possesses this surprisingly urban quality, a quality that Montecastellesi describe as "civilized."

That Montecastello's "civilization" is my central theme means that I have made a selection among many realities; another observer might well describe the same place with a very different emphasis. Like every ethnographic study—even the most descriptive—this one is the product of the theoretical and personal perspectives that guided the observations, their organization into a description, and the attempts to explain them. Ethnographic data do not consist of objective facts waiting to be collected. They are shaped by the observer's frame of reference, both initially and as it changes in response to the events observed. The "facts" of Montecastellese life and my ordering of these facts must therefore be seen in relation to the orientations I have brought to this work.

My study of Montecastello began in 1960 with fieldwork undertaken for a Ph.D. thesis in anthropology. At that time the civilized Western world, despite its proximity and familiarity, was relatively new to ethnographic study. My interests turned toward Italy. I had long been fascinated by the contrasts among Italian cities evident in their architecture, city plans, social patterns, and life styles. Moreover, Italy seemed to me a potentially important area for the emerging anthropology of complex societies.

Most of the work being done in Italy at that time was in the South. For ethnologists this was the most "folk-like" area of the nation, while for applied social scientists there was the persistent "problem of the South." The material on Southern Italy was of theoretical interest as well. For instance, Friedmann's concept of *la miseria* (1953) and Banfield's "amoral familism" (1958) raised the controversial issue of the significance of "ethos" in underdeveloped societies. Furthermore, when Redfield attempted to define recurrent "peasant attitudes and values" in the course of his "excursion into problems of peasantry as a human type," he found that each of his generalizations was contradicted by findings from Southern Italy (Redfield 1956:60–73). The cultivators there, it seemed, despise rather than revere the land, value leisure above work, have a taste for commerce, and show other "unpeasantlike" attitudes. The apparent contradictions raised tantalizing questions about the variability of peasant societies.

Outside of the South during the 1950s, sociologists were beginning to study the industrial development of Northern Italy (see Barbano and Viterbi 1959; Rapport, Cappannari, and Moss 1957; Rossi-Doria et al. 1959). The familiar contrast between the progressive North and the backward South was pointed up once again, but this contrast submerged a vast central region, the very heart of much that is "Italian civilization." Despite recurrent pleas for comparative data, Central Italy was virtually ignored by social scientists until the end of the decade, when Tullio Seppilli and his colleagues at the Università degli Studi di Perugia studied sex and family roles in a community near Rieti and began other projects in the area (Seppilli 1960).

Since so little was known of Central Italy from an anthropological perspective, I planned my fieldwork as a holistic descriptive study of a community. The central focus of the study changed several times during the field period, emphasizing first the life crises of women, then the social processes related to fertility, then demographic change in general, then the background of peasant emigration, and finally the agricultural system itself. The Ph.D. thesis emerged as a study of the social context of the *mezzadria* system of share-farming and changes in the ways it functioned. In retrospect, I believe that these transformations of the problem reflect a bias toward topics amenable to measurement. It was only much later that I appreciated how much my initial description of Montecastello had pruned out some of the most revealing facets of the community.

I returned to Central Italy only in the summer of 1971. As I reread my notes in preparation for the visit to Montecastello, it was the styles of interpersonal behavior that impressed me most: the conversational games, the gossip, the joking, the forms of sociability and daily interaction, and all the other details that were so much a part of Montecastello. Throughout was an insistent theme: the town represents not only a settlement and a cluster of functions, but a way of life, which is celebrated in the idea of *civiltà* (roughly translated, the "civilized"). The visit to Montecastello revealed that much that had been thought of as civiltà had changed, but the changes themselves brought into sharper focus the patterns I had learned about ten years before.

I began to think about the foundations of civiltà, and in the summer of 1973 and again in the spring of 1974 I returned to the area primarily to look for additional historical material. In the course of this work, I detected unmistakable echoes of civiltà appearing as early as the communal age of the twelfth and thirteenth centuries. When this book was nearly completed, a new synthesis of communal history appeared, which focused on the *vita civile* of medieval Italy (Hyde 1973). Hyde's picture coincided at many points with my guesses about some of the sources of Montecastellese civiltà, to which I had come by a very different route. The "vita civile" I describe for Montecastello emerged through traditional anthropological fieldwork, as did the clues to my analysis of it. If the parallels between my account and Hyde's are genuine, they offer encouragement for an increasing collaboration between anthropology and history.

The results of any field study are in part the product of the predilections and criteria that guided the choice of the site. It seems likely to me now that Montecastello's quality of civiltà influenced my decision to work there. When I came upon Montecastello I felt an immediate affinity to the place, perhaps an urban person's sense of familiarity and relief at finding urbanity unexpectedly in the countryside. Fortunately, Montecastello also met the several criteria I had established.

Some of those criteria were implicit ones, the assumptions of the community-study method itself. The idea that the strategic unit of study is a community tends to favor certain kinds of settlements: those that are well-delimited, self-contained, and that include specific complements of the expected institutions; located off the major thoroughfares, yet not completely isolated; and of a size that lends itself to participant-observation. Since these considerations make some communities seem more "anthropological" than others, it is likely that, at least until recently, the literature on complex societies has been based mainly on a rather special selection of settlements. For better or worse, Montecastello fits the pattern.

I began the process of choosing the community by delineating the larger cultural region that I hoped the particular site would exemplify. On the assumption that agricultural organization is highly correlated with other aspects of culture, I used as guides various agrarian-economic schemes for marking out agricultural zones of Italy, especially that of the Istituto Nazionale di Economia Agraria (Medici 1956: 3–15). The region of "Central Italy," as defined primarily by agricultural criteria, extends over the sub-Apennine hills of Emilia and the hills and plains (excluding the mountain zones) of Tuscany, Umbria, the Marches, Lazio, and the Abruzzi provinces of Teramo and Pescara (see Figure 1). As of 1960, the economic base of this region was an agriculture of nonmechanized family-farms raising mixed crops and livestock. The mezzadria system of share-farming predominated (covering 47 percent of the productive land area), but peasant proprietorship (20 percent) and wage-labor cultivation (23 percent) were alternatives (Medici 1956: 190, 196, 199, 204). The characteristic form of settlement outside the major cities was, and is, the community with a nucleated town surrounded by dispersed farms.

Within this general region the choice was narrowed to the province of Perugia in Umbria, which showed an intermediate degree of modernization and resembled the region as a whole in its distribution of types of agricultural organization. As in the wider region, industry in the province was limited. It consisted of small and medium-sized concerns located in the city of Perugia and scattered among the larger towns of the plains, devoted mainly to foodstuffs, tobacco, textiles and clothing, and building materials (Bellini 1959: 55–56). However, this province is not a microcosm of all of Central Italy any more than a particular community can be a microcosm of a larger area. The findings of this study are most relevant to central and western Umbria; they apply to a lesser extent to the Tuscan hills, and to a lesser extent still to the peripheries of Central Italy.

In looking for a community I had three specific criteria in mind. First, I sought a place that reflected the agricultural and settlement pattern of the province and that had retained at least the main outlines of the traditional social structure. Second, I wanted a situation that revealed something of the social processes that were important in Umbria, such as the rural exodus, the agricultural crisis, and changes in women's roles. Fi-

Figure 1   Italy, showing the agrarian-economic zone of "Central Italy" in white (after Medici 1956)

nally, I hoped to find a community that contained, within a size conducive to study, the major dimensions of ecological, agrarian, and social variation represented in the province.

Montecastello seemed a good choice on many grounds. In size it was a reasonable compromise. The parish, which may be considered the effective community, had a population of less than 2,000 in both town and countryside. Given this size, I was able to have personal contact with most people of the town and at least to identify the rest of the population through a census of households. The fact that Montecastello was the seat of a small commune (*comune*, the administrative unit) ensured that important institutions would be represented, and it facilitated the use of statistics that are compiled by commune. The economy of Montecastello was primarily agricultural and the mezzadria system predominated; still, there was some variation in forms of settlement, land use, and agricultural organization, and the range of altitude made for ecological differences. (I later learned that far from being unusual, this variation within a community was the result of deliberate policies in the histories of the communes.) Above all, Montecastello included a diversity of social segments: several occupational categories, a wide range of social strata, and persons of every degree of education and sophistication. Finally, it had a recorded history of at least seven centuries, and considerable documentation was available.

Although there are many other places much like it in Umbria, Montecastello was not selected because it is "average." It is not necessarily at the midpoint on various social-economic measures of the region (cf. Wylie 1957: viii–ix), nor is it statistically representative of a larger universe. It was chosen precisely because it is *not* average. In particular, the presence of several landowners who form the core of a local upper class is not usual in contemporary communities of this size, but it provides a revealing perspective on Umbrian rural social structure. The special characteristics of Montecastello make it *diagnostic* of processes in the wider region but not typical in any statistical sense.

My husband and I lived in Montecastello from September 1960 to September 1961. We rented an ancient house in the center of town and introduced ourselves as having a dual purpose for settling there: he to devote himself to his painting and I to write a study of daily life in a small Italian community. Despite our frequent references to my work, few people ever regarded it as anything other than the amusement of an idle American wife. In the beginning I did little to discourage this definition, because it enabled me to collect spontaneous and personal information. However, as I tried to move into more structured procedures, it presented difficulties. For some people, it gave credence to the rumor that we were spies—if only they could figure out what there was in Montecastello worth spying on! That such a situation raises ethical problems is obvious.

At first the fieldwork consisted exclusively of participant-observation. Montecastellese hospitality opened most doors, and we made friends with several families, including a fairly diverse selection of the town population. I was taken into the women's visiting and sewing circles; my husband was absorbed into the group of young married men, and as he took up bocce and billiards he was included in the mixed-age men's playing groups. Our main guides to the ways of Montecastello were our housekeeper, a middle-aged woman of peasant origin who proved to be a remarkably shrewd social observer, and a retired bureaucrat who was an amateur local historian. While my informants were drawn from most social strata and occupational categories, they are not a random selection. To varying degrees they have the special qualities of informants everywhere, including an ability to objectify their own lives and an inclination to associate with strangers.

The major source of data was innumerable casual conversations, both private and public, with individuals and with groups. This approach was supplemented by more formal procedures: mapping spaces and recording rounds of activity; extracting census and demographic data from the records of the town hall and checking them through direct observation and questioning; conducting structured interviews on specific subjects, including life histories and family histories; and devising a technique for studying prestige. Government statistics and other official data on the local economy and population were useful, and the communal archives yielded some valuable material. However, the most significant information always came through immediate involvement with people and events: we learned about feuds through becoming embroiled in some; about government at the local level through hassles with the bureaucracy; about local politics through having my presence manipulated by various factions; about dowries and weddings through helping a bride with her preparations and problems; and about pregnancy and childbirth through my own pregnancy toward the end of the year.

Montecastello presented two special problems for participant-observation. First, there was the physical and social separation of town and countryside. While it was possible to know the town intimately by living there, the scattered farm families had to be approached individually and formally. Gradually I was able to work through town contacts, sharing their networks into the country, but I was always regarded as someone of the town. The second problem was the political factionalism of the community. To the extent that we were identified with the coalition of the Center-Right—inevitable for us as "rich Americans"—our access to the Left was hampered. However, our political identity was complicated by the fact that I was sponsored by Perugian academics associated with the Left. Eventually I learned to capitalize on the ambiguities, in the same way that I learned to use constructively the uncertainties of many Montecastellesi about what to make of us as Jews.

Fieldwork of this kind and publication of the results present ethical dilemmas that I do not claim to have resolved. The very nature of anthropological method means that the most telling data will always come from situations in which the anthropologist cannot solicit people's informed consent to be the objects of study. Similarly, in deciding whether to include or omit material for publication there is, above all, the obligation to protect informants' confidences, but at the same time there is the obligation to provide the data that will allow others to evaluate one's analysis. I have tried to preserve the anonymity of individuals by changing names and initials (except in historical references) and by omitting many specific details. However, the place names are real. I think the Montecastellesi prefer that their name be known.

Acknowledgments

MANY FRIENDS and colleagues have contributed to this work in the course of its long gestation. To the people of Montecastello I am deeply grateful for unfailing hospitality, help, and friendship. Most of them have played a part in creating this book, but I owe special thanks to Franco and Mara Brachini, the family of the late Antonio Capociuchi, Ermes Innocenzi and family, the late Renato Ippoliti, Nello and Ada Latini, Gino Margaritelli, Piero and Clara Pierantoni, Cesira Spazzoni, and—above all—Marina Tomassi. I am also indebted to the officials and staff of the commune for facilitating my collection of data.

Several Italian scholars gave generously of their time and knowledge. Tullio Tentori helped me to initiate the study and continued to lend his assistance in many ways. Tullio Seppilli introduced me to Umbria and offered me use of the facilities of the Istituto di Etnologia e Antropologia Culturale at the Università degli Studi di Perugia. He and his colleague Luigi Bellini gave me invaluable help in selecting the community. Paolo Abbozzo of the Istituto di Economia e di Politica Agraria made available data on land tenure in Montecastello. On my later trips to Italy, I had the good fortune to meet two historians who provided guidance through the archives of Todi and Perugia: Giorgio Comez and Don Mario Pericoli. Thanks are also due to the personnel of the Archivio dello Stato di Perugia and other public and church archives cited in the book.

My late husband, Mel Silverman, contributed greatly to the field study. He shared the joys and difficulties of fieldwork and helped gather material that would otherwise have been inaccessible to me. The sketch-maps of Montecastello and the woodcut used on the book-jacket are his work.

Conrad Arensberg, who fostered my development as an anthropologist, has directly and indirectly influenced this book. I have also benefited from discussions with a number of colleagues, including Ernestine Friedl, Gloria Levitas, Mervyn Meggitt, Joyce Riegelhaupt, Jane Schneider, Peter Schneider, and Stuart J. Woolf. Raymond Grew read an early version of the book and offered ideas that I have drawn on freely. More important, he led me to rethink my material and to ask some of the historical questions that guided subsequent work.

The National Institute of Mental Health financed the field study through a predoctoral fellowship (MF-11,068) and research grant (M-3720). A fellowship from the National Endowment for the Humanities during 1973–74, as well as a sabbatical leave from Queens College of the City University of New York, enabled me to complete the project.

My greatest debt is one both intellectual and personal. It is to Eric Wolf.

Contents

CHAPTER 1

◆ ◆

The Quality of Civiltà

TRAVELERS in the central hill regions of Umbria and Tuscany have long been struck by the impress of town life upon the countryside. The social centers of gravity everywhere, even for the country people, are the towns. They range in size from villages to small cities. Many of them are administrative seats, but some carry on only remnants of past functions. Each one, however, is the nucleus of a rural domain, a *contado*. These are not the agrotowns of Southern Italy. Often much smaller, the Central Italian town contains a population of mostly noncultivators; whether landowner, bureaucrat, shopkeeper, artisan, or laborer, as townsmen they are clearly distinguished from the *contadini* of the surrounding countryside. The styles of town life bear traces of the sophistication born of a long urban history. Even the peasants, for centuries settled on the land and still today uneasy in town, show the urban influence, what Emilio Sereni described as *"un che di cittadino,"* something of the townsman (1968:176). What this town life consists of, where it comes from, and how it affects not the cities of historical fame but the smaller centers and their countrysides—these are the questions behind this book.

The people of Montecastello are conscious of this quality of town life, indeed they glorify it. The term that most accurately sums it up is *civiltà*. The Montecastellesi refer to themselves as *gente civile*, though they are careful to point out that some of them are more civile than others and many of them are not civile at all. Signs of civiltà appear at once in the physical aspect of the town and in the forms of hospitality shown to the outsider. If one remains long enough to learn what life in Montecastello is like, and listens to people talk of it, one finds that "civiltà" carries many meanings. But however it is to be interpreted or explained, the ideology of civiltà provides a wedge into the complexities of town life.[1]

There is no exact equivalent of "civiltà" in English. It is close to "civility," but broader in meaning. It is related to the "civic" and the "urbane," but is not quite either of these. It is more like "civilization," but not quite so broad or so grandiose. In general, it refers to ideas about a civilized way of life. It must be understood in terms of a range of meanings rather than a precise definition, but it always implies an *urban* way of life. The various specific meanings draw on quite a wide range of the patterns of civilized social life in Umbrian, Italian, and Western civilization, but civiltà assumes a certain selection of patterns; some are extolled in ideology but not others. Furthermore, civiltà may refer now to a wider sphere (such as the Italian nation), now to the local manifestations that are considered specifically Montecastellese. Like the term *paese*, which means one's "country"—whether village, town, region, or nation—"civiltà" can describe different degrees of inclusiveness.

If "civiltà" is translated loosely as "civilization" in the sense of "civilizedness," it is not the anthropologist's use of "civilization" to define certain kinds of societies, those with cities, state organization, and literate traditions. "Civiltà" is an ideology *about* civilization. Such ideologies must be defined in native terms, for the aspects of civilized social life that are significant in an ideology vary in different cultures. To ask what the Montecastellesi mean by "civiltà," or what some Sicilians or Spaniards or Germans might mean by their notions of "civilization," is to ask what it is about being part of a civilized society that those people talk about, worry over, exalt, or deplore.

Concern with being civilized is a familiar theme in anthropological studies of complex societies, particularly in the Mediterranean world and in societies deriving from it. Patterns reminiscent of civiltà have been described for hinterlands far from the cities where they seem most appropriate. For instance, Ernestine Friedl found that the Greek village of Vasilika reproduced many of the urban qualities characteristic of Athens (1961), and Marvin Harris documented the emphasis upon *movimento* in a small Brazilian mining town (1956). For anthropologists it has never been self-evident that people should value being civilized. This may be because our fieldwork in civilized societies began in the rural areas and small communities. Since our theory defined such areas as "periphery" (in relation to a "center", usually in the city), we found it noteworthy that people of the periphery might claim civilization and urbanity, cultural attributes of the center. Yet we still know little about how and why such ideologies are disseminated into hinterlands and perhaps transformed in the process.

If many cultures have ideologies about being civilized, their specific content varies. One might ask, therefore, why a particular ideology contains its own emphases, its elaboration of certain qualities rather than others. To ask why is to inquire into the relation of ideology to other phenomena. In looking at the case of Montecastello, I think it can be shown that the several elements of civiltà can be related to patterns of social behavior that are the products of certain political and economic conditions. In other words, I see ideology as rooted in social action and, in turn, the material basis of such action. If civiltà is an ideology about town life, then tracing its roots may expose some of the processes that have shaped town—and country—in this part of Central Italy.

When Montecastellesi talk of what it is about their town that is good or bad, and when they compare it with other places, they make a number of assumptions about the nature of town life. In talking about towns, they are also talking about people, that is, the aspects of human behavior that are identified with town life. Their premise appears to be that it is in towns (or cities, or villages like towns), or living in the manner of the town, that man is most "human." The words "civiltà" and "civile" express this idea in a general way. However, no single term or self-conscious ideology corresponds to the complex of underlying assumptions. What I call "civiltà" is an analytic model, my attempt to make these assumptions explicit and find connections between them. The model is in part a composite of the different uses of the terms "civilta" and "civile," but it is broader in scope; it is a summary of the many ways in which Montecastellesi express values about town life and townsmen. Like any analytic model, this one is intended as a tool for understanding, and it must be judged on the basis of how useful a tool it proves to be.

If one explores the range of meanings that may be intended when someone is said to be civile, it becomes evident that the concept as used in Montecastello has many senses. It means certain personal attributes, such as genteel behavior, courtesy, and generosity. It means making a good appearance: observing the correct formalities and etiquette in social interaction, and guarding one's "good face" or *bella figura*. It means talking eloquently and arguing well. It means having command of written language, familiarity with the idioms of government, and an appreciation of formal "culture." It means participating skillfully in the public life of the piazzas and bars. It means showing concern for one's inferiors while maintaining the demeanor appropriate to one's position. It means dressing, dwelling, speaking, and behaving in the manner of the city, while appreciating the country. It means having access to more important places while demonstrating civic pride in one's own paese. It means cherishing glories of the past while believing in progress.

These meanings reflect criteria for evaluating townsmen, but they are clearly associated with class distinctions as well. In fact, some uses of the term *"signore"* (and *"signorile"* and *"signorilità"*) in Montecastello are closely related to the idea of being civilized. While "signore" is specifically a social-class designation, much that defines a "true" signore is part of an ideal of civilized town life, for only a signore can possess the full complement of civile qualities, and only one who is civile can be a true signore.[2]

The language through which Montecastellesi express these values has a built-in ambiguity. The terms "civiltà" (a noun) and "civile" (an adjective) seem to be used in slightly different contexts; their ranges of meaning are overlapping rather than identical. Nevertheless, to attempt to differentiate them sharply would be to distort their actual looseness.

In this book I use the term "civiltà" and the phrase "the civil life" to express two different stances: the first reflects the point of view of the actors, the second that of the observer. I use "civiltà" for what I think are the Montecastellesi's ideas and values about being civilized. For instance, I discuss a changing ideology of civiltà—different definitions and overtones attached to the concept at different times. I also talk of Montecastellesi making judgments about people's "level" of civiltà—"civiltà" being a summary of certain criteria that the Montecastellesi themselves seem to use. ("Civile," used as a simple adjective, describes anything the Montecastellesi would evaluate as civilized.)

By "the civil life," in contrast, I mean an outsider's view of the patterns of behavior through which civiltà is enacted and the social context in which they occur. I am using this phrase in a more mundane and commonplace sense than is usually attached to the expression "la vita civile" in the historical literature. I am thinking of such things as manners of meeting and greeting, modes of arguing politics in public, and ways of expressing community identity. I am obviously not talking of a vita civile in the sense of an artistic florescence under civic sponsorship. The common thread that runs from the civil life of the medieval communes to contemporary Montecastello is the town-centered organization of Central Italian society. I ask what the continuities might be and how they manifest themselves in everyday interaction even today.

In a general way, the elements included within the idea of civiltà fall into two categories. First, there are qualities that pertain mainly to the local context. Some concern local relationships, especially as these involve persons of high status: showing generosity, fulfilling obligations appropriate to one's rank, and displaying a combination of authority and concern for those over whom one has authority. Other qualities point to public behavior in general, the self-presentation and performance one makes before a local audience. Finally, there are qualities that describe membership in a community: identifying with the community and expressing some commitment to it; assuming responsibility for public projects; and showing civic feeling and pride in whatever can be considered Montecastello's distinctiveness.

A second general category consists of those elements of civiltà that refer mainly to a larger society and a wider sphere of civilization. The specific qualities demonstrate familiarity with this larger world and the capacity to function in it. This includes having the means to move back and forth to the urban centers, and showing evidence of such contact through the personal attributes, information, and values one possesses. Physical contact alone is of little value, however, unless one also has effective social contact and the ability to operate in urban centers. Thus, qualities that indicate possession of the skills of the larger society are important: literacy, understanding of the tools and techniques of bureaucracy, and formal education. Linguistic skills are especially significant: control of the dialect and conversational styles of the city, the ability to produce some of the non-utilitarian information that makes up *cultura*, and above all, skill in discourse and argument. Other qualities concern mastery of the formalities of urban life—the manners of drawing room and street appearances. Furthermore, it is a mark of civiltà to demonstrate active membership in the larger sphere through patriotism to the nation, fidelity to the universal church, and personal association with the glories of Italian civilization.

The second category probably resembles closely the qualities that define being civilized throughout the Mediterranean world. The emphasis upon local commitments appears widely in various forms of *campanilismo*, but usually this is divorced from urban values. In civiltà, however, the two aspects are intertwined. Civiltà is not merely a parroting of city life, or is it only a matter of local identity or of elite behavior within the community. In fact, each aspect qualifies the other. On the one hand, to be civile in a local relationship or performance requires some command of the ways of the larger society. On the other hand, to be considered civile when operating in the larger arena (e.g., as a functionary in a national institution) requires that one recognize local obligations. It is perhaps this combination of both aspects that characterizes Central Italian ideologies about civilized life.

This catalogue of the elements of civiltà is a statement of the possible range of the concept. In actual use, different qualities are significant in different situations. First of all, individuals vary in what they emphasize. For instance, a landlord who has the means to be a patron to a peasant and stands to gain by it might underline the importance of upper-class obligations, while an artisan who helps organize local events might stress civic participation. Then too, the qualities that people draw on in evaluating others depends upon who is being evaluated: when a signore is criticized for being *poco civile*, the qualities at issue are different from those that define a laborer as poco civile. Moreover, what is considered civile differs with the context: the same person might appeal to the importance of local tradition in criticizing the priest but deprecate local tradition in evaluating a Carnival dance. Finally, the emphases in defining civiltà change over time. Thus, evidence of connections with the larger society might not always have been as important as it has been in the past century, while local commitments have been increasingly played down.

In fact, the range covered by the concept and the flexibility of its definition may be the key to its adaptability and its persistence. If certain qualities arise out of earlier conditions and come to be called "civile," they can drop out in favor of other qualities appropriate to later periods. At the same time, new elements incorporated into civiltà are supported by the aura of ideological continuity. For example, a political program for mass education can claim the banner of civiltà, which has always stood for literacy and citizen participation, though in the past these were extended only to the privileged few. The looseness of definition also allows inconsistencies between ideals and reality to be tolerated without threatening the ideology itself. Thus, a *padrone* (a mezzadria landlord) who does not act the patron yet is urbane or cultivated may still be considered civile. Furthermore, real changes in social structure can be accommodated. A successful entrepreneur of humble origin can be defined as sufficiently civile to be an acceptable husband for a landowner's daughter, and it can be left to their children to learn the subtleties and confer the family name with undeniable civiltà. So long as the ideology is not too carefully spelled out, it can serve very different ends. It can be used to urge the acceptance of some change or to defend a traditional arrangement, and it can do both at once.

It is not clear when the terms "civiltà" and "civile" began to be used in Montecastello, since the kind of evidence that would document the matter is scanty before the late eighteenth century. The two terms, which probably have a separate though related history, appear with many of their modern meanings in Italian writings from the thirteenth century on (see Battaglia 1961: III, 210–14). The expression "la vita civile" also dates from this time. The common denominator of its various meanings is participation in public affairs; it refers to man as a member of a politically organized society, but it is far more inclusive than the modern sense of "citizenship." Dante described it as one aspect of human nature, in opposition to "the contemplative life," which he considered the more excellent and more divine (Battaglia 1961: III, 213). Then, in fifteenth-century Florence, la vita civile became an ideology about the life of the complete gentleman-citizen. Hyde suggests that this ideal, "the model citizen, governing his own affairs in town and country and dutifully participating in the affairs of the state," actually described the social and political life of the communes that came into existence three centuries earlier (Hyde 1973:8).[3]

More important than the origin of the terms, however, is to trace the various elements that make up civiltà. The concept as used in Montecastello in contemporary times is the product of accretions and recombinations over a long history. It is likely, as Hyde's analysis has shown, that social patterns may come to be elaborated into ideology only at a later time and that the ideology may persist long after the social patterns have changed. It is also likely that the patterns included under the ideological umbrella of civiltà derive from different periods and different sets of conditions. For example, in the nineteenth century civiltà became the expression of a carefully limited openness to "modernization," but this involved a reinterpretation of elements formed out of other historical experiences rather than a break with the past.

The major concern of this book is to show how civiltà is grounded in social realities. This is not to say, however, that there is a stable equilibrium between ideology and society. On the contrary, a central point of my argument is that civiltà is a fluid ideology that in the course of Montecastellese history has been manipulated and often recast by certain groups in pursuit of their interests. Thus, an ideology like civiltà enters into social action as well as expressing it. It enters into action not only as explicit symbols but also as implicit assumptions that guide individual behavior; yet ideology does not constrain behavior, or explain it. This study of Montecastello attempts to trace connections between the content of civiltà and particular social, economic, and political structures. But I hope it will also show that civiltà is neither a simple mirror of Montecastellese society nor a straitjacket upon it.

In seeking the sources of civiltà in the history of Montecastello—as it can be reconstructed and as it is reflected in contemporary social structure—I follow two clues. One clue is that many of the elements of civiltà describe elite behavior and elite values. The data from Montecastello show that until very recently, the main carriers of civiltà—those who propounded its ideology and acted out the civile styles—were a local, predominantly landowning elite. Therefore, I look at the characteristics of the members of this elite and their local roles and relationships: the agricultural system that underwrote them; interclass relationships and the role of the elite within the community; and the changes over time that have affected the composition, economic base, and social functions of the elite. But if civiltà is an ideology with elite overtones, consistent with a social structure dominated by an elite, it also affects the lower strata of the population and the life of the town as a whole. Thus, the study of civiltà takes in the whole community, not just a segment of it.

A second clue is furnished by the history of Montecastello's relations with larger powers. A recurrent theme is the claim for autonomy, especially with respect to the nearby larger town of Todi. In some instances the claim refers to the civiltà of the community, presumably to demonstrate its capacity for self-government. The linking of autonomy, skills of self-government, and civiltà suggests some functions that the patterns of civile behavior might have played in the political history of Montecastello. Following the unification of Italy, when autonomy was no longer an issue, civiltà continued to be significant but in other ways. Since World War II, on the other hand, the terms of integration into the nation-state have changed fundamentally, as has the civil life. Thus, I look at the changing relationship of the community to larger polities.

The civil life and the ideology about it are thus results of several processes in Montecastellese history. These may be summarized in terms of major phases. The first coincides with the age of the communes, from the twelfth to the early fourteenth centuries, and the period of the *signorie* (lordships) that followed. Though there is little evidence on Montecastello's internal organization during this period, it was affected by the politics of the area and the patterns of communal life, which are known for Todi and other towns. As the documentation on Montecastello improves, it appears as a miniature commune itself. As in the larger towns, some of the social relations and styles of public life that came out of the commune persisted as political control passed to despots, territorial states, and finally a centralized nation-state. The communal period produced an elite with ties both in the city and the small town, at ease in the institutions of local government, merging aristocratic values with a taste for bureaucracy. This period put a premium on skills in oratory, written language, the law, and political maneuver. It gave form to ideals of citizen participation and civic pride. The diplomatic activity of the period may have played a special part, in fostering a role for personal cultivation and etiquette.

A second phase begins in the sixteenth century. Montecastello's political situation was strengthened by the consolidation of the Papal States, and it shared in the growing commerce in agricultural products. Most importantly, a process of colonization of the countryside began, one which continued into the twentieth century. Peasant families were settled on the land, on farms which they created and cultivated under mezzadria share-contracts. This settlement under the mezzadria system gave rise to the town-country relationship implied in the civil life. On the one hand, the interdependence of town and country was reinforced, for the town remained the functional center for the whole community. Town-landlord and peasant were drawn into ties based on the mezzadria contract, and the landlord's role took on aspects of patronage. On the other hand, the separation of town and country set off a contrast between the life of the town and that of the peasantry outside.

The end of the eighteenth century saw the advent of new forces, both economic and political, which intensified with the unification of Italy about 1860. The landowning class of Montecastello, incorporating into its ranks high-status new arrivals to the community, assumed positions of mediation between Montecastellesi and the nation-state. Knowledge of and ability to operate within the larger society became the major hallmarks of civiltà, but they remained tied to local relationships. The political events of the nineteenth century initiated processes of change which eventually altered the distribution of land ownership and power. However, the local elite survived and maintained their pivotal role until the Second World War.

In the years after the war, accelerating changes impinged upon every aspect of community life, but in general they occurred within existing structures. In 1960 the agricultural system was still essentially intact though in serious difficulty; class relationships still reflected prewar realities; and some of the population still maintained traditional community activities. Yet evidence of transformations under way was all about. The ideology of civiltà was voiced, but often with the regret that it was passing. It was, in fact, invidious comparisons with the past and conflicts engendered by the changing times that pointed up some of the phenomena related to civiltà. In describing Montecastello in 1960–61, I attempt to show both how it reflected the conditions out of which civiltà emerged, and how those conditions were changing. A redefinition of civiltà was also in process, and there are hints of what that would involve. (In this description of Montecastello the present tense refers to the situation in 1960–61; the "contemporary period" indicates the time from World War II to this ethnographic present.)

By 1971 Montecastello seemed to have crossed another historical threshhold. The civile styles persisted, but their social context was different in important ways from that of a decade earlier. These differences are summarized in chapter 8. If the time of the field study appears in retrospect as the end of an era, this may be more than the bias of nostalgia. The beginning of the 1960s may be considered, on many grounds, a turning point for Montecastello, and for Umbrian rural society in general. In his recent historical geography of Umbria, Henri Desplanques identifies 1960–61 as the start of a comprehensive transformation. "Everything was overturned: the social structures, the systems of cultivation, the types of land use, the habitat itself. Never had the countryside known such a mutation" (1969:10). It remains to be seen how this transformation will affect the pattern of town life revealed in Montecastello.

CHAPTER 2

The Community

UMBRIA is a landlocked region, embracing the slope of the Apennine chain to the east and a country of hills and riverine plains in the center and west (see Figure 2). About 70 percent of the total area is included in the administrative province of Perugia; the remainder comprises the province of Terni in the southwest, which contains Umbria's largest city and its only heavy industry. The province of Perugia is cut through the middle by river valleys which form an inverted Y, whose joining point lies just east of the city of Perugia. From the northwest, the Tiber flows through its narrow upper valley, turning due south below Perugia into an undulating course to form the broader middle valley, which extends as far as Todi. The southeastern arm of the Y is the still wider Umbrian valley, an enclosed basin which describes an arc through the plains of Assisi and Foligno to Spoleto. These valleys are the areas of intensive agriculture, the main routes of communication, and the sites of recent industrial development. The hills rise on all sides, in some places becoming rugged mountains. It is the area of low and middle hills, between 200 and 500 meters, that is the characteristic setting of the kind of community described in this book.

Montecastello is located in the Perugia-Todi basin, some forty kilometers from the provincial capital. The visitor coming by automobile or motorcycle from Perugia or Rome would follow the Via Tiberina. If he were traveling by public transportation he would take the Umbrian Cen-

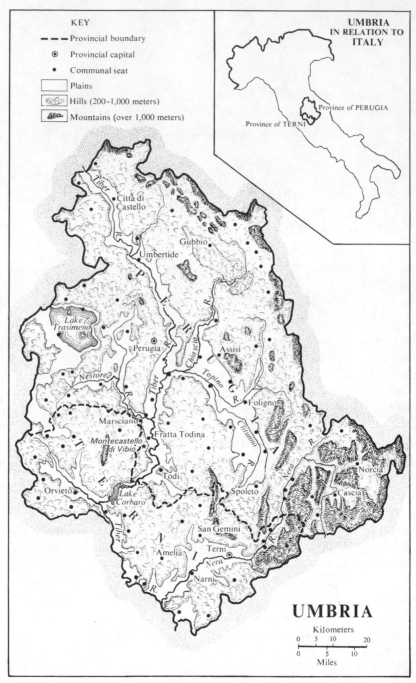

Figure 2   Umbria

tral Railroad, which would bring him to a station in the neighboring
commune of Fratta Todina. There he would wait for the bus that twice a
day makes the trip between the station and the village of Doglio in the
hills above Montecastello; at other times he might telephone to Montecastello for the sole taxi. From the railroad station, he would travel
through the fertile Tiber Valley, passing the tobacco factory and several
prosperous-looking farms. After a kilometer he would turn into a smaller
road, cross a stream that forms the commune boundary, and traverse the
plain of Montecastello. This would soon bring him to the hamlet of
Madonna del Piano, a strip of new houses along the road. Just beyond is
the crossroads, where he would begin the curving climb from the 180-
meter altitude of Madonna del Piano to the town of Montecastello at
425 meters.

The town is visible almost halfway from Perugia on a clear day, but as
the traveler approaches the hilltop, its walls and towers come into focus.
As he passes stone farmhouses, wheat fields and olive groves, and foun-
tains where peasant women scrub their laundry and fill their water jugs,
he can sense the subordination of the slopes to the castle above. Occasionally there is a cluster of more elaborate farm buildings: this is a *fattoria*, the coordinating center for several farms. Scattered along the way
are shrines where flowers or candles show traces of a recent visit. At the
last sharp turn of the road is the cemetery; surrounded by a high stone
wall and rows of cypress trees like those at the edge of town, it seems a
Montecastello in miniature. From here foot traffic reaches the town
quickly by a steep path, but the main road follows a long circular
route below the "modern" section of Montecastello, the area just outside
the walls.

The town may be entered from the north through a narrow opening
between the most imposing *palazzi*. The main gateway, however, is on
the south side. The road to it leads along the western wall—past several
new houses, the football field, the new elementary school, and the public
gardens. The bus and other motor vehicles park outside the gate near the
bocce ground. From here there is an extraordinary panorama of the
Montecastellese countryside, the river valley, and the surrounding hills
topped with castles and towns.

To the modern eye Montecastello seems like a stage set, and indeed it
forms a stage on which the civil life is enacted. As the visitor walks
around it, he encounters all the settings essential to a civilized way of

life. He can literally walk around it, for the physical plan is circular. The main streets are arranged in an irregular spiral that climbs in altitude toward the center, with narrow alleys cutting across it (see Figure 3). However, there is no clearcut social center, for unlike many Italian towns in which one piazza concentrates administrative, religious, and marketing functions, in Montecastello these are dispersed in several places. In fact, there are three town squares of approximately equal importance.

At the spatial center of the town is the Piazza of the Monument. The monument commemorates the sons of Montecastello who died in World War I, and this is the locale for ceremonial expression of the community's membership in the Italian nation. On national holidays secular rituals are performed here, and religious processions making the round of the town stop at the monument too. At one side of the piazza is the civic tower, the *campanile*, which contains a chiming clock and the bells that in Montecastello, as throughout Italy, are a symbol of the community (as the word for parochialism, "campanilismo," suggests). The bells serve as a town crier, announcing school times and public events such as church functions, processions, and secular meetings, as well as marriages and deaths. But these bells are special to the Montecastellesi, for there are three, which are shown off in the lively and distinctive festival ring. The bells are cited almost as part of the name of the community in one of the sayings most frequently quoted, which begins: *"Montecastello dalle tre campane . . ."* [1]

The Piazza of the Church, the religious center of the parish, is a general gathering place for the community whenever church events are held. On holidays (but rarely at other times) it is filled with crowds before and after services and, even during the mass, clusters of men remain in the square. The piazza also contains the *spaccio*, at which small groups assemble on other days. A café and the local concessionary of salt and tobacco, the spaccio is also a center for communication with the outside world, for it sells newspapers and periodicals and has the only public telephone in town.

When the Montecastellesi speak of "the piazza" they generally mean a third square, the Piazza of the Holy Cross, also referred to as the Piazza of the Market. The itinerant food peddlers who come occasionally on weekdays show their wares here, and on holidays one or two local men set up stalls with clothing and various small articles. Political rallies and secular dramas take place in this square too. At one end is the *chiesina*, a

Figure 3   The town of Montecastello: (1) *Piazza of the Monument;* (2) *Piazza of the Holy Cross;*
(3) *Piazza of the Church;* (4) *parish church;* (5) *chiesina* (little church); (6) campanile (*civic
tower*); (7) spaccio; (8) *town hall;* (9) *Monument to the Fallen;* (10) *recreational societies;*
(11) *bar;* (12) *food stores;* (13) *bakery;* (14) *post office;* (15) *pharmacy;* (16) *household-goods shop;*
(17) carabinieri *headquarters;* (18) *old elementary school;* (19) *new elementary school;* (20) *middle
school* (avviamento); (21) *infants' school* (asilo); (22) *theater;* (23) *football field;* (24) *dance
platform;* (25) *shrine of San Giovanni;* (26) *Porta Tramontana* (north gate); (27) *Porta del
Maggio* (south gate); (28) *parking area;* (29) *public gardens;* (30) *main road;* (31) passeggiata;
(32) *path to the cemetery;* (33) *vegetable gardens*

small sixteenth-century church that is closed most of the year but comes
alive during Holy Week. Like the marketing, political, and other secular
events that are held in this piazza, the Holy Week festivities draw many
people into active participation. Thus, this square, more than the others,
is a place of the "people," less tied to the formal institutions of church
and state.

The *comune* or town hall is the center of administrative business of the community: one goes there on official matters, the tax office and medical clinic are located there, and the bureaucracy resides there. Spatially, however, it is rather isolated from the main hubs and paths of social activity. Official business is conducted at other places too. The post office provides not only mail and telegraphic services but also various banking facilities, and most importantly, it disburses government pensions and allotments. Montecastello has a barracks of the *carabinieri* or national police, staffed by a marshall and four or five carabinieri. There is an elementary school in the town (as well as four others throughout the commune), and in 1959 an *avviamento* school covering the sixth through eighth grades was opened in an ancient house near the town hall.

Several locales in the town are gathering places where men carry on the public discourse that is so important in civiltà. Each one has a more or less steady clientele and a character of its own. The café that is generally referred to as "the priest's bar" is in the basement of the parish house and is formally organized as a branch of ACLI, a national Catholic worker's association. It attracts mainly artisans and laborers who identify themselves as non-Communists. A second bar (the CRAL), which is affiliated with a national recreational society, draws its membership mostly from the upper levels of local society. A third is a commercial bar run by ex-peasants and patronized primarily by lower-class workers and peasants who come into town on holidays. All the bars of Montecastello are places where men play cards and billiards and carry on endless discussions. However, women and children enter freely on specific errands, and nowadays spend whole evenings watching television in the bars.

In addition to the bars, the two largest food stores are places where people congregate, drawing out their frequent shopping trips to talk over events of the day. The bakery is also important; besides selling bread, it has a wineshop for men and a public oven where women can gossip and see the food others are preparing. The pharmacy and the post office next door are informal meeting places for the professional people of the community. As in some other locales, individuals who work there seem to attract a following of certain regulars.

The town contains a much larger number of commercial establishments than would seem to be required by a community of this size. Small shops all over town sell various combinations of foodstuffs, fabrics, shoes, clothing, hardware, and household items. These are all minute enterprises employing only family labor. At the expense of what is undoubtedly over-servicing and marginal profits, the community seems to maximize the number and variety of permanent sites at which there is simultaneously commercial exchange and public social interaction. Though the formal data on local commerce apply to the commune rather than just the town, they substantiate this impression. According to the 1961 census, there were 27 permanent places of commercial activity in the commune (ISTAT 1964). An earlier survey found 17 locales for the distribution of foodstuffs alone (MLP 1959:167), serving a population of perhaps 500 who regularly purchase a large part of their food.

The building that evokes the greatest pride of the community is a small but quite elaborate theater. Accommodating some 300 people, it was until 1950 the site of elegant and eminently urbane performances and dances. Though now closed because of its state of disrepair, some Montecastellesi talk of restoring it. More than any other single locale it manifests the idea of civiltà, evidence of Montecastello at its best.

The north and south entrances to the town are favorite places of outdoor congregation, and these ideal observation points provide limitless topics for conversation. Since the interior of the town is usually cool and damp, throughout the day groups form "to take the sun" in the area around the walls. These groups are usually single-sexed and roughly age-graded. At several spots women gossip while doing handiwork. The older men favor the southern parking clearance, where there is likely to be a bocce game under way. The younger people gravitate to the public gardens, planted by the town a half-century ago on what was once the moat; children run and play there, while adolescents stroll, exchanging confidences. Along the western wall, women do laundry, tend vegetable gardens, and raise chickens and rabbits. The western rim of the town is also important as a holiday area, for the road leading between north and south gates becomes the route of the *passeggiata*, the formal holiday stroll.

The new section outside the walls seems to concentrate more modern patterns of socializing. The area, called San Giovanni after a shrine erected there a generation ago by a local landowning family, began to be built up after the war. The inhabitants are mainly middle-level families of artisans and clerks who have been moderately successful, for families of older money have palazzi inside the town. San Giovanni is the site of football games, the modern way in which the population celebrates community identity, and in 1960 a dance platform was built in the area. The proprietor of one of the bars has plans to move there, recognizing that while the main stream of social traffic is within the town, San Giovanni is the likely area for the upwardly mobile of both town and countryside to build new houses.

Here, then, are all the public places required for the civil life. "Civiltà" implies locales for certain kinds of activities: for the institutions of Church and State and their local manipulation, for public discourse, for socializing in organized events and informal encounters, for indulging in cultura, and for expressing community identity. Within almost minimal space, the town of Montecastello contains the full range.

"Civiltà" refers primarily to public life, but some aspects are acted out inside the houses. Most of the town houses are large stone structures, often repaired and modernized over the centuries but little altered on the outside; a few show traces of former splendor. A whole house may be occupied by a single family, or it may be divided into two or three apartments of perhaps three to five rooms each. The living quarters are always a story above street level, while the ground floor is used as a shop, storehouse, or garage. This separation of living space from the public street means that to enter someone's home—even that of a relative or close friend—is to pay a call, requiring a degree of formality.

Almost all daily activity of the family takes place in the kitchen, and everyday visitors are received there; in winter, it is the only room that is kept warm. However, the family's public identity, its collective civiltà, is conserved in the *sala*, which is used only on special occasions—for entertaining important visitors and for major family celebrations. Here the furniture is formally arranged: a large table stands in the center of the room, chairs are lined up carefully along the walls, and at one side is a cabinet containing sweet liqueurs and ware for formal service. The bedrooms are private retreats, but those of married couples also display the items of furniture that are part of marriage exchanges. Perhaps the only really private area is the lavatory, if there is one, which is not shown to visitors unless it has been modernized and made into an elegant place.[2]

The walls surrounding the town mark off quite sharply the domain of civiltà, for in social behavior as in settlement pattern there is a clear distinction between town and countryside. Still, the separation has been softened somewhat with time. The public gardens, the formal walk, some of the recreational spaces, and the parking area now spill out

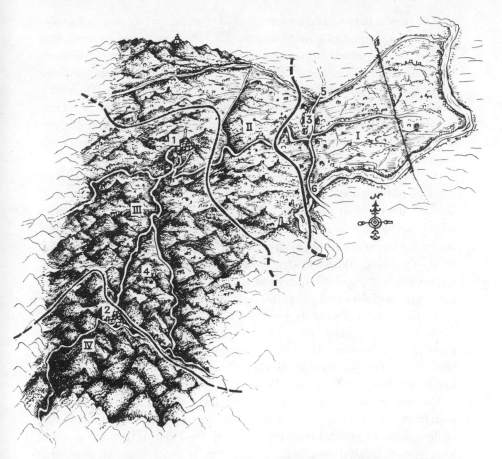

Figure 4   The commune of Montecastello: I-II-III-IV—altitudinal zones; (1) the town of Monte-castello; (2) Doglio; (3) Madonna del Piano; (4) Poggio San Quirico; (5) bridge over Torrente Faena and road to Fratta; (6) bridge over the Tiber and road to Todi; ++++++ railroad

beyond the walls. Moreover, the San Giovanni extension is expanding down the slope and almost faces the nearest farm.

The commune contains another nucleated settlement, Doglio (see Figure 4). Doglio and its countryside are not part of Montecastello parish and they have a rather separate history; thus, for purposes of this study Doglio was not considered part of the community of Montecastello. Doglio contains the major provisions for the ordinary round of life of its own inhabitants (under 200 as of the 1961 census) and for the surrounding dispersed population (about 400): a church with a resident priest, a school, stores, bars and other recreational centers, and its own cemetery. However, Doglio looks to Montecastello for a few specific functions, such as formal administrative business and health services.[3] Although similar to Montecastello in its physical structure, Doglio is more rustic in appearance, for it lacks the paved streets and large palazzi of Montecastello. In fact, much of its population consists of agricultural workers. Doglio is clearly a village, while Montecastello—with only a slightly larger population—is more aptly described as a "town." The Italian term "paese," of course, covers both.

Within the territory of Montecastello parish are two other settlements, hamlets: Madonna del Piano and Poggio San Quìrico. Each had a population of under 40 in 1961 (ISTAT 1965), and each included a church, a school, and a cluster of houses; however, they are quite different. Madonna del Piano originated around a little church at the crossroads and is steadily growing. With a food shop, a bar, some artisan workshops, a political club, and regular holiday church services, it is a subcenter for the large farm population of the plain. San Quìrico, in contrast, is merely an expanded fattoria. Primarily serving the area held by a single landlord, the hamlet includes only the family of the *fattore* (the estate manager) and a few peasant families. Its church is essentially the private chapel of the landowning family. Except for the school, the people of San Quìrico look to the town of Montecastello as their community center.

The major portion of the community (over three-fourths of the total population) live on farms dispersed across the countryside. The territory of the commune extends from the banks of the Tiber to the high wooded hills around Doglio, covering a wide range of environmental diversity. This range may be indicated grossly in terms of altitudinal zones (see Figure 4).

Zone i. The plain takes in an area from about 140 to 200 meters. It forms a broad, fairly level strip of the best-watered, most fertile land, enriched by deposits from the slight annual inundation of the Tiber. This zone produces the highest yields of grain and forage, supports the greatest density of livestock, and grows the few specifically industrial crops in the area. The advantages of the zone have increased since the war, as much of this land has been irrigated by water pumped up from the river. However, the plain is susceptible to several environmental hazards: occasional floods, excessive humidity and fog throughout the winter, and frost, especially the treacherous late spring frosts, for although the plain is the zone with the highest mean temperature it is also characterized by marked fluctuations and temperature inversion.

Zone II. The low hills, from 200 to 300 meters, form an intermediate zone. It shares, to a lesser degree, both the advantages and hazards of the plain. As in the higher hills, the slopes (in the range of 10–20 percent) present problems for working the land, but they also hold less humidity.

Zone III. The middle hills extend from 300 meters, roughly the fog line, to about 500 meters. Though the climate is more moderate and less unpredictable here than in the lower altitudes, the average productivity for seed crops is lower. (The situation on one fattoria in this zone was improved during the 1950s with the construction of an artificial lake for irrigation.) Zones II and III together form the range of the olive.

Zone IV. In the territory of Doglio parish is a zone of high hills, from approximately 500 to 650 meters. Beyond the optimal range for vines and olives, and with a relatively small proportion of arable land, this zone has nevertheless had some importance in the past as woodland and sheep pasture.

For administrative convenience the rural area of the commune is divided into four *frazioni*. Of the three that make up Montecastello proper, one corresponds to Zone I, while the other two cover both Zones II and III. In informal usage, areas are more often designated by the names of the fourteen *contrade* of Montecastello parish, divisions which have some ritual significance. The most important unit of organization in the countryside, however, is a social one—the circle of neighbors (*vicini*) surrounding each farm, within which there is exchange of labor and certain other obligations.

Most families living in the countryside work farms that are operated as integrated and self-contained units. Typically, a single family lives in a farmhouse that is separated from other houses; sometimes, however, a few houses cluster together, or a single house is divided for two families. The land worked by a household generally includes at least a vegetable garden near the farmhouse, but the fields are often dispersed in three or more plots at some distance from each other. For example, one farm in Zone II has a field adjacent to the house, a second in the plain (where crops requiring irrigation are raised), and a third (with olive trees) in the uplands toward the town.

Most of the farmhouses are substantial stone buildings, sometimes hundreds of years old, and often large enough for the families of ten to

twenty that once were common. The farmhouse is the center of the great
variety of activities that are combined on each farm. In the farmyard are
haystacks and protected areas for storing animal feed and wood; the
kitchen garden is nearly. Several structures are built onto the house: pig
sties, coops for poultry and rabbits, sheds for carts and large equipment.
At one side of the house is the large outdoor baking oven, and near it,
the henhouse. Often the farmhouse includes a tower, the *palombara*
where pigeons are kept. The ground floor of the house contains cattle
stalls, haybins, a tool storage area, and the wine cellar. On the upper
floor, which typically is reached by an exterior staircase, is the living
area for the family, as well as one or two storerooms. Family activity
centers in the large kitchen, around the hearth and the table in the
middle of the room. There are bedrooms for each married couple and
their infants, which—as in the town homes—display the furniture acquired at marriage. The sala, reserve of the town families' civiltà, is
generally absent in the farmhouse plan.

As Desplanques has pointed out, the Umbrian farmhouses reflect the
design of the houses in town, after which they were modeled (1969:482;
see also Bonasera et al. 1955). Nevertheless, in the view of many Montecastellesi, the traditional farm represents the antithesis of civiltà. It is
possible to reproduce a degree of civiltà in the hinterlands by improving
the amenities of a house and decorating it in the style of the town. In
general, however, distance from town is a rough measure of place within
the sphere of civiltà.

Population and Economy

As of the end of 1960, the community of Montecastello included 1,885
individuals living in 465 households.[4] Table 1 shows how the population
is distributed among the major sections within the community in terms
of total numbers, sex and age groups, and marital status of the adult population.

Some general features of the population and some gross differences
among the sections of the community are evident. Average household
size is considerably smaller in town than in country. In this as in most
demographic characteristics, the plain resembles the town more closely
than do the hill zones. In the community as a whole the proportion of

Table 1   Population Characteristics of Montecastello, 1960

	Montecastello Town	Plain	Low and Middle Hills	Total Community
Population	345	581	959	1,885
Number of households	112	151	202	465
Average household size	3.1	3.8	4.7	4.1
Sex Distribution				
Male (%)	47.5	48.9	51.0	49.7
Female (%)	52.5	51.1	49.0	50.3
Age/Sex Distribution				
Age distribution of				
males (%)				
birth to 15	17.8	14.8	23.3	19.6
16 to 45	36.2	48.9	50.1	47.2
over 45	46.0	36.3	26.6	33.2
Age distribution of				
females (%)				
birth to 15	15.6	24.2	24.7	22.9
16 to 45	47.2	44.5	45.5	45.5
over 45	37.2	31.3	29.8	31.6
Marital Status/				
Sex Distribution				
Males over 16 never				
married (%)	19.3	26.6	29.9	27.0
Females over 16 never				
married (%)	25.0	13.7	15.1	16.5

males and females is approximately equal, but in the town (and to a lesser degree, in the plain), females are more numerous than males, while the reverse is true in the hills. The age-sex distribution shows a number of town-country differences. The proportion of children is higher in the countryside than in town, reflecting the higher levels of fertility of the country population. The town, on the other hand, has a relatively greater number of people of both sexes over 45 than does the country. Perhaps most significant is the fact that men in the most economically productive age group, 16 to 45, are more numerous in the country than in the town. Finally, the marital status distribution shows that the town contains a much higher proportion of women who have never married than does the country, while the countryside has a larger number of un-

married men. The reasons for these differences will become apparent as
the economic and social structure of Montecastello is described, but in
general they reflect the absorption of manpower by the agricultural system.

The economy of Montecastello is based upon agriculture, which directly or indirectly supports most of the population. In the town itself
there are few people who actually work the land. This is the domain of
the landowners and the professionals, clerks, merchants, artisans, and laborers. In the countryside live agricultural administrators and a small
but increasing number of nonagricultural workers, but most of the
country people cultivate the land—as *mezzadri* (share-farmers), owner-
cultivators, or salaried laborers. The largest and most clearly defined of
these categories consists of the mezzadri, who will be discussed in detail
in the next chapter. The term "owner-cultivators" covers various kinds
of peasant proprietorship in the commune. One such variant is made up
of peasants who own integrated farms on which each family has its
house. Most frequent in the lower altitudes, such holdings derive from
fairly recent purchases of farms formerly worked under the mezzadria
system. Another kind of owner-cultivator consists of those holding plots
of land rather than whole farms. Since the land provides only partial
subsistence in such cases, these families combine different economic activities. In Doglio, still another form occurs, perhaps representing an
older peasant proprietorship that survives in Umbrian mountain regions.
Here cultivators live in the village and work scattered plots in the area
surrounding it. The category "salaried laborer" is relatively small but
quite diverse, covering semi-skilled employees on *fattorie* as well as permanent hired hands on mezzadria farms, and including workers paid in
cash, in produce, and in combinations of the two.

The number of people involved in various categories of economic activity is summarized in Table 2, which is based on 1961 census data for
the commune. These data show that about 70 percent of the active population (over age 10) are engaged in agriculture. However, these figures
underestimate the agricultural labor force, for many of the housewives
contribute to it, while persons with other occupations and children still
in school also do farm work at times.

The labor force in "industries and manufacture" includes several people who work in the only industry in the area, the tobacco factory in
Fratta. Until 1961, when new sorting methods were introduced, the

Table 2   Labor Force of the Commune According to
Branch of Economic Activity, 1961

Branch of Economic Activity	No. of Persons	Males	Females
Agriculture	639	620	19
Industries and manufacture	68	57	11
Construction	92	92	0
Transport and communications	27	27	0
Commerce	29	20	9
Services	31	11	20
Public administration	21	13	8
Credit and insurance	2	2	0
Total active population	909	842	67
Seeking first occupation	10	7	3
Housewives	790	0	790
Pensioners	79	56	23
Students	207	114	93
Other	93	49	44
Total inactive population	1,179	226	953
Total resident population over age 10	2,088	1,068	1,020

SOURCE: ISTAT 1965.

plant also employed over 200 women for seasonal work, including about
thirty from Montecastello, mostly peasants. Most of the individuals employed in industries and manufacture are artisans serving local needs; in
addition, a few women do piecework for textile concerns. The census
lists thirty "manufacturing units" in the commune: five devoted to food
products (such as mills and bakeries), eleven to clothing (tailors, dressmakers, knitters, and shoemakers), six to woodworking (carpenters), and
eight to mechanical products (smiths and mechanics) (ISTAT 1965). The
category "construction" refers to the large and rapidly increasing number
of masons and building-trades laborers. The number of persons engaged
in "commerce" reflects the proliferation of minute enterprises already referred to. Only one or two merchants are involved in extralocal commerce, selling agricultural products. Finally, the categories "services"
and "public administration" together describe the small army of bureaucrats, teachers, policemen, and professionals employed locally by the
municipal and national government.

An overview of Montecastello's primary economic activity may be ob-

Table 3   Utilization of Land Area, Agrarian
Zone of Todi, 1955

Utilization	Percent of Area
Total Agricultural Area	
Arable	74.0
Specialized tree cultivation [a]	.5
Permanent forage	4.1
Woods	14.8
Total productive area	93.4
Uncultivated and unproductive area	6.6
Total Area	100.0
Arable Area	
Wheat	44.1
Other cereals	5.7
Maize	7.0
Industrial cultures	2.2
Legumes	3.7
Potato	2.5
Forage	34.8
Total Area	100.0

SOURCE: MLP 1959:131.
[a] Olive, vine, fruit trees.

tained by considering the major emphases in agricultural production.
The patterns of land use in the area are suggested by the summary in
Table 3, which applies to the agrarian zone of Todi (including Montecastello).[5] Three-fourths of the land is arable; this includes clean-tilled fields
as well as land combining field crops with olives and vines, for specialized cultivation of these important products is rare. Permanent pasture
land takes up only a small proportion of the land, but woodlands (which
provide forage as well as fuel) amount to 15 percent of the total. The
major crops are wheat and various types of forage, together accounting
for 80 percent of the cultivated land. Among the minor crops, maize is
the most important.

Comparing these 1955 data with similar information for 1929 suggests
the main trends of the decades preceding the field study. The amount of
arable increased during that period, as did the proportion of arable devoted to forage crops, while the area in woods and uncultivated land
decreased (MLP 1959:131). A comparison of production figures for the
two years indicates that the amount of wheat produced almost doubled

and that there was a great increase in the industrial crops, especially tobacco; however, the production of other cereals, grapes, olives, maize, potatoes, and legumes was reduced (MLP 1959:139). In the livestock economy, the production of cattle and swine increased, while sheep and goats became less important (MLP 1959:26).

Wheat dominates Montecastellese agriculture. It is the subsistence staple and the primary income-producing crop for both peasants and landowners. Production has steadily increased since the beginning of the twentieth century, when improved methods of crop rotation and fertilization were introduced. However, the relatively low yields (compared with national averages) restrict Montecastellese wheat to nearby markets.[6]

Wine grapes are raised throughout the countryside, although the low and middle hills are the most favorable zones. Vines are cultivated in the fields, and usually raised onto trees. The local varieties are not highly prized and production is primarily for local use, but many landowners sell some surplus. Until recently, several proprietors made their own wine for sale, but most now sell the surplus grapes to a cooperative cellar that has been instituted in the area.

The olive is cultivated in the middle hills, usually in association with wheat. It is both a subsistence essential and a source of income for many proprietors. However, production has declined considerably since a disastrous frost in 1956 destroyed almost a third of the trees. While such frosts have occurred in the past (the previous one was in 1929), this time market competition from imported peanut oil tended to discourage replanting.

Forage crops are second only to wheat in importance today. "Artificial meadow" (lucern, clover, and sainfoin) was introduced at the beginning of this century, causing a minor revolution both in the livestock economy and in methods of crop rotation. In addition to these crops, several cereals are also used for fodder: barley, oats, rye, vetch, and sorghum. Since the forage crops are integral to all regimes of rotation used in Montecastello, as well as supporting the commercially valuable livestock, they always take up at least a third of the tilled area.

Maize was first grown in the area in the late eighteenth century and its cultivation was expanded steadily throughout the nineteenth. Before World War I it still occupied as much as a third of the total area, often forming a two-year rotation cycle with wheat. Maize was the dietary staple of the peasants and it served a variety of other uses, providing fodder, fuel, and bedding. Today, greatly reduced quantities of maize are grown, primarily in the lower altitudes, as feed both for the livestock and for poultry.

Over the past few decades various industrial crops have been added to the productive complex of many farms in the lower altitudes, where they provide a supplementary source of income. Tobacco was introduced in the 1920s, and the opening of the tobacco factory stimulated its expansion wherever land could be sufficiently irrigated. Although tobacco is several times more profitable than wheat per unit of land, it requires both capital investment and intensive labor; moreover, it is vulnerable to the dual uncertainties of weather and state control. Thus, tobacco production has leveled off.

To the extent that other crops are grown specifically for the market, they are even more dependent upon irrigation than tobacco. Sugar beet has for some time been grown throughout the countryside primarily for animal fodder, but it became an industrial crop for some irrigated farms in the plain after the last war. Its main destination is the sugar refinery in Foligno, which supplies the Perugian candy industry. Tomatoes, commonly grown in vegetable gardens for family needs, are now raised on irrigated land for sale to the canneries in Perugia. However, production varies considerably, with the fluctuation in prices. Similarly, cauliflower is beginning to have commercial significance.

A great variety of other crops is raised in small quantities: broad beans (fave), green beans (fagioli), chick-peas, lentils, potatoes, peas, squash, cabbage, broccoli, artichokes, lettuce, spinach, onions, garlic, herbs, several kinds of fruits, and others. These are combined in many different ways to serve multiple purposes. In addition to feeding the family, several serve to renew the land or are used for animal fodder; these are cultivated in the fields. Others are grown in the garden near the farmhouse (and in the gardens around the town walls, which townspeople lease from the commune). Small surpluses of all these crops may also be sold locally.

Cattle are today the single major source of cash income for Montecastellese proprietors. Still vital for agricultural work and transport, their main commercial use is production of calves for meat. Calves are generally sold at the weight of two or three quintals, some to local butchers but most to outside breeders who raise them to a greater weight. Older cows are used for traction, in place of the oxen that were common before

World War II. (Bulls have also been replaced, for the most part, by artificial insemination.) There is very little milking of cows, and only one farm sells milk—a small quantity that flavors the town's morning coffee.

Cattle are stalled and never put out to pasture. Feeding them remains the incessant problem of local agriculture. Before the new forage crops were introduced, the main source of fodder was trees, and the number of animals that could be kept was strictly limited. Today, the limit is set by the yield of the forage crops. In general, farms of the plain can support about one head per hectare of arable land on the farm.

The expansion of forage cultivation around the time of World War I made possible a considerable commerce in work oxen. The breeds raised locally included both the Perugino and the robust Maremmano. Purchased as yearlings, the oxen were used for work, then resold at six or seven years of age. Only animals defective for work were butchered. With the spread of tractors after World War II, work oxen rapidly lost their importance in the regional economy, while at the same time the market for meat expanded. These factors stimulated a shift toward calf production, for which the Chianina breed is favored.

Pigs are raised on every farm for both subsistence and sale, and their production has increased steadily. Unlike cattle, pigs are slaughtered for direct consumption by both landlord and peasant, and even nonagricultural families may raise a pig. The animal slaughtered at Christmas furnishes pork provisions for year-round use. In addition, the piglets taken to the Saturday market in Todi throughout the year are a modest but significant source of income.

Sheep were formerly important for several products—lamb, cheese, wool, and manure—and most farms kept several head. However, as pasture has been converted to arable and as the overall economy has emphasized income-producing activities, the number of sheep has been greatly reduced. Those that remain are primarily in the middle hills, where they are pastured on olive land. These sheep furnish some cheese (the *pecorino*) and, more importantly, lambs taken to market in the spring and slaughtered for Easter.

Each farm raises a variety of courtyard animals: chickens, ducks, geese, pigeons, guinea hens, and rabbits. They are consumed by the peasant family on holidays, and until recently they ended up on the landlord's table as well. In addition, many peasant women sell eggs and poultry to townspeople, which gives them a small cash income.

The changes in the agricultural economy reflect an increasing emphasis upon production for the market. This has been facilitated by steady advances in agrarian technology, particularly in the recent postwar period. By 1960 mechanization was making inroads; there were eight or ten tractors in the community, and sowers, harrows, reapers, and other machines were becoming common.[7] Other developments have also been important for the move toward commercialization: the introduction of selected seed, chemical fertilizers, insecticides, balanced livestock feed, irrigation installations, and specialized equipment for industrial crops. However, these advances have been incorporated to very different degrees by different landowners, and there is still great variation among zones and among individual farms. Moreover, commercialization has taken place within the same general productive complex. The increase in income-producing crops and animals remains a shift of emphasis rather than a fundamental departure from traditional agriculture.

At the same time, farms are becoming less self-sufficient. The technological improvements mean more articles that must be purchased. On the other hand, consumption needs can no longer be fully met by farm production. Increasingly, food items are purchased, either to supplement home production or to satisfy new tastes—items such as pasta, oil, tomato conserves, cheese, coffee (replacing barley coffee), and sugar (replacing honey). Virtually all families buy fabrics, clothing, and linens; home-grown and home-manufactured hemp, linen, and wool have disappeared. Furthermore, many services formerly paid for in grain from the threshing floor (those of the blacksmith, the physician, the veterinarian, and the various religious specialists) are now paid partly in cash. In addition, new needs deriving from the postwar Italian consumer culture are rapidly spreading among the country people. Yet the peasants' increasing dependence upon the market has taken place within an economic structure geared to self-sufficiency. The problems created by this situation will be discussed in chapter 3.

The Annual Round

It is evident that Montecastello comprises an extremely diverse population, a complex of economic activities, and a variety of living standards and styles. Yet this diversity exists within an integral institutional framework, and it is played out, in part, in the common arena of the town.

Thus, it is possible to speak, in a general way, of the life of the community. This section gives a brief sketch of the seasonal patterns of work and sociability as manifested on the public stage—the changing scenarios of social life that appear over the course of the year. To a large extent, this round is regulated by the agricultural cycle, which affects not only the countryside but also the town. For town and country, though always distinct, live in mutuality: they are tied together in many ways, and people in each area are constantly made aware of the other.

The agricultural year begins and ends in the fall, the cycle of wheat beginning before the other main crops are harvested. During the early fall the wheat fields are prepared for planting while the last vegetables are gathered. The dryness of summer rapidly gives way to the season of heavy rains, of fog that covers the valley in great clouds, and of sudden cold spells which sometimes strike before the harvests are done. The *vendemmia* (the grape harvest) comes in late October, and the town witnesses peasants bringing cartloads of grapes to the landowners' cellars. Many men make their family's supply of wine, and as the wine matures their friends congregate to taste it and to discuss the relative quality of different vintages. The main topic of conversation in the town now is politics, and as election day approaches the discussions and public forums become more heated. Evenings and holidays are livened by outdoor rallies and organized entertainment in the clubhouses. This is the hunting season too, and men engage in this passion at every opportunity, bringing home the much-prized small birds and an occasional hare. Everyone prepares for winter: peasants try to increase their supply of livestock feed, and most families must accumulate firewood, either collecting it from their own farms or buying it from the fattorie with woodlands. In the countryside, late fall sees both the last harvest—the olives—and the major planting: wheat, forage, and several secondary crops. In the town, above the fog, these last days of warm sun bring people outdoors, and there is a great deal of informal socializing around the walls.

By December, the community begins to turn inward for winter, and informal social activity shifts to indoor and more private locales. If the planting has not been delayed by excessive rain, the work of the farms slows down, and the longer evenings allow time for the *veglie*, visits exchanged among the farms. In the town too, the social scenes center around the family hearth, where neighbors and friends gather informally for games, suppers, and impromptu dances. All the farms and many town families have pigs to slaughter; men of each household prepare hams, bacon, and fresh sausages that are cooked over the hearth during the evening. The Christmas festivities fit the season's tone of familial and neighborly gatherings, and the birth of the Christ Child is celebrated almost as a family event.

The New Year holiday ushers in a more public round of socializing with organized parties and dances. The pace of these events builds up throughout the weeks of Carnival. Finally Carnival is "put to death," and then Lent harnesses the socializing. February and March see an increase in agricultural activity: the wheat, vine, and olive land is hoed; spring crops are planted; vines are pruned; and the lambing season begins.

Public social activity, now in a more religious mood, is resumed with the Easter holidays and the arrival of true spring. Holy Week assembles the community in an intense series of ceremonials, and throughout April and May there are frequent processions both within Montecastello and to other places nearby. The content of much of this ritual concerns the growing crops: adequate rainfall is now critical while the danger of hailstorms increases, and late frosts may still occur. Agricultural work accelerates: the wheat is weeded, the first cut of forage is made, the summer-long gathering of fresh feed begins, maize is planted, and vines are sprayed. As the season continues, the farm tasks require more people working together. For instance, several workers in a row weed a field or cut grain; if the family is not large enough, neighbors exchange help. The cattle fairs, held on fixed dates throughout the summer at various places in the region, also begin at this time. In the town, spring weather brings people back to the outdoor gathering places. The talk-groups at times become larger and livelier than usual, for the spring holidays see return visits of some of the temporary labor emigrants.

Summer comes with St. John's day (June 24). In the countryside the wheat reaping has begun, there is a second cut of forage, and the secondary cereals are harvested. The intensity of both labor and socializing increases, until the climax of the agricultural year—the threshing of the wheat in July and August. On one farm after another, large groups of neighbors assemble for the work, and relatives and friends of both landlord and peasant come for the festive meal that follows. The town population grows in summer, and there are more high-status people around— landowners who come from the city for the harvest season, former Montecastellesi who return to family palazzi, and kinsmen of the townspeople who enjoy the "good air" of Montecastello. With the arrival of these visitors, dances and other public entertainments become more frequent, and as the threshing comes to an end peasants appear at these events in increasing numbers.

Now the daily routine is modified by the heat of day. Midday meals are followed by long siestas, and the streets and outdoor sitting places remain deserted until evening. Then the walls, the house steps, the piazzas, and the tables set outside the bars fill up, and animated conversation continues until late into the night. Public ritual is infrequent in summer until mid-August, when a Montecastellese festival coincides with the national holiday week. This is the time when social contact between Montecastello and the outside is at its peak, with more visitors coming to town, and with many Montecastellesi going to the seashore or other vacation places.

The beginning of September sees the re-formation of the local population. The heat of midday subsides and throughout the town conversational groups again gather outdoors during the day. In the countryside, the late-summer vegetables and fruits are picked, forage is planted in the cleared wheat fields, land is plowed. Work routines of the nonagricultural population become more regular after the interruption of summer; children are made ready for the reopening of school; hunting and politics again dominate men's talk.

This yearly round incorporates a shorter-term cycle—the alternation of a festival routine with the routine of everyday life. The festa is a rather frequent event, including every Sunday and at least twenty other days throughout the year. A day of festa is distinctly different from ordinary days in the sights, sounds, and smells of the town. The day begins somewhat later than usual, announced by its characteristic noise, which continues throughout the day—the murmur of people walking and talking, accompanied at frequent intervals by the bells ringing in the festa. Most people do not work, and chores are done early to leave as much time as possible for the social activity of the day. The clothing worn on a festa also marks the day as special; almost everyone tries to look like a lady or gentleman, and the usual distinctions in dress among various social categories are somewhat muted. Except during meal times and in very bad weather, the town is crowded with people from the country, and the piazzas, bars, and other congregating places are filled. Most of the country people go to the morning mass, but many townspeople wait for the late-afternoon service ("the mass of the signori," some call it). After mass people mill about in the piazzas and along the streets; men transact business as they talk; and the little market is alive. Then, quite suddenly, the streets are deserted, and everyone goes home to a dinner which includes more extravagant foods than those on the daily menu. The meal is followed by a rest, and public activity resumes late in the afternoon. This is the time for formal strolls through town and along the passeggiata, and is usually when the special events of a particular festa are scheduled. As darkness nears, the bars become crowded with men playing games and people watching television, while women visit neighbors and kin. Supper is a brief interlude, and socializing on the streets and in the bars continues until late in the evening.

This festa pattern, varying slightly with the season, is repeated on all holidays. It forms a common ground on which the special content and activity of each holiday are superimposed. Some of those specific features, the major events of the ceremonial cycle, are described in chapter 6.

Styles of the Civil Life

If one looks more closely at sociability in the town of Montecastello, one can see the acting out of the dimensions of civiltà that were set forth in the last chapter. Obviously, some behavior that is defined as "civile" is accessible only to an elite, and some only to a kind of elite that scarcely exists any longer. Yet in a more general sense, the idea of "civiltà" aptly characterizes the social life of the town. Patterns inherited from the past have been reworked by contemporary conditions and modified by their diffusion to diverse social categories, but they still define a distinctive kind of town life. This section describes some of the styles of social behavior which communicate the quality of civiltà.

TALKING

Some months after my arrival, I met an old peasant woman near her farm just below the town wall. She asked me how I liked being in Montecastello and what I thought of the place now. Without waiting for my answer, she gestured toward the town above us (which framed her face while she talked) and declared: "*Chiacchiera!* That's what they do. That's what it's all about, there." And she nodded in satisfaction, having summed up the way of life in the town.

Chiacchiera, gossip or idle talk, is a mocking reference to what is indeed almost a way of life in Montecastello—indulging in talk for its own sake. Conversational styles of men and women differ, as do those of different classes. While verbal expertise is important to all, it is the men's talk in public that is most characteristic of the civil life. This kind of talk is developed as a skill, even an art, of discourse, argument, and verbal play. It takes place in the piazzas, the bars, the clubhouses, at the bocce grounds, in the spectator stands at the football field, interspersed with work or business in stores or workshops, and wherever several men may be gathered. The best talk requires a minimum of five or six men, for there must be at least two or three participants to take turns at speaking while the others form an audience. The most active participants tend to be solid citizens—heads of families, middle-aged, and of the higher social strata—but much depends upon individual skills.

The topics of talk are enormously varied, ranging widely over matters of general interest and taking in far more than the local scene. In fact, part of the skill of discourse at its best involves connecting particular cases and events with some broader context. The favorite subjects are politics, food, romance, sports, and people and places—especially arguments about the nature of different groups and ways of life, in which the Montecastellesi try to define their own uniquenesses and commonalities in relation to other people. ("We Italians are . . .; it is our nature to do . . .; the Germans, instead, are . . ." and so on.) However, any topic can be picked up if it lends itself to a development of different aspects and opposing positions.

A talk session often begins as a casual exchange, building up as the talk elaborates and an audience gathers. Once a subject is introduced, someone might follow it up by making a declaration: "I think like this: If . . . would happen, then. . . ." The speaker often develops a number of related points, and finally ends in some general statement: "After all, we Italians understand food, not like those. . . ." The audience follows this presentation and makes its judgment, with appreciative comments or ridicule. Others then counter by spinning off opposing points and developing other arguments, concluding with some generalizations of their own. The audience evaluates the performance by agreeing with one or another of the positions. The point in all this is clearly the verbal game rather than the conclusions reached.

The style and content of women's talk follow a different pattern that is more akin to gossip than to the discourse of civiltà. Among women, talk is not elaborated as a skill in itself or as public performance. It differs little from private settings to public ones. Women's conversational groups are usually smaller than men's, often consisting of only three or four persons. The makeup tends to be fairly stable; generally, some kinswomen and neighbors form a core of regulars who are joined by other participants at different times. Two contexts are most characteristic: women talk while working at their tasks (a common scene is a group sitting in a circle and sewing), and while taking holiday strolls about the town, arm in arm. A few older women of high status engage in verbal acrobatics like the men, but generally women's talk takes more the form of a running commentary. The manner of presentation tends to be indirect, and exchanges often begin as if they were continuing an earlier conversation. Typically, one woman starts with a casual comment about some person or event, and the main issue emerges gradually rather than being set forth.

The subject matter is more personal and more individualized than the men's, with less elevation of particular cases into generalizations. The favorite topics are the events of the female life cycle—courtship, marriage, birth, and child care. However, there is also detailed examination of individuals' behavior. The most biting comments point up the discrepancies between what various people are supposed to be and what they show themselves to be: the woman who puts on airs but is not really a signora, the cleric who does not behave like a man of God, the bride of questionable reputation who claims to be a virgin. Thus, the women's conversation serves as a forum for relating the behavior of actual people to the definitions of social roles.

FORMALITIES OF DAILY INTERACTION

As we were settling into local life, people offered us hospitality, gifts, and assistance of various kinds. If we hesitated to accept, we were encouraged with further insistence accompanied by the statement *"Non fate complimenti!"* (Don't stand on ceremony). We usually accepted gratefully and, we thought, graciously. As we tried to extend favors in return, such as a drink or some food in our house, we found that people regularly refused; we would repeat the offer, then let the matter drop. Soon we learned that on both counts, our ready acceptance of offers and our slight insistence on behalf of our own offers, we were behaving in an uncivilized manner. Offers needed to be refused three times before they could be accepted. The urging that we not stand on ceremony was actually instruction to do the contrary. On the other hand, the Montecastellesi learned to adapt to us; before long, our offers were accepted after only one tentative refusal, in the expectation that we would too readily withdraw them.

The smallest details of interaction in Montecastello are permeated with *complimenti*, "ceremony" of the kind described above. Good manners are defined in terms of the mastery of such formalities.[8] Greeting and addressing others involves an important etiquette that governs the order of greeting, the choice of grammatical forms, and the manner of speech and attitude. Titles are used for every adult who is not a very close relative, an intimate friend, or distinctly a social inferior. A woman is addressed as "Signora" or "Signorina," a man by the highest honorific he can claim—"Professore" or "Dottore" if he is educated, "Sor Giovanni" if he is a member of the elite but not a professional, or by the title of his occupation ("Ragioniere" to an accountant, "Sarto" to a tailor, "Barbiere," and so on). In the course of polite conversation, the title of the person being addressed is repeated as often as possible. Similarly, even casual exchanges are dominated by expressions of greeting and by polite phrases lavishly scattered through the conversation. There is a correct mode of entering other people's houses and of receiving others into one's own. Serving food and drink properly and accepting service from others involves a complicated procedure. Matters of business are also handled with a certain etiquette; for instance, in talking about or exchanging money, each party makes a point of denying any material interest.

These observances define proper behavior at all times, and formalities exist (though of different kinds and to different degrees) in all classes and in relations both within and between classes. Lapses are appropriate only among close kin and the most intimate friends, and clearly the etiquette acts to preserve the distance that already exists in other relationships. In the Montecastellesi's own view, such formalities are at the core of what is meant by "civile" behavior.

PUBLIC APPEARANCES

One evening I joined a group watching television in a local bar. The main interest of the evening's schedule was a popular quiz program. A tense moment in the show came when a contestant was faced with a difficult question, on which a large prize depended. The answer he gave was wrong. My own reaction was one of regret for the lost fortune, but that of the people around me was different. They were saying to each other, with expressions of disgust: "*Ha fatto brutta figura!*" (He has lost face, i.e., made an ugly appearance).

The concern with one's *bella figura,* or "good face," is ever-present as a quite self-conscious guide to behavior. The concept is a measure of personal integrity, but it has little to do with one's essence, character, intention, or other inner condition; rather it centers upon public appearances. To acquire and preserve bella figura require being impeccable before the eyes of others. Physically, one must be as immaculate and elegant as possible; if not at all times, given the necessities of work, then at least when engaging in social interaction after work. One must always present a pleasant face to the world, regardless of the negative emotions that may simmer behind it. One must carefully observe the formalities already described; even an unintentional violation will cause a person to bemoan, *"Ho fatto brutta figura!"* One must show oneself to be knowledgeable of the proper order of rights and obligations in social relations. (A butcher's wife once lamented to me about the brutta figura she had made for erring in a judgment of two of her customers' relative social rank and awarding the last available pork chop to the wrong one.)

This emphasis upon appearances is central to the notion of civiltà, and it extends readily to the lower strata of the population. Like honor for the Southern Italian, it can be translated into symbolic counters that are available even to the poor and uneducated. Thus, people who would hesitate to claim civiltà on other grounds take care to defend their bella figura.

ORGANIZED SOCIABILITY

During the Carnival period, a group of young adult men of the town discussed their schedule of activities for the final week. On Thursday an organized supper at the CRAL, followed by dancing. On Friday a formal dance in the large meeting-room of the town hall, organized by a local committee for the benefit of the Red Cross. On Saturday a dance at a town about an hour's drive away. Early Sunday, a drive to Rome for a football match with a return drive in the evening, and that same night a dance at the recently opened platform in San Giovanni (not a highly valued affair because of the large number of peasants expected, but nevertheless something to do). On Monday—nothing yet, so they would have to "organize something." On Tuesday, the last night of Carnival, a dance at the theater in Todi. On Wednesday, the festivities in Montecastello for the death of Carnival, to be followed by a spaghetti supper in the wineshop. We listened to the schedule in amazement, for all of the men would be working full days at their jobs and would be able to sleep only a few hours each night. As the week went on, some of the men did, in fact, rigorously pursue the schedule, their determination increasing as their exhaustion mounted and their enjoyment clearly diminished.

Carnival week is an unusual time representing a peak of public social activity, and few people engage in the Carnival events with the exertion of the men described above. Yet the pattern of organized sociability is important throughout the year for a substantial part of the town population. There are formal clubs which arrange social occasions, and many holidays provide excuses for parties, excursions, or other happenings. Even without a ready excuse a casual gathering of people might call for the local accordionist and organize a dance, or a family might invite several others for an evening of *tombola* (a game like bingo). This activity represents a range of inclusiveness, from events that take in only a limited clique to those that are community-wide.

The younger people explain this activity as a way of alleviating the boredom (*noia*) of routine life in Montecastello. As cars and motor scooters are increasingly available, they underline their attitude with a new kind of event—the practice of collecting a group to attend a dance or simply to have coffee in one of the larger towns nearby. However, older people insist that traditional Montecastello, in the days when it was *truly* civile, had the liveliest round of social events in the area—"one did not need to go anywhere else for entertainment."

All the occasions referred to here require the full play of formalities, sometimes to the point of self-parody.

One evening, I attended a public dance at the new dance-platform. The dance was commercially operated, and a small admission was charged. The people present included a wide range of the local population, from upper-level townspeople to peasants. All the rituals of formal dances (chaperonage, formalized requests for dances, correct dancing positions, the offering of refreshments at the bar, etc.) were carefully and, for the most part, rather self-consciously observed. At one point a highly respected professional man of the town asked a peasant girl to dance, a girl barely out of adolescence, whom he knew casually. He bowed to her slightly and said, "*Balli, Signorina?*" A woman who was standing with me, watching this, erupted into giggles. The dottore had addressed the girl in the familiar, as was appropriate to their relative status, but accompanying it with the formal "Signorina" and the ceremonious bow only heightened the incongruity of the situation.

In addition to the formally organized social activity, informal socializing is regularly elevated into an event in itself. A walk around the town with a few companions may be prepared for and carried out as if it were a formal social occasion. Indeed, this activity is the favorite holiday pastime, institutionalized as the *passeggiata*. The Montecastellesi dress up in their best and, arranging themselves into small groups, walk back and forth along the route looking at each other, greeting each other, exclaiming over each other's children, and generally reveling in the sport of public meeting. To a lesser extent, a spontaneous street exchange may be treated in the same way. Not only are occasions for formal and organized sociability maximized, but routine social intercourse is also elaborated into an occasion whenever possible.

HOSPITALITY, HOSTILITY, AND HUMOR

In the early months of the fieldwork, I marveled at the ease with which we were able to settle into community life, establish rapport with a wide range of people, and maintain relations of cordial acquaintance with everyone else. Then, during the fourth or fifth month, we began to encounter a series of inexplicable difficulties in various relationships, until one day, much to my alarm, I realized that we had acquired a number of "enemies." It was only some time later that I understood this meant that our time as strangers, to whom hospitality must be extended, had come to an end, and that we could now become part of the hostilities, feuds, and embroilments that are normal to community life.

The change in behavior toward us was subtle and disconcerting, for the Montecastellesi are very adept at the forms of hospitality, including the careful presentation of good will to the outsider. People's behavior toward strangers (at least those who seem to be of relatively high status) is quite explicitly guided by their self-definition as "gente civile." Hospitable behavior involves, at a minimum, greeting the stranger cordially or showing readiness to respond to a greeting, observing rigorously the formalities of deference, and showing friendliness and good intentions. Wherever possible, the stranger should be invited into one's home, ushered into a suitable place for receiving guests, and offered a drink or food (the offer to be repeated until he accepts). Hospitality also requires avoiding any talk that might be construed as offensive to the stranger, and any talk that might reveal unpleasantness in the host's own life. Rationalizing hospitality as a means of easing and welcoming the stranger, Montecastellesi use these formalities to conceal all possibly damaging information about themselves.

It was as hard to learn about hostility directed to others as about hostility directed toward us, because the Montecastellesi are extremely careful about expressing hostility openly or directly. Gradually, we began to get reports of one family's conflict with another, but always from third parties. Direct interaction between the hostile parties often revealed no evidence of discord; at most, a degree of coolness and distance would be maintained. If the breach were really serious, the parties would cease to speak and would avoid recognizing each other in public. On the rare occasions when hostility erupted in a direct encounter, other people expressed ridicule and disdain, even while recognizing that one or another of the parties was justified. Open conflict is evidence of a lack of civiltà.

This wariness in dealing with hostility is matched by a sensitivity to hostile overtones wherever they might conceivably occur. People frequently inquired into conflicts they assumed we were involved in, but of which we were unaware. Similarly, while almost everyone was eager to express himself on the subject of politics in general, most were cautious about asserting their specific loyalties; they would explain that one must be careful about offending others, or that enemies might be listening.

Perhaps the most common way in which hostility is expressed is in the veiled and deflected form of humor. Pranks, teasing, and joking go on constantly. A frequent sight is a group of men jovially goading some half-witted or otherwise vulnerable lower-class individual; though people enjoy even more the human failings of those of higher class, they are understandably cautious about showing it in public. Humor is used to talk about sex, male-female differences, and the interaction between men and women—in a kind of persistent and overtly good-natured battle of the sexes that is unquestionably grounded in real hostility. Humor is used by married men to taunt the bachelors and vice versa. It is used to characterize people who practice a particular occupation by persons of other occupations. It is used by laymen to talk about the clergy. It is the mode for expressing (and exaggerating) differences between the Montecastellesi and other peoples or other places. Sayings, verses, and stories—always humorous and often vicious—describe the qualities of various communities, regions, and nations. In general, humor seems to be a mode of intercourse between persons of different social and economic categories, of different sexes, communities, or nationalities—persons among whom there is real divergence of interest yet among whom an overt expression of hostility cannot be tolerated.

These forms for the treatment of strangers and for handling hostile relationships are part of what is defined as civile behavior. Like the bella figura, however, they extend more widely through the population than the explicit concern with civiltà.

INVOLVEMENT IN THE WORLD OUTSIDE

On more than one occasion I joined animated conversations already in progress in which people were dissecting and evaluating the private lives of individuals (such as the details of their childbirth and their family problems). I assumed such persons must be intimately known to the speakers, only to discover that the subjects of conversation were the royal family of Iran or the Kennedys. Many women who had never been beyond the immediate region not only filled local scenes with talk of international society but effectively reproduced some of its ways—for example, in their holiday clothes carefully copied by local dressmakers from magazine pictures of the latest Paris fashions.

The concern with the world beyond the community constitutes a framework within which styles are introduced, valued, perpetuated, or discarded. This concern has obviously intensified in recent years with the vast increase in possibilities for contact with other places, both directly through expanded means of transport, and indirectly through radio and television, newspapers, and magazines. However, the pattern of receptiveness to styles from the outside is not recent. The larger world has long been brought into the community through the local upper class, whose familiarity with major centers was, in fact, one of the defining features of their civiltà. In the past as at present, many townspeople seem to have shared an intense interest in outside fashions, events, and personalities, and a readiness to learn from them. In addition, movement back and forth between Montecastello and urban places was and is a highly valued activity in its own right. Local routines are thus constantly punctuated by reminders of a wider scene; reminders that come in the form of references to that larger world, the incorporation of modes of behavior from it into local activities, and increasingly, the actual comings and goings of the population.

CHAPTER 3

———— ◆ ————

The Mezzadria System

THE CIVIL LIFE is grounded in town, but it presupposes an integral organization of town and country. The countryside is the dependent territory of an urban-like center whose influence permeates the country. On the other hand, the townsman's own civiltà incorporates a degree of familiarity with the country and certain sentiments about it. This interdependence is both the source and the product of the dominant institution of Montecastellese agriculture, the *mezzadria*. This agricultural system forms the background of the civil life—supporting it economically, providing a structure of town-country relationships, and defining roles that shape the ideology of civiltà.

The Organization of Production

The term "mezzadria" refers to a contractual relationship between a cultivator and a landowner or other holder of rights over land, on the principle of dividing both expenses and products half-and-half. However, in the form that it takes throughout this region of Central Italy, the so-called classical mezzadria, it constitutes a whole system of production. In 1960 about two-thirds of the land area in the commune was in mezzadria tenure. The remaining third was divided, approximately equally, between land in peasant proprietorship and enterprises employing salaried labor. The land owned by peasant proprietors is for the most part in small holdings that are more intensively cultivated than the mezzadria land. The land held in salaried-labor enterprises refers primarily to parts of large estates; some of this land is in extensive cultivation, but much consists of woods and unproductive land.

In the sense that the mezzadria entails a division of produce in kind, it is a form of sharecropping, but it is distinguished by three essential elements. The unit of land worked is an integrated farm committed to polyculture; the labor unit is a family who live on the farm; and both landowner and cultivator actively participate in the operation of the enterprise. Thus, the mezzadria must be differentiated from those share systems in which land is granted as separate plots, in which the cultivators do not live on the land, or in which they are contracted for as individuals. Similarly, it should be distinguished from forms of sharecropping in which a landowner confers the farm and simply collects a share-payment rent for it, leaving decisions and investments to the cultivator; and from those in which a proprietor or a subcontractor manages the entire enterprise and provides all investment, limiting the cultivator's participation to the actual labor.[1] Other characteristics of the mezzadria, such as the long duration of contracts and the fixed apportioning of the division, also define it among sharecropping systems, but it is the farm, the family, and the specific roles of landlord and peasant that mark a distinctive Central Italian agricultural organization. The system is far more uniform than the large and diverse area it covers would lead one to expect. Nevertheless, specific details vary locally and over time. The description here is of the mezzadria as practiced in Montecastello during 1960–61.

The land is granted and worked in the form of a relatively self-contained farm, which is maintained over time as a unit and is operated as a single enterprise. Ideally, the farm comprises a variety of resources: arable land (including plots at different altitudes and some irrigated land where possible), olive trees, vines, fruit trees, meadow, pasture land, and woods. Typically, land is dispersed in at least three or four plots, but the various resources are exploited in a closely integrated manner. In addition to the land the farm must include, by the terms of the mezzadria contract, a farmhouse, animal stalls, sheds, and a well or cistern. In Montecastello as in most of Umbria, it also includes livestock; in other areas the livestock are owned in common. In addition, certain large items of equipment are considered part of the fixed capital that makes up the farm.

While the individual farm is a viable unit in itself, proprietors who have at least eight or nine farms situated contiguously generally operate them as part of a fattoria. The fattoria organizes the production and marketing of all the farms. It contains equipment and services for the common use, such as tractors and other machinery, silos, tobacco drying-sheds, sometimes a steam-driven thresher, and perhaps stud animals. It also includes a wine cellar, an oil mill, and sometimes a grain mill. The fattoria is under the direction of an agent or fattore, who usually has some training in agrarian technology; one of Montecastello's fattori even has a university degree in agronomy. In Montecastello, there are three such fattorie, each comprising ten farms. Landlords whose property includes fewer farms, or whose farms are dispersed, may employ a fattore who circulates among the separate farms. Smaller-scale owners in Montecastello generally direct the agricultural enterprise personally, while those who do not live locally usually manage with an agent who handles the sale of animals and supervises the main harvests.

The size of the farm is limited by two factors: it must be large enough to support a family without major dependence upon outside staples; yet it must be within the labor capacity of that group, given the available technology. The actual distribution by size of the mezzadria farms in Montecastello is shown in Table 4, which includes separate breakdowns for the total area of the farms and for the arable area. The range in size is from under 2 hectares (mainly farms in the plain, whose land is intensively cultivated) to about 30 hectares (farms in the higher zones, generally including land in pasture or woods). Ninety percent of the farms have between 2 and 15 hectares of arable land. The median size of farms (considered either by total area or by arable area) is between 7.5 and 10 hectares.[2]

The farm has a unitary identity, marked by its traditional name, which is distinct from that of the current peasant or landowner. It is valued, sold, and inherited as a unit, and is so transferred to other families of mezzadri. From time to time plots may be added to or detached from a farm; occasionally whole farms are broken up and new ones created. Such changes, however, are limited by the necessity that a farm include a combination of resources, buildings, and equipment that requires an initial capital outlay and that, once built up, is not readily divisible.

Table 4 Size and Arable of Mezzadria Farms by Location, 1960

Location of Farm						Total Size of Farm (hectares) [a]							
	.5–1.9	2.0–3.4	3.5–4.9	5.0–7.4	7.5–9.9	10.0–12.4	12.5–14.9	15.0–17.4	17.5–19.9	20.0–24.9	25.0–29.9	30.0–34.9	Total
Plain	3	4	10	7	11	7	5	2	0	0	0	0	49
Low & mid. hills	7	7	16	26	15	15	11	4	3	5	0	1	110
High bills [b]	0	2	4	4	13	7	3	6	2	4	1	0	46
Unknown [c]	0	0	1	3	0	2	1	0	1	0	0	0	8
Total	10	13	31	40	39	31	20	12	6	9	1	1	213

Location of Farm						Amount of Arable Held by Farm (hectares)							
	.5–1.9	2.0–3.4	3.5–4.9	5.0–7.4	7.5–9.9	10.0–12.4	12.5–14.9	15.0–17.4	17.5–19.9	20.0–24.9	25.0–29.9	30.0–34.9	Total
Plain	3	4	11	6	12	7	4	2	0	0	0	0	49
Low & mid. hills	7	7	19	28	16	17	9	6	1	0	0	0	110
High bills [b]	0	3	4	7	14	7	7	2	2	0	0	0	46
Unknown [c]	0	1	0	3	1	3	0	0	0	0	0	0	8
Total	10	15	34	44	43	34	20	10	3	0	0	0	213

[a] Including land in arable, arboriculture, pasture, woods, and unproductive land.
[b] Frazione of Doglio.
[c] The location of eight farms was not indicated in the available data.

Wills and arrangements among heirs recognize this integrity of the farm within the legal requirement of partible inheritance. Whenever possible, inequalities of shares are compensated for through cash payment or other nonland assets rather than the breaking up of a farm. One case will serve as an example.

B.E. owned three mezzadria farms, two of about 10 hectares each and one of about 5 hectares. He had four sons, three of whom were married. Before his death, B.E. divided his property among his sons, leaving for himself the usufruct (the rights to all the income) for the rest of his life. One farm was given to each of the married sons. The son who received the smallest farm was also given a piece of property in town. The unmarried son was given money and notes equivalent in value to the shares of the other sons. Neither the father nor any of the heirs considered the possibility of dividing any of the farms. At the same time, the family house in town was divided, giving one son ownership of the top floor and another son the two lower floors.

This inheritance practice acts as a brake on fragmentation of land. Nevertheless, over the past several decades there has been a steady decrease in the size of farms. It can be estimated that the average farm size in Montecastello at the beginning of the twentieth century was 15–20 hectares. Following the introduction of artificial forage, landowners often found they could realize greater income by dividing a large farm (say, 20 or more hectares) into two smaller farms.[3] The steadily increasing peasant population until World War II assured sufficient labor to work the additional farms. The main problem was in the capital needed for a new house and farm equipment. Since the war, other factors have encouraged a breakup of farms: technological improvements that have made possible more intensive cultivation, and the accelerating emigration of peasant labor. Even where capital is sufficient, however, the division of farms does not go on indefinitely if they continue to be worked in mezzadria, for a limit is set by the minimum area required to support a family.

The labor force of the mezzadria farm is a peasant family. According to the contract they must live continually on the farm and are responsible for all labor required for cultivation, harvest, first handling of the products, and care of the animals. The whole family is bound by the contract that the *mezzadro*—the head of the family—enters into, and family labor cannot be diverted to other enterprises without explicit consent of the landlord. In addition to the labor of the family itself, there may also be a hired helper who lives with the family, the *garzone*. The mezzadro organizes and directs the work of the household and has legal control over the disposition of family resources, both material and manpower. The mezzadria family has long been among the largest of any occupational category in Italy. However, a declining birth rate since about 1930 and the emigration of young adults since the last war have reduced its size. Table 5 summarizes the mezzadria labor units in Mon-

Table 5   Labor Force of
Mezzadria Farms, 1960

Number of Workers per Farm	Number of Farms
2– 2.5	32
3– 3.5	43
4– 4.5	44
5– 5.5	37
6– 6.5	22
7– 7.5	17
8– 8.5	10
9– 9.5	4
10–10.5	2
11–11.5	1
12–12.5	1
Total	213

tecastello at the time of the study. The number of workers (defined as adults fully employed on the farm, boys being considered one-half a worker) on mezzadria farms ranges from 2 to 12, with the median at about 4.5 and an average of just under 6.

In addition to their own labor and that of the occasional garzone, the peasant family utilizes other sources of labor at peak periods. Extra workers may be hired for specific activities, such as the olive harvest, and paid in produce; these workers, many of them women, are generally members of other mezzadria families whose farms lack a field in the olive zone. However, since most labor is absorbed by the mezzadria system, extra hands are scarce. Thus, the primary source of labor beyond the family is the system of reciprocal work-exchange, the *aiutarella*. Neighboring families (vicini) send some of their members to help out when needed, and when tasks require a large number of hands the vicini pool their labor and move from one farm to another. In either case people keep track, at least roughly, of the number of man-hours given and owed.

The mezzadria system is feasible only if a general balance is maintained between the size of the peasant family and the size of the farm. The balance that holds for contemporary Montecastello is indicated in Table 6. The labor unit increases with the arable area of the farm—from about 2.5 workers for farms under 2 hectares, to 7 or more workers on farms over 15 hectares. However, the larger the farm, the fewer the workers per unit area. A general balance between land and labor holds over time because of the possibility for families to change farms. Varia-

Table 6   Labor Force of Mezzadria Farms by Arable Area of Farm, 1960

Area of Farm (hectares)	No. of Farms	Median Area of Farm (hectares)	Median No. of Workers per Farm	Ratio of Median No. of Workers to Median Area
0.5– 1.9	10	1.5	2.5	1.67
2.0– 4.9	49	4.0	3.0	.75
5.0– 9.9	87	7.0	4.0	.57
10.0–14.9	54	12.0	6.0	.50
15.0–19.9	13	15.5	7.0	.46
Total	213	7.0	4.0	.57

tion in a family's labor capacity may be adjusted to by certain modifications in the choice of secondary crops, or the landowner's possible reassignment of fields among his mezzadri; but significant change in the size of a family usually results in either the peasant's or landlord's termination of the contract.

Expanding families have access to larger farms. So long as the farms remain nonmechanized, it is often more advantageous for a sizable peasant family to cultivate one large farm than to disperse to two smaller farms. Labor can be more efficiently coordinated, and there is less capital investment per person. At the same time, the diversity of crops in combination with animal husbandry can absorb the labor of a large family the year round. When a household becomes too large for any available farm, it divides and one segment may take over another farm. On the other hand, if the family loses some of its workers, it may be compelled to move to a smaller farm.

Although a certain amount of movement among farms is essential to the mezzadria system, until recently it was common for a family to remain on the same farm for decades and often for generations. The Montecastellese countryside had a long period of steady population growth from the end of the eighteenth century until after World War II. As good land became more scarce, the additional labor went into more intensified working of the farm a family already occupied. Since about 1950, however, the exodus from the land has meant more frequent changes and a better choice of farms for those who remain. The remaining families, with fewer hands, have increasingly favored farms that can be worked most easily and most productively on the basis of the improved technology. This has resulted in a net movement down from the higher to the lower altitudes.

The mezzadria system incorporates a logic of production based on considerations at two levels. The landowner operates in a commercial economy, selling livestock and most of his share of the produce. For the most part this is small-scale commerce in limited regional markets, and there is little incentive for him to maximize productivity through greater investment and specialization. On the other hand, the cultivator is concerned with family subsistence. The result is an extreme diversification of production on each farm. Each one repeats in fairly standard combination the whole range of subsistence and cash products. Each farm has a third to a half of its area in wheat, another third or more in forage, several other field crops, olives, vines, a number of garden vegetables, and several kinds of animals. The main variations from one farm to another occur in minor products and industrial crops. In general, however, efforts are made to minimize and compensate for the special ecological features of a farm, rather than treating them as possibilities for specialization. The standard peasant response to the question of what a farm raises is "a little of everything."

This variety reflects the mezzadria system's basic requirement that each farm provide self-sufficiency for the peasant family. To this end too, crops are raised at the extremes of their environmental limits, and farms include fields in different zones at some distance from each other. Variety is also increased by combining different products on the same plot. The most important aspect of this is the pattern of arboriculture. Fruit and nut trees, olives, and trees whose leaves provide fresh animal feed are grown in cultivated fields. Moreover, grapes are raised among the crops, the vines trained over trees which have been planted in widely spaced rows both within the fields and along their borders. Raising the vines on trees makes them less vulnerable to humidity and frost, making it possible to extend grape cultivation to the plains. It also protects the vines against damage by animals and provides some defense against the spread of phylloxera. At the same time, the supporting trees are valuable in themselves. Elm was introduced early and had some commercial importance as a source of timber, but maple (*lo schiuccio*) soon became the preferred vine support, its leafy branches cut for forage. In the eighteenth century mulberry was added, supplying the growing household industry of silkworm raising.

This thoroughgoing nonspecialization of the mezzadria farm represents economy for the peasant. A great diversity of products can be obtained from a limited amount of land; livestock can be fed with little pasture; one fertilizing serves for several crops. Most of all, polyculture spreads the risks. As Desplanques has pointed out, the Umbrian climate permits a wide variety of cultigens, but its instability and the many seasonal dangers mean that each crop may be struck with disaster (1969:73). There is a degree of insurance in not depending upon any single product and in having fields in different climatic zones.

The strategy toward farm self-sufficiency also accounts for much of the mezzadria's resistance to modernization of the agricultural economy. Throughout the nineteenth and early twentieth centuries the mezzadri expanded maize cultivation, contrary to all norms of good agrarian technique. Productivity was low, other crops suffered, and pellagra was endemic, but—as peasants said—a hectare of *granturco* filled the stomach more than other cereals, forage, or fallow. Wheat persists today for similar reasons, given the fact that labor is now more at a premium than land. Wheat provides a more dependable subsistence with less labor than potentially more profitable crops like forage or tobacco.

It is not peasant conservativism but realism that has inhibited greater commitment to commercial production. The industrial crops were taken on as additions to the polyculture complex, and their expansion is limited by the demands of that complex. Thus, the fact that tobacco is labor consuming, particularly during the peaks of the wheat cycle, means it is uneconomical for a small family. Moreover, the costs of industrial crops (not only the initial capital investment but the ongoing expenses that the peasant shares) must be weighed against the dependability of income.

The mezzadro confronts several capricious forces: natural disasters of weather and plant disease; market fluctuations and state regulations; and the uncertainty of ever seeing cash returns once the landlord has calculated the year's accounts. Wheat is the one cash crop that has been successful in the long range, for it is predictable in its requirements and risks, fairly stable in price, and sure cash in hand for the peasant.

If the landowner has more to gain and less to lose than the peasant by moving toward greater specialization, he too is constrained by the imperative that the farm feed its labor force, and he too is concerned with minimizing risk. The landowners of Montecastello depend upon the safety of their capital and the relative security of their income; few are in a position to make substantial investments or take on considerable risks for the possibility of greater profits. Conflict of interest with the mezzadro emerges mainly where the relative contributions of capital and labor are at issue. Thus, the landowner complains that the mezzadri are unwilling to do the work required for tobacco or sugar beet, while the peasant protests that the land is inadequate and the owner refuses to invest in improvements. In fact, the rationales of both are complementary, and both are enmeshed in the limiting conditions of family-farm production.

Where the classical mezzadria predominates, the contrast between landlords and mezzadri—one oriented to the market and the other geared to family subsistence—is striking and tends to eclipse other economic roles and relationships. However, the mezzadria never absorbed all land or all labor in Montecastello, or anywhere in the mezzadria area. There were always many people, including mezzadria landlords and peasants, who owned bits of land that they worked themselves or leased out under contracts other than mezzadria. In addition, the agricultural labor force always included, along with the stable mezzadri, a floating population—men who for some period of time might form part of mezzadria families, and at other times might hire out as *garzoni* or day-laborers or join the groups of migrants who worked on the harvests in the Maremma, the Tuscan coastal plain.

At the same time, mezzadri were not necessarily excluded from other economic roles or from involvement in the market. The contract's prohibition on work outside the farm was often not enforced, especially when a farm could barely sustain the family. In fact, landowners frequently employed their mezzadri for wages on odd jobs (at a rate that was always considerably less than the going wage) or helped them find supplementary work. On the other hand, mezzadri themselves sometimes hired labor, both on a long-term basis and for specific tasks.

Moreover, peasants moved in and out of the mezzadria system. In times of prosperity, when there were improved opportunities for wage labor elsewhere, mezzadri tended to leave marginal farms; in difficult times they would return to mezzadria. Finally, although the system formally defined marketing and account-keeping as functions of the landlord, there is ample evidence that mezzadri were generally well aware of market conditions in the area, familiar with the concept of agriculture as a business, and often adept at mental bookkeeping. Indeed, it is a consequence of the mezzadria system that the peasant is kept at once in contact with the market and marginal to it.

Landlord and Peasant

Central to the mezzadria system of production is the definition of a relationship between landowner and cultivator. Through that relationship and its ramifications, the mezzadria forges links between town and country. The rights and duties of landlord and peasant are specified in an explicit contract that forms the outline of a broader, informal relationship. This section describes the contractual tie between landlord and peasant as manifested in Montecastello during the period of the field study.

The mezzadria contract defines an association between the grantor of a farm (*concedente* or padrone) and the head of a peasant family (mezzadro or *colono*) on the principle that one party provides capital and the other party labor, while investment and returns of the enterprise are divided half-and-half. The Italian agricultural census of 1961 classifies this association as an enterprise in which an entrepreneur confers the landed capital and "identifies himself" with a cultivator. This distinguishes it from agricultural enterprises in which the entrepreneur remains detached from the labor force, which is constituted by wage laborers and/or sharecroppers (ISTAT 1961b:16). The term "identifies" is not only the rationalization prevailing among defenders of the mezzadria system, who think of it as a partnership; it also describes the fact that investment and operations are shared between landlord-entrepreneur and mezzadro.

The landlord provides the major capital and the direction of the enterprise. His responsibility is to furnish the farm, pay all taxes on it, maintain it, and pay for all improvements on it. He also provides some major items of large equipment (such as seeding and mowing machines) and livestock. (In this area, if the mezzadro contributes to the purchase of an animal, he is paid an annual interest on his share.) The proprietor advances all capital as needed. Usually this includes the colono's part of those expenses which are supposed to be shared; the sums are debited without interest to the colono's account until the end of the year. In addition, the proprietor is obliged to supply (also as a loan without interest) whatever food or money is required to support the peasant family if the harvest is poor, or at other times of special need. The peasant family provides all the labor and a minor portion of the nonlanded capital. The mezzadro furnishes the tools, the oxcart, and usually the small machines such as plows and harrows. Operating costs of the enterprise are divided in half: seed, fertilizer, animal feed, insecticides, vine sprays, machinery upkeep, fire and hail insurance, various taxes, veterinary services, and other expenses. Both produce and cash income are divided, theoretically in a ratio that reflects the contributions of each party. In 1948, the official share of the colono was raised to 53 percent, with 47 percent going to the landowner. However, other formulas may be negotiated in special circumstances.

The landlord is defined as the director of the enterprise, and if there is a fattore he is the landlord's representative. The law states that the director must "observe the rules of good agrarian technique," but this is clearly one of the less enforceable provisions. The mezzadro is supposed to be consulted, though the extent and manner of this consultation are unspecified. In some fattorie, the heads of all the peasant families used to meet regularly in a kind of council; for the most part, consultation was and is informal. The degree of participation of both landlord and peasant in the decisions of the enterprise varies a good deal. On the fattorie where skilled fattori are permanently resident and there is some effort to expand commercial production, both landlords and peasants have a less active role than the fattore. However, the fattoria is only an organization superimposed upon separate farms, which remain the essential units of production, and each mezzadro retains some control over his own farm. In the case of farms that are not in fattorie, the degree of autonomy left to the peasant depends upon where the landlord lives and how much he is inclined to be involved. In most cases, the landlord lives in the community or comes there often, and he in fact manages the enterprise. Even so, the colono generally has an active part in decisions about production, and he is in charge of day-to-day operations.

The contract holds for at least one year. It is renewed tacitly from year to year unless notice (the *disdetta*) is given by either party before the end of February. In accordance with the 1948 law, the proprietor may dismiss the peasant only with "just cause," which includes serious non-fulfillment of the contract, an illegal act by the colono against the landowner, an insufficient number of working hands, or the proprietor's intention to work the land himself or to convert it to some other allowable use. In effect, these restrictions virtually prevent the landlord from dismissing a family (a quite common event in times and places in which labor was in oversupply). The peasant family is not restricted from leaving the land, provided ample notice is given and all terms are fulfilled. Legally, individual members of the family may not leave without consent of the landowner, but the shortage of mezzadri now makes it difficult for padroni to withhold consent.

News of the availability of a farm or family travels by word of mouth, and either the landlord or the colono may approach a likely prospect. The new colono and his family take over the care of the animals and their feed in July. They gradually assume charge of the crops for the following year, while the outgoing family continues the harvests. The departing colono retains the use of a storeroom in the farmhouse until after the last harvest—the olives. When the final accounting is made the following March, he is compensated for any investment he has made in the permanent equipment of the farm.

The financial status of the enterprise is recorded in the *libretto colonico*, the yearly account book maintained by the proprietor or his agent. At the beginning of the year, the inventory of the farm is consigned to the colono. The monetary value of all the livestock (*scorte vive*) is calculated on the basis of prices in the July fair at Doglio, and the sum is debited to the colono. The value of the *scorte morte* (hay, feed, manure, etc.) is also calculated, according to the official standards set by a provincial commission; one-half of the value is marked to the debit of the colono. During the year, every sharable expense, special investments by either party, and all cash income are recorded in the libretto. Also marked are any sharable losses, such as the death of an animal. At the end of the year, the colono's account is settled. The current value of the existent livestock and other scorte is recalculated as a credit; 53 percent of the income is credited, and one-half of the expenses is debited. The previous year's debt or credit (if it was not paid in cash) is added.

The difference between the income recorded in the libretto (mainly from the sale of animals) and the expenses recorded in the libretto (both livestock and farm expenses) is the colono's credit for the year. The credit is generally paid in cash today, but it used to be common for landlords to retain a portion of the credit against future debts. If the difference consists of a debt for the peasant, it is always applied against the following year. Until recent years, the peasant would also be credited with the so-called *conguaglio* (payment of balance), a variable monetary allotment which was supposed to compensate for any departure from the ideal equality of investment and profit, the specific amount being determined by bargaining each year. This payment was eliminated in Montecastello when the share of the colono was increased to 53 percent.

The crops are divided in kind at the time of each harvest. The division may vary from the usual ratio by mutual agreement, particularly for crops which require unusual investment by either party; for example, tobacco is divided with 60 percent going to the colono. An abbreviated description of a wheat harvest which I observed illustrates how the division is carried out.

A member of the landowner's family attended the threshing. He arrived at the farm by automobile and was greeted deferentially by the peasant family, the neighbors of surrounding farms (there as part of the aiutarella exchange), and other friends and relatives of the family. . . . Some twenty men worked at the threshing machine, while the women prepared the food for the day and carried wine and water to the men. The padrone sat in the shade and presided over the scales. As each sack was filled from the thresher, two men carried it to the scales, and the padrone adjusted the quantity of grain in the sack to equal one quintal. The filled sacks were set aside. All present kept count of the number of sacks and speculated on the final number, lamenting over the poor prospects in comparison with last year's abundant harvest. The colono of the farm did not work himself but he assigned tasks, oversaw the threshing, and observed the weighing. When 100 quintals were obtained, a loud whistle was sounded from the thresher, a signal for jubilation and renewed effort. . . . When the threshing was done, the whistle sounded again. While the men rested in the shade and joked with each other, the padrone calculated the division in the presence of his fattore, the colono, and an educated adult son of the peasant family. From the common pile of sacks, the required amounts were set aside for the seed and for other shared payments. The rental of the thresher was calculated and paid.[4] The remainder

was divided on a 53:47 ratio. . . . There followed a festive dinner provided by
the peasant family. The padrone sat at the head of a table with the fattore,
members of their families, honored guests, and the man in charge of the
thresher. The colono and the neighbor men sat at a low table in a shed. The
women served and later ate together in the kitchen. . . .

In former times, the grain scattered on the threshing floor, one or two
quintals, would be left for the colono; today, it is collected and divided.
This change is regarded as indicative of the fact that the mezzadria has
become a more businesslike association, rather than a system of customary obligations and mutual favors between landlord and peasant. Similarly, the colono used to send a portion of every dish of the meal to each
member of the landowning family who could not attend—a practice now
rare.

The next day, the colono would deliver the landowner's sacks to his
warehouse, provided it was within the distance specified by law. Of his
own portion, several sacks would supply the family's bread and pasta for
the next year, others would pay debts and donations of various kinds,
and the remainder would be sold for cash. As required by law, both
landowner and peasant would sell some of their wheat to the Consorzio,
an official agency that serves to regulate the market. Most likely the peasant would sell all his surplus at once, but the landowner would try to
hold his until the following spring, when prices would be higher. In the
past, the landlord had the right of first refusal on the peasant's share.

In addition to the fundamental terms of the contract, there are sub-
sidiary rights and obligations. The peasant is entitled to cultivate a plot
of land as a family vegetable garden, to take wood from the farm for family use and to raise a certain number of pigs, fowl, and other courtyard
animals without sharing the profits. In the past the colono had to make
various gratuities to the proprietor. Until the early twentieth century,
these consisted of substantial payments and unpaid labor. The colono
shared the land taxes and paid the proprietor fees for the house, the garden, and each work animal. He was required to plant a certain number
of trees each year, to dig ditches, and to perform other work that sometimes amounted to minor land reclamation. He provided transport services, sawed firewood and drew well water for the padrone's household,
and supplied feed for his stables, while the peasant women did the
laundry of the padrone's family.

The last of the colono's obligations to be suppressed were the *regalie*, gifts of fowl and eggs in specific quantities (according to the size of the farm) at fixed times: capons at Christmas, hens at Carnival, eggs at Easter, and geese or chickens at the festa of mid-August. The land-owners explain these payments as compensation for the damage to the farm and consumption of produce by the colono's poultry. To the peasants and their political champions, these gifts symbolize the servitude of earlier days. In fact, the regalie were always treated as distinct from the division of expenses and profits, and they were presented as offerings to the padrone rather than in the spirit of a contract. Yet in 1961, many people in Montecastello still regarded the regalie as a fundamental part of the mezzadria relationship, though they had been legally optional since 1948. They are no longer obligations, and political pressures require the peasants to denounce them, but similar gifts are still made quietly to persons who can bestow favors, including landlords.

The official mezzadria contract specifies only the basic terms, and there is considerable room for variation in the way they are implemented. Specific arrangements may be written into the contract or left to verbal agreement. At the same time, actual practice may depart considerably from the formal terms. Until the last century, the peasant had little protection against a landlord's arbitrary changes or violations of a contract. Following national unification, the mezzadria was included in the Civil Code, and there has since been increasing standardization of contracts and stricter adherence to the terms. Nevertheless, before literacy was common among the peasants, landowners frequently manipulated the accounts in their own favor, and some still try to withhold payments or neglect to credit all the colono's services. On their side, peasants may keep small amounts of the secondary crops out of the division. Some provisions of the contract are virtually unenforceable, such as the post-war law requiring that 4 percent of the landlord's share must be reinvested in the farm. How the contract works out depends on the economic and political context at any given time. If contemporary landowners still have the advantages of their higher status, these are balanced by the increasing scarcity of agricultural labor and the growing political power of the peasants.

The landlord-peasant relationship outlined by the mezzadria contract has fundamental bearing on the civil life. In the first place, it implies a setting in which landowners are close to their land in terms of both residence and involvement, often forming local elites in the centers around which their farms are dispersed. That the landlord is defined as having an active role in the management of the farm assumes that he is present much of the time, either living in the immediate area or keeping a part-time residence there. An absentee landlord can be represented by a fattore, but where such an agent acts as a long-term substitute he tends to become a quasi-landlord in the local social system. (Indeed, the history of the area includes success stories of fattori who came into possession of substantial estates, aided by the absence of a landlord's close supervision.) If neither landowners nor their representatives had been nearby, it is likely that the mezzadria would have been converted into a form of tenancy or sharecropping in which the peasant retains major charge of the farm. It has been suggested that this did, in fact, happen in eighteenth-century France: that landlord absenteeism gave the *métayers* effective control over the land and led to their becoming tenant farmers or peasant proprietors (Bandini 1945:389).

Absentee landlords have been common enough in the mezzadria areas of Central Italy, particularly among owners of large properties. Alongside them, however, there was generally also a considerable number of medium-scale, locally resident landowners. Moreover, "absenteeism" usually meant that the landlords lived in the larger cities of the region; many of these absentees kept villas on their land or palazzi in the small towns. To a large extent this was a consequence of the political context. In contrast to France, where the court acted to centralize commercial and industrial activity, the history of Central Italy is one of regional states, a large number of vigorous urban centers, and continuous interaction between city and country.

Thus, the mezzadria system is consistent with the presence of local or partly local landowners in many small and large towns. But the landlord-peasant relationship also creates the lines of connection between those towns and their surrounding rural areas. The mezzadria involves landlord and peasant in continuing, personal interaction in the operation of the farm. It also defines roles for each that go beyond the business of the farm. The padrone is supposed to be guide and protector of the peasant family, a source of capital, and a recourse in crisis. The colono, in turn, owes him loyalty and respect. The relationship is based on the existence of a social differential between the parties, but it also spells out the forms in which that differential is expressed. How the pattern of the mezzadria is elaborated, and how it imbues class relationships in general, will be discussed in chapter 4.

The Mezzadria in Historical Perspective

To understand the part played by the mezzadria system in molding civiltà, it is necessary to trace its development over time.[5] The "classical mezzadria," considered as a total organization of production, appeared in the Montecastello area in about the sixteenth century, but its emergence in Tuscany was much earlier. Contracts that resemble modern mezzadria pacts in many ways existed as early as the ninth century and became numerous in Tuscany by 1200 (Luzzatto 1948). Such contracts were applied to true family-farms in promiscuous cultivation by the mid-thirteenth century, and by this time too, the contributions of landlord and tenant were often similar to the patterns of recent times (Jones 1968:223–27, *passim*).

Many scholars consider the roots of the mezzadria to be even earlier, in the Roman *colonia partiaria* or share-tenancy.[6] During the Roman period, much of the Tiber Valley was farmed in family-sized units under this system, which took a variety of forms. However, it was probably more akin to rental (with rents paid in kind in some proportion of total production) than to the mezzadria, since the proprietors—based in Rome—remained essentially detached from their land.[7] Most coloni were apparently freemen initially, but during the late Empire they were legally attached to the land.

In the early Middle Ages, this area may have seen the manorial system (the *curtis*) that prevailed in much of Northern and Central Italy (see Luzzatto 1967; Jones 1966: 395–402). An increasing amount of land was absorbed by great estates of the church and lay nobility, and both former slaves and free peasant proprietors became dependent tenants. Estates (which were not compact but rather an agglomeration of holdings scattered around a manor farm) were divided into two parts: a demesne (the lord's land) and land granted to the tenants in small farms. The coloni paid the lord only minor shares of their own crops, but they owed a large proportion of their time (often half or more) to work on the demesne. The manorial system began to break down in the tenth or eleventh century, a time of general economic revival and population increase.

The nobility and the abbeys attempted to attract cultivators by offering concessions, and more land was brought under cultivation. This agricultural expansion was intensified with the rise of the urban communes, which progressively brought the surrounding countryside into their own territories, incorporating the nobility and establishing new settlements.

The commercial revolution of the communal period transformed tenurial relations in the countryside. Customary bonds tended to be dissolved and replaced by free agrarian contracts and leaseholds: "free" in that they held for a specific period of time rather than in perpetuity, provided for rents rather than dues, and had terms established by the market.[8] In Tuscany, the predominant kind of lease from the thirteenth century on was for share rent *a mezzadria*, namely for half of specified crops. The terms of such leases were highly variable, but features of the later mezzadria were common from the beginning. Often they covered a variety of crops, as well as livestock; defined a joint enterprise between owner and tenant; and included detailed conditions concerning the mezzadro's labor and other obligations and the landlord's contributions of capital and credit. To an increasing degree from the fourteenth century on, mezzadria leases in Tuscany were associated with *poderi*, consolidated farms adapted to the labor of a family, on which the peasants were required to reside. By the fifteenth century, most estates in Tuscany were grouping these farms into managerial units—fattorie.

From their early development in central Tuscany, mezzadria contracts and the associated forms of rural settlement and farm management spread to many areas of Central Italy and the Northern Plain, though the timing and variations involved in that spread are little known. In Umbria, the leases of the thirteenth and fourteenth centuries that have been studied were not mezzadria (see Desplanques 1969:176 ff.). Most common at the time were *livello* (long leases at fixed rent, paid either in cash or kind) and, particularly on church lands, emphyteusis (long-term leases at a small periodic rent, carrying obligations to cultivate or improve the land). Except for scattered instances, moreover, the leases applied to separate parcels of land rather than whole farms. It was only in the sixteenth century, particularly the second half, that the "complete" mezzadria became widespread in Umbria.

The mezzadria system was essentially an invention of townsmen, both urbanized nobles and the commercial bourgeoisie that grew with the ascendancy of the communes. At the same time, many ecclesiastical and feudal lords were drawn into the mezzadria, as the expansion of the commercial economy increased the necessity to make their properties earn more (Luzzatto 1948:81). Town statutes, written by landlords, actively encouraged the mezzadria and defended the interests of proprietors.[9] These urban landowners never abandoned their mercantile activities, but the land represented a profitable investment. Share contracts were especially attractive to them, since these were an effective means of keeping land under cultivation and of realizing increasing returns on investments in times of inflation. Until the mid-fourteenth century, and again after the plagues, the growth of the cities encouraged capital investment in the land. However, the flow of urban capital into agriculture varied at different times and places, and it was always more true of Tuscany than of Umbria.

If the mezzadria did not necessarily bring capitalization, neither did it inevitably mean agricultural development or better conditions for the peasantry. On all counts it seems to have been steadily less successful as it spread to marginal areas. Even in its Tuscan heartland, the expansion of the mezzadria from the fourteenth century on occurred at the expense of smallholders who were dispossessed and forced into tenancy by high taxation and other financial pressures (Jones 1968:231).

In Umbria, as elsewhere, the mezzadria became a means by which urban landlords sponsored a transformation of the hinterlands: it became what Desplanques has called "an instrument of rural colonization" (1969:180). Several factors might account for the process by which the Umbrian countryside was settled, new land brought under cultivation, and existing parcels combined into farms. Following a century or more of devastating plague and warfare, the late fifteenth century began a period of marked population growth (Braudel 1972:402). Related to this was the increasing security of the countryside with the growing supremacy of the Papal State, which was virtually achieved by the middle of the sixteenth century. Furthermore, the general economic situation throughout Europe encouraged the investment of available capital in the land: markets were closing, industry was in crisis, banks had failed (Sereni 1972:224). Share-farming offered a safe investment, particularly as the influx of silver from the New World touched off inflation. For anyone with money, a mezzadria farm could provide secure—if modest—profit, as well as an ingenious means of increasing the value of an investment— peasant labor. With the contracts stipulating labor requirements for planting trees and improving land, the colonization process brought a steady expansion of vines, olives, and other arboriculture, as well as drainage, terracing, and other systematization of the land.

This process was evident in Montecastello at least by 1600, and it continued at varying rates there into the twentieth century. (The maximum occupation of land in Montecastello appears to have been reached in the 1920s.) If population figures are any guide, the rate seems to have slowed down toward the middle of the seventeenth century and then picked up again at the end of the eighteenth century. For Central Italy in general, the seventeenth century saw the beginning of a "refeudalization." Various forms of property entailment were revived, and there was an increasing concentration of land in the hands of a new aristocracy, one created out of the commercial and manufacturing success of preceding centuries (Sereni 1972:248–50). As we shall see later, the Montecastellese data show no evidence of an aristocracy at this time. However, it is likely that the area shared the general trend toward a crystallization of the mezzadria into terms that meant less security and lower returns for the peasant (Desplanques 1969:178). Still, the stability of the farm unit represented an advantage as compared with the situation of many peasants elsewhere, notably in the South. Neither the growth of large properties nor later reforms aimed at them threatened that stability or altered the farms themselves.

Whatever the variations in patterns of property, commercial and professional men of the towns and cities continued to find the mezzadria an attractive investment. As Bloch has commented, "no safer remedy against monetary fluctuations could have been devised" (1970:147). But there were more subtle factors too. The larger proprietors built country villas and declared a sentimental attachment to their land and their peasants. More important was the mezzadria's appeal for the petty bourgeois, small-town men who were always the most numerous among mezzadria landlords. Bloch has described this phenomenon in explaining the spread of the French *métayage* from the sixteenth to the eighteenth century; he might well have been speaking of Umbria.

> It was not merely that their estates were too meagre to attract leaseholders from among the capitalists; it was also, and above all, because for many reasons this type of lease suited their outlook and way of life. The small town merchant or notary liked to eat food grown on his own land; he delighted in the crusty bread . . . made in his domestic bakehouse with flour from corn

grown on his *métairie;* his wife could produce unrivalled delicacies for his table from the eggs, poultry and pork which were the minor incidents of the lease, set out in great detail in the contracts. Whether he was living in town or in his house among the fields, he found it pleasant to see the *métayer*—his *métayer*— coming to him cap in hand, obliged to render him the various services, not far removed from *corvées,* so carefully stipulated in the agreements, and the subject of his condescension. . . . Under the system of *métayage* a whole section of the urban population was kept in direct contact with the soil, linked by genuine ties of personal dependence with the men who tended it. . . . (Bloch 1970:148).

Thus, once the mezzadria was widespread in Central Italy, it acted to connect town-based landowners, both large and small, with the countryside.

Toward the end of the eighteenth century, Northern and Central Italy saw an economic revival and an increasing influence of capitalism in agriculture. The effects on the mezzadria varied in different areas. In some, like the Po Valley, the mezzadria farms were forced out and the peasants absorbed by new capitalistic enterprises. This process, beginning in the irrigated plain, was eventually repeated in many dry areas of the North. Central Italy, for the most part, experienced the developments of the 1750–1850 period within the mezzadria organization. In Tuscany, new crops and new agricultural techniques were adopted, legal reforms eliminated the last feudal privileges, and "enlightened" proprietors joined in attempts to improve the lot of the mezzadri. Sereni sees these trends as intrinsic parts of an "Italian-style" capitalistic development of agriculture. In this process of development *all'italiana*, new modes of production were incorporated into a traditional structure of relationships, with the landowning class acting as the driving force of selective progress (1972:291, 343–44). Within the Papal States, the process was retarded until after unification, but it followed the same lines. Despite this delay in technological and social progress, the Montecastello area reflected the general economic acceleration of the late-eighteenth/early-nineteenth centuries: population grew, the mezzadria expanded, and agricultural commerce increased.

Not only did development all'italiana in Central Italy preserve the mezzadria, but articulate (and politically powerful) landowners regarded the system as the linchpin of the society and essential to its progress. For instance, an English Parliamentary representative who prepared an economic report on the area in the 1830s recorded this statement of a large landowner (whom he described as one of the most intelligent men in Tuscany):

> And where is the remedy [for the current "impoverishment" of landed propri-
> etors]—in the destruction of the *mezzeria* system? Impossible. In the first place,
> nothing in the world can be more deeply rooted, and the will of man is power-
> less in such matters; the system is essentially connected with our existence; it
> is the absolute condition of our being; the physiological necessity of our coun-
> try. . . . (Bowring 1837:44).

In Umbria the unification had mixed effects on the mezzadria. It opened up the region to the advances that had already been achieved in Tuscany, but it also brought the region into national markets in which it could not compete. The mezzadria farms were especially vulnerable to a series of agricultural crises in the last decades of the century. By the end of the century, the number of mezzadria contracts was decreasing, and processes that in other areas were bringing about a proletarianization of mezzadri now began to spread to Umbria (Sereni 1968:289–94). In the 1890s Socialist party organizations and peasant leagues met with success among the mezzadri of Emilia and Romagna, but Umbria remained tranquil. The landowners credited this fact (quite correctly, as will be seen) to the close ties between padrone and mezzadro. Nevertheless, 1902 brought Umbria the first organized strike of mezzadri, initiating a wave of strikes that continued sporadically for a few years (Procacci 1972:131–37). Though these strikes were abortive and had only limited objectives, they succeeded in alarming the proprietors. Thus, in 1907 the Accademia dei Georgofili, the landowners' association of Tuscany, ac-knowledged the need for certain reforms "that would not change the na-ture of the contract but would adapt it to the new times" (Bandini 1957:78–79). As a result, several of the traditional obligations of the peas-ants were eliminated from the pact.[10]

In the early twentieth century, the continuing development of the na-tional economy intensified pressure on the mezzadria. In places like Montecastello, however, the system was buffered by the adoption of various technological improvements and by a steady increase in popula-tion. Then, following World War I, there was a resurgence of militancy among mezzadri, led by both Catholic and Socialist organizations ("white" and "red" leagues). In 1919 and 1920 the peasants won several improvements in the contract: increased shares of industrial crops; re-duced obligations in paying for threshing labor, pesticides, and certain other expenses; compensation for extra labor rendered to the landlord; and the introduction of the conguaglio (Gennari 1949:268–69; MC 1947:221–22). These concessions, as well as the general threats to proprietors posed by the Socialist electoral victories of 1920, enhanced the support that the landowning classes gave to the Fascist movement. In Romagna and the North many mezzadri also joined the Fascist leagues; in these areas the mezzadri formed a "middle peasantry" who felt their interests threatened by the *braccianti*, the landless day-laborers. In Tuscany and Umbria, however, the mezzadri lent little support to the Fascists (Snowden 1972:278–79, 287).

After the Fascists came to power in 1922, the mezzadria was officially declared a realization of the ideals of the Corporative State: collaboration between capital and labor, and solidarity between opposite social categories. The regime attempted to encourage the system, extending it to newly reclaimed lands and favoring the conversion of wage-laborers into mezzadri. In fact, under Fascism the number of mezzadri increased: in the agricultural census of 1936, 20 percent of the nation's agricultural workers were mezzadri, as compared with 15 percent in the previous census of 1912 (Acerbo 1961:151–52). Similarly, data comparing 1921 and 1931 point to about a 20 percent expansion in the mezzadria labor force and a 30 percent increase in the number of mezzadria families (Lorenzoni 1938:244–46).[11]

Even more significant was the action of the Fascist government to "stabilize" the system through the 1933 Charter of the Mezzadria. The Charter halted any further changes in terms and defined an official fixed pact, formulated by the Tuscan landowners' association (Bandini 1957:145). The mezzadria relationship (which the Civil Code of 1865 had rationalized as being simultaneously a leasing of land and a labor contract) was redefined as a partnership. In reaffirming a strict fifty-fifty division of all products and expenses, the Charter eliminated most of the concessions which the peasants had won after the war. The terms of the Charter were carried over into the Civil Code of 1942, and most of them were formally still in effect at the time of the field study (D'Agata 1956; see Franchi et al. 1973: arts. 2141–63).

The years immediately after World War II were a time of turmoil for rural Italy, and agitation over the mezzadria system was part of a general movement for the reform of agrarian contracts. The mezzadria had special difficulties, however, such as the problem of assigning value to livestock in light of the inflation and currency devaluation. In 1946, a major eruption among the mezzadri was forestalled when Prime Minister DeGasperi arbitrated a temporary settlement that granted some concessions to the peasants. Further changes were included in the "mezzadria truce" of 1947, which was codified into law in 1948 and 1950. In general, however, the postwar changes in the contract amounted to modifications in the details of the system, while the fundamental organization and the essential principles of the mezzadria were maintained intact.

The postwar conflict surrounding the mezzadria brought into relief several issues that had long been debated in controversies over the system. In 1947, a multiparty government commission headed by the agrarian economist Manlio Rossi-Doria investigated conditions in Italian agriculture and concluded that the mezzadria system was in "crisis" (MC 1947:219, 222–30). The report points up a number of problems. First, there are the related questions of whether the system can be made to raise productivity; whether it can provide adequate income to the peasant and just compensation to the landowner; and whether it can be effectively applied to the widely varying conditions occurring within the mezzadria areas. Second, there is the inconsistency between the partnership theory and the definition of the proprietor as director of the enterprise. Moreover, the problem of direction becomes more acute as the technical competence required for agriculture increases. Third, there is the problem of assigning financial responsibility and initiative for the major improvements demanded by modern agrarian technology. The final conclusion of the report was that the mezzadria contract need not be abolished but rather had to be made adequate to current conditions.

Though the structure of the mezzadria institution was virtually unchanged until the 1960s, its actual functioning in the postwar period effectively altered the equilibrium between landlord and peasant. The amount of working capital required increased steadily as technological advances were incorporated. Originally a minor quantity compared to the value of the farm itself, these expenses are, of course, shared by both parties. The contradictions this situation creates are suggested by one informant's comment: "Only one proprietor in Montecastello fertilizes rationally, but then, his peasants are always in debt." Furthermore, the mezzadro's participation in the direction of the farm changed as a result of the new technology. On the more progressive fattorie the peasant's control was in effect reduced; on individual farms, on the contrary, the

mezzadro generally took on a more active role, as technology outdis-
tanced the landlord's expertise. At the same time, as the peasants were
increasingly drawn into a cash economy, returns from the farm could not
keep up with wants. One middle-aged mezzadro expressed the problem in
this way:

> The life of the colono is not bad. It is secure. Certainly there's no worry of
> starvation. We have plenty to eat and to provide for our needs. But what we lack
> is money. If we want a thousand lire in our pocket, we don't have it. . . . We
> would like to have money for entertainment, to move around a bit away from
> home, for an emergency, for a child to dress nicely and have schooling, to pro-
> vide for a child's marriage, to save for the future, to better ourselves.

From the landlord's point of view, the changes in the mezzadria equilibrium amounted to a steady deterioration in his own position. Indeed, the
postwar period brought both greater expenses for the landlord and a
smaller share of the returns.

By 1960 the stresses in the mezzadria system were evident in Montecastello. The mezzadria was the central political issue. The parties of
the Center-Right held out hopes of government assistance for the proprietors, while the Communist party slogan of "The land to those who
work it!" found great appeal among the mezzadri. Peasant militance was
demonstrated not only in votes for the Left but also in the harvest strikes
that were organized each year by the provincial union of mezzadri. In
1961 posters in Montecastello called on the peasants to refrain from
"threshing, carting the grain, and delivering the landlord's portion."
Most mezzadri avoided threshing on the main day of the strike, and
some participated in the demonstration held in Perugia. However, no
one could afford to leave the grain unthreshed for long, and the strike
resulted only in slight inconvenience for the landowners.

The peasants' most direct response to the crisis was to leave the land
in increasing numbers, despite the limited alternatives available. Between 1950 and 1959, there was a net decrease of mezzadri (working
members of mezzadria families) from 1,200 to about 1,000 in the commune; during 1960 there was a further net reduction of almost 50 persons, a 5 percent loss in one year. This decline was due wholly to out-
migration and shifts to other occupations in the community. (The rate of
movement was greater than the figures themselves suggest, since the
mezzadria population had a positive rate of natural increase.) The loss
represents a decline both in the number of mezzadria contracts and in

the number of workers on each farm; mainly it is the young adults of the family who leave, while the old remain behind on the farm. Some of the ex-mezzadri became peasant proprietors, whose numbers in the commune increased from 369 to 482 between 1955 and 1959. A few became agricultural wage-laborers. Without question, most left agriculture and left Montecastello as well.[12]

The mezzadria system has always had built-in mechanisms for adapting to changing contitions. Several of these were brought into play in Montecastello in efforts to deal with the crisis within the structure of the institution: families changed farms; farms were divided; hired hands were taken on by families diminishing in size; landlords purchased labor-saving machines; concessions were offered and agreements made to modify the terms of the contract; premiums were paid for crops requiring intensive labor, or such crops were eliminated. However, landlords were already considering alternatives to the mezzadria. Larger-scale proprietors talked of combining several farms into cattle-raising, vineyard, or single industrial-crop enterprises based on wage labor. Small landlords thought of planting olives, which requires little labor, or allowing cultivated land to revert to pasture for sheep and hiring shepherds. One landowner tried a different solution, when six years after his colono left he was still unable to find another. He hired a laborer to live on the farm with his family and work it under the mezzadria pattern, but at a fixed salary. The arrangement did not last, however, for the owner found his profit too low, which he attributed to the inferior quality of the labor.

The mezzadria system persisted into the 1960s in Montecastello essentially because there had not been any drastic change in the productive complex and because the regional economy could absorb only limited amounts of ex-peasant labor. Fundamental shifts in local agricultural organization were soon to come. In 1964 a new law—a product of the Center-Left national coalition—spelled the eventual end of the mezzadria system (Law of Sept. 15, 1964, n. 756). The official purpose of this law was to achieve "more equitable social relations" in the practice of agriculture and a more harmonious development of the economy. Unofficially, its aim was to speed up the de facto decline of the mezzadria by increasing the pressures on landlords to sell out.

The 1964 law prohibited new mezzadria contracts from being entered into, though existing contracts could continue—in effect, as long as the peasant wished and as long as the family could work the farm. The mezzadro's share was increased to a minimum of 58 percent; the 50-50 division of working capital and all expenses other than labor was retained. In addition, the law redefined the landlord-peasant relationship in several ways. The mezzadro was to collaborate fully in the direction of the enterprise, including its marketing activities, and any disagreement between the partners was to be decided by a designated provincial official. The peasant was entitled to carry out—and be compensated for—innovations and improvements, even over the opposition of the landlord (provided they could be justified). The landlord could no longer prevent members of the peasant family from leaving the farm or working elsewhere. Finally, all gifts and other forms of "extra" payments of peasant to landlord were declared illegal, regardless of any previous agreements. Other laws passed both before and after this one complemented it with the establishment of credit facilities to enable peasants to buy land (see Corvisieri 1972). In particular, a 1965 law was aimed at converting mezzadri into peasant proprietors. It required the landowner to give preference to the mezzadro when selling a farm, and it set up a machinery for controlling the price and conditions of sale.

These legal steps to eliminate the system accelerated the processes already described that were leading to its demise. By the time of the agricultural census of 1970, only about a third of the land area of Montecastello was still worked under the mezzadria (ISTAT 1972:30). Changes on the remaining mezzadria farms are almost as significant. The factors that had been modifying the roles of landlord and peasant since World War II intensified during the 1960s, compounded by the 1964 changes in the contract, while developments in the wider economy diminished farm self-sufficiency. Where the mezzadria continues, in practice it often comes to resemble straight rental, with peasants increasingly independent of the landlord and more closely involved in the market. Thus, the agricultural system that contributed to the civil life in Montecastello is rapidly becoming a thing of the past, but it leaves its imprint on behavior and values in the present.

The social organization of agriculture within the mezzadria system reflects the interpenetration of town and country that is intrinsic to the civil life. A sharp contrast between townsman-citizen (*cittadino*) and excluded countryman (*contadino*) coexists with important relationships that tie them together. Town dwellers—merchants, professionals, bureaucrats, and others—are also involved in the countryside and in a sense have made it their own. On the other hand, the peasant who is alien to the town is at once identified with it and a product of it, manifesting some of the characteristics of townsmen.

While we have seen a functional relationship between the mezzadria system and civiltà, the causal connection between them is more complex. The system surely grew out of the intimate ties between town and country that are very old in this area. But the mezzadria in turn provided the specific form that these ties have taken over the past 350 years. Moreover, the mezzadria underwrote civiltà at the local level. It supported a class of prosperous landowners, kept them close to the locality, and furnished models for their behavior and ideology. The next chapter looks at these landowners, the main participants in the civil life of Montecastello.

Montecastello, from the southwest.

Men's talk: the Piazza of the Church.

Women's talk: outside the walls.

Dividing the wheat harvest on a mezzadria farm.

Closing a deal at the Loğno cattle fair, with aid of a middleman (center).

View to the south. Mezzadria farms, the Tiber (center), Todi on the horizon.

A young *mezzadro*.

A landowner.

CHAPTER 4

The Carriers of Civiltà

AT LEAST FROM the time that the mezzadria system became widespread in Umbria until about World War II, Montecastello was dominated by a local elite. Always consisting of a core of families who owned farms in the surrounding countryside, this elite enacted the civil life in the town. Their role in the community, their style of living, and the values they professed provide many of the elements in the ideology of civiltà. Though their position was seriously undermined by the time of the field study, their influence was still apparent, permitting an ethnographic perspective on the social context of civiltà. In this chapter, I bring together the themes of land ownership over time, the changing role of the elite, and the significance of civiltà in defining social status.

Land Ownership

The history of landholding in Montecastello forms the background of the elite who came to be the carriers of civiltà. Data specifically on Montecastello are only indirect and intermittent before recent decades, but various clues may be pieced together into a hypothetical reconstruction.

Montecastello first appears in documents around the thirteenth century as part of the rural district (contado) of Todi. The forms of land tenure and the distribution of land in Montecastello at the time are un-

known; popular accounts of local history refer to "feudal" lords, but little
can be said of what that means. It is clear that a good deal of land
belonged to the Abbey of San Lorenzo, located about a kilometer from
the town, whose existence is attested since at least the eleventh century.
Probably most of the land, however, was held by nobles and other secular owners. These were citizens of Todi and at least part-time residents
there. Nobles "of Montecastello" are mentioned among the prominent
citizens of Todi, and according to the city statutes of 1275, only citizens
(whether by origin or by incorporation) were allowed to buy land in the
contado. At any rate, Montecastello figures in the commercial transac-
tions of the commune of Todi, and there can be little doubt that it
shared in the process of commercialization of land of the communal
period.

As already suggested, in Central Italy landed property and agricultural commerce were largely controlled by city men from an early date.
In Umbria this control came about less through the flourishing of new
classes based on manufacturing and trade (as in Tuscany) than through
the landed nobility's moving into the cities and becoming involved in
commercial activity. As Desplanques puts it, "the rural nobility took
over the city, in a certain way became *embourgeoisés*" (1969:121). Certainly
land was held by citizens of all classes in the urban communes—in Orvieto, for instance, two-thirds of the heads of urban households owned
some land in 1292 (Waley 1969:24, 28). Still, bourgeois land ownership
was probably much less significant in Umbria than in Tuscany. The communal period saw some advance toward a wider distribution of property
in Umbria as elsewhere. In the fourteenth century, however, many new
owners were forced out, and there was a reconsolidation of noble holdings, a development similar to that in Tuscany, but again, within a more
static economic context (see Jones 1968). Nevertheless, by the sixteenth
century some places had witnessed a considerable movement of property
from the old nobility to smaller-scale owners of other classes (Desplanques 1969:150). Large holdings of nobles and ecclesiastical corporations continued to dominate Umbria as a whole (apart from the mountain
zones), but much land close to the towns was in smaller properties that
circulated mainly among the local bourgeoisie.[1]

In Montecastello itself there seems to have been a shift from noble to
bourgeois holdings by the mid-sixteenth century, for in the documents
of that time (the earliest to survive in the Montecastello archives), refer-

ences to nobles are rare. There had also been a shift in the locus of landowners from Todi to Montecastello. The prominent figures of the sixteenth century appear as a local elite; they were not citizens of Todi, and
they plainly had an economic base independent of Todi. A record of a
1557 tax assessment on wealth (*beni*) in Montecastello, summarized in
Table 7, suggests that most privately owned land was in local hands.
Over 85 percent of the tax on individuals was asessed on Montecastellesi;
the nonlocals—persons who owned land in Montecastello—were all from
Todi and other adjacent communities. This tax was assessed in proportion to the value of a family's property, based on the current land register (*catasto*); special grants of tax reduction or exemption were recorded
separately. Although there are obvious sources of error in such data, the
tax figures can be taken as an approximate picture of the distribution
of landed wealth. It seems that half the persons on the list (apparently
half the household heads of the community) owned little or no property,
but there was a fairly wide spread of small and medium landowners.
The dozen most prosperous households together held about a fourth
of the private wealth in land. The proportions of land held by the church

Table 7 Distribution of Taxable Wealth by Amount of Tax, 1557

Amount of Tax (scudi)	Locals				Non-Locals	
	Taxpayers		Total amount of tax		No. of	Total amount
	No.	%	scudi	%	taxpayers	of tax (scudi)
0– .5	146	48 ⎤	36.5	11 ⎤	33	8.3
.5– 1	69	22 ⎬ 85	51.8	15 ⎬ 46	4	3.0
1– 2	45	15 ⎦	67.5	20 ⎦	5	7.5
2– 3	18	6	45.0	13	3	7.5
3– 4	15	5	52.5	15	3	10.5
4– 5	2	1 ⎤	9.0	3 ⎤	2	9.0
5– 6	5	2	27.5	8	0	—
6– 7	1	—	6.5	2	1	6.5
7– 8	3	1 ⎬ 4	24.5	7 ⎬ 26	0	—
8– 9	0	—	—	—	0	—
9–10	1	—	9.5	3	0	—
10–11	0	—	—	—	0	—
11–12	1	— ⎦	11.5	3 ⎦	0	—
Total	306	100	341.8	100	51	52.3

SOURCE: A.C.M., 1. Data for Montecastello parish. Only secular and private taxpayers are
included in the table.

and by the community cannot be determined from these data, but the
abbey certainly continued to be the most important non-private owner.
The extent of its property is indicated only in a much later document, a
survey of 1751; at that time it amounted to over 10 percent of the total
land area of the community, which meant perhaps 15–20 percent of the
cultivable land (A.C.M., 2).

In Umbria as a whole, the seventeenth and eighteenth centuries
brought a general increase in the holdings of large noble and church estates. The Napoleonic regime expropriated and sold off some ecclesiastical lands, but the *catasti* of the early nineteenth century show there was
still a high degree of concentration of property in the province (Francesconi 1872; Desplanques 1969:124). In Montecastello, however, it was
medium-scale, bourgeois proprietors who seem to have been the main
beneficiaries of the political developments and the colonization of the
countryside under the mezzadria system. Accounts of the early nineteenth century repeatedly refer to several local families as those who held
"most of the land." One Montecastellese family, the Pettinelli, was particularly successful, for they obtained emphyteusis rights over the abbey
lands and eventually came into their full possession. A Pettinelli held the
emphyteusis at least by 1808 (A.C.V.), but it is likely that the family
acquired it before 1798. In that year the mayor reported to the new
French administration (which was preparing to suppress the major religious corporations) that the territory of Montecastello contained no sizable ecclesiastical property nor any corporation with more than eight
priests (A.S.P., 2).

The situation as of 1826 can be seen through a tax assessment roll
summarized in Table 8. The figures representing taxable wealth (*estimi*)
were based on a census of landed property; the category of private taxpayers refers to legal personalities owning land (who might be groups of
co-owners as well as individuals), but in most cases these were household
heads. Less than 20 percent of the landed wealth was held by church
corporations, a figure which suggests that ecclesiastical land ownership
played a smaller role in nineteenth-century Montecastello than in many
other Umbrian communities.[2] Very little of the land-wealth (under 3
percent) was in public ownership. Other evidence indicates that there
were virtually no common lands in Montecastello by this time and that
pasturage rights of all kinds had disappeared (Desplanques 1969:162).
Possibly the success of the landlords in bringing land under private con-

Table 8   Distribution of Taxable Wealth, 1826

| Amount of Taxable Wealth (scudi) [b] | Private Taxpayers | | | | | | Church Corporations [a] | | | |
| | Locals | | | | Non-Locals | | Local | | Non-Local | |
	Taxpayers No.	Taxpayers %	Total wealth scudi	Total wealth %	No. of taxpayers	Total wealth (scudi)	No.	Total wealth (scudi)	No.	Total wealth (scudi)
0– 100	77	43.	3,625	4.	13	625	4	200	1	75
100– 200	26	15.	3,900	4.	4	600	3	450	4	300
200– 300	17	9.5	4,250	4.	3	750	2	500	2	500
300– 400	13	7.	4,550	5.	1	350	3	1,050	0	—
400– 500	5	3.	2,250	2.	0	—	2	900	1	450
500–1,000	16	9.	11,400	12.	8	5,900	6	4,100	2	1,500
1,000–1,500	8	4.5	9,740	10.	1	1,010	1	1,020	1	1,060
1,500–2,000	4	2.	6,900	7.	1	1,780	1	1,960	1	1,990
2,000–3,000	4	2.	10,460	11.	1	2,650	0	—	0	—
3,000–4,000	6	3.	21,340	21.	0	—	0	—	2	7,730
4,000–5,000	1		4,460	5.	0	—	1	4,670	0	—
5,000–6,000	0		—		0	—	0	—	0	—
6,000–7,000	1	2.	6,000	6.	0	—	0	—	0	—
7,000–8,000	0		—		0	—	0	—	0	—
8,000–9,000	1		8,730	9.	0	—	0	—	0	—
Total	179	100.	97,605	100.	32	13,665	23	14,850	14	13,605
Total taxpayers (%)	72.				13.		9.		6.	
Total taxable wealth (%)			70.			10.		10.5		9.5

Bracketed subtotals (Locals): Taxpayers % { 86.5 }, { 5 }; Total wealth % { 31 }, { 41 }.

SOURCE: A.C.M., 8. Data for Montecastello parish.

[a] Including also public corporations (of minor significance).

[b] The value of the scudo at this time is suggested by the daily wage of laborers, which ranged from .15 to .30 scudi in this area (Bowring 1837).

trol was related to the fact that they were a local group in active charge of their properties. As Table 8 shows, 85 percent of the secular land-wealth was in the hands of Montecastellesi.

The distribution of property among local owners points to a somewhat greater concentration than in the sixteenth century, for the top 5 percent now held 40 percent of the wealth, compared to about 30 percent in 1557. (The fewer names on the roll may mean either that many household heads in 1826 owned no property at all, or that household size had increased greatly with the spread of the mezzadria system, or both.) The largest property was that of the abbey, held in emphyteusis by two Pettinelli brothers, one of whom also had a separate holding of almost 4,000 scudi. The other major owners are familiar names of local history (often referred to as the "old" landowning families). However, it is not possible to trace their holdings to 1557, since the earlier register did not list surnames.

At the time of the unification, most cultivable land in Montecastello was in mezzadria farms. The distribution of farms in the commune (including Doglio) may be inferred from a tax roll listing persons who owned work animals in 1868. Table 9 shows the ownership of farms

Table 9   Farms Paying Tax on Oxen, 1868

Number of Farms	Peasant Ownership no. of owners	Mezzadria Tenure			
		Private Ownership		Church Ownership	
		no. of owners	total no. of farms	no. of owners	total no. of farms
1	18	23	23	2	2
2		14	28	1	2
3		2	6	0	0
4		5	20	1	4
5		0	0	1	5
6		1	6	0	0
12		1	12		
Total	18	46	95	5	13
Total owners (%)	26.	67.		7.	
Total farms with oxen (%)	14.5		75.		10.5

SOURCE: A.S.P., 4. Data for commune.

equipped with oxen. How many other farms there were without oxen, and how much land was cultivated as individual plots rather than as part of a farm cannot be determined from these data, but it is unlikely that the amount was of any great significance. About 85 percent of the farms with oxen (namely, those equipped with the basic means of production) were in mezzadria tenure. Most of the mezzadria farms belonged to private owners, predominantly locals. By far the largest holding (with at least twelve farms) was that of the Pettinelli heir. Other families who made up the local elite owned two to six farms—medium-sized holdings of about 30 to 100 hectares. Half the mezzadria landlords were modest proprietors with only a single farm. The church property was held by a confraternity (five farms), the Bishopric of Todi (four), the seminary in Todi (two), and the parishes of Montecastello and Doglio (one each).

An immediate effect of the unification was the expropriation of most of the ecclesiastical land. In Montecastello, however, only a limited amount of land came onto the market in this way. The parishes were allowed to keep their land (subject to governmental supervision), and the farms of the confraternity were turned over to the commune to support a public charity. After the unification, too, some land that belonged to the community was sold off to private owners. Most of this land was an inheritance from a Montecastellese landowner of the mid-seventeenth century, and it had been leased out to provide income for the commune. The 89 small parcels involved were acquired by about half as many individuals, local landlords for the most part, as well as some peasant proprietors (A.C.M., 9).

A more profound effect of the unfication was in the modification of inheritance law. Before the nineteenth century landowning families had at least an ideological preference for primogeniture.[3] The wealthier ones sometimes employed the institution of the *fidecommesso:* by a declaration in the will, all or part of a patrimony was bound to a man's own descendants through a rule of primogeniture, and sale of the property was prohibited. The fidecommesso was abolished briefly under French rule, but from 1815 until unification it was again legal. The extent to which it was used in Montecastello is uncertain, however. During the first half of the nineteenth century, there is good evidence of primogeniture only for the Pettinelli. To judge by the holdings of brothers and cousins included in the tax lists of 1826 and 1868, it would appear that the common practice among Montecastellese landowners was unequal division among sons but not strict primogeniture. Females were excluded from inheritance but were dowered by the father or his heirs.

The Napleonic code, with its provisions for partible inheritance, was introduced into the Papal States in 1812; though abrogated two years later, it became the basis of the Civil Code of 1865 (Limpens 1956:94–98). The new law required that a large portion of the patrimony (the *legittima* or legitim) be divided equally among all children. As practiced in Montecastello, this meant that equal, major shares were given to all sons, while daughters received minor portions—the minimum share to which they were legally entitled. All or part of a daughter's inheritance was provided as a dowry, which was sometimes in land. In the twentieth century, there has been an increasing tendency to minimize the distinction between sons and daughters in allocating property outside the rights of legitim. Contemporary families generally follow the principle of equal division among all children; in practice, however, inequalities may result from the special claims of certain children, the changing fortunes of a family during the course of the parents' lifetimes, and the fact that sons are usually more closely involved in the management of the patrimony than are daughters.

The partible inheritance laws and the inclusion of women in the legitim contributed to a subdivision of patrimonies because they coincided with a period of high birth rates and declining death rates. The birth rate in Montecastello remained in the range of 25 to 30 births annually per 1,000 population until just before World War I and started to decline only in the 1920s (its present level being in the range of 10–15 per 1,000). Inheritance by affinals also played a part in breaking up family holdings, particularly when there were no surviving children. A widow or widower would sometimes inherit property that would then pass to his or her kin or to the kin of a subsequent spouse.

As has been seen, the period after unification brought new opportunities for entrepreneurs but also new pressures on the mezzadria landlords. The agricultural crises of the 1890s must have been particularly difficult for the smaller landowners. The histories of landowning families suggest that debt and the mortgaging of land were common during this period; the evidence of economic pressures often appears in the guise of stories of gambling, unwise investment, and *troppo buona volontà* (too much good will), namely guaranteeing loans for other people.[4] In the late nineteenth century new family names appear among the references to

Montecastellese landlords: some were from Todi and other neighboring towns, others were Montecastellesi who had been peasant proprietors or artisans in the previous generation. At the same time, the increasing mobility of professionals and bureaucrats meant that more and more, people who inherited land in Montecastello lived elsewhere. Absentee ownership increased also as a result of events following World War I. The concessions won by the peasants, the postwar inflation (in which the prices of agricultural products lagged behind the general rise in prices), and the strikes and unrest in the countryside from 1918 to 1922 forced out some landowners who were already in a marginal position, and created opportunities for purchasers based in Perugia and Rome.

The intersection of these several processes may be illustrated by the history of the Pettinelli family.

The 1826 tax roll lists two sons of E.P., who had obtained the emphyteusis of the abbey lands. The emphyteusis was in the name of "the Pettinelli brothers," but the elder, F.P., was apparently the sole heir of E.P.'s own patrimony and eventually the sole (or major) heir of the emphyteusis. Two other Pettinelli brothers, cousins of F.P., were joint owners of a smaller property; only one of these brothers, G.P., left descendants.

F.P. had three sons and four daughters, who were dowered. The eldest son, S.P., was the major heir when F.P. died around the middle of the century, but the other two retained rights in the emphyteusis. The youngest died without descendants, and his property reverted to his two brothers, S.P. and E.P. S.P. was the first *sindaco* (mayor) of Montecastello after the unification and by far the wealthiest landowner on the tax list of 1868.

S.P. was married to the daughter of an innkeeper from a nearby town; they had no children. When S.P. died, his property passed to his wife and his brother. The widow married N.F., a carter from Marsciano; they too were childless. She died first and left her wealth to her widower. Upon the death of N.F., the inheritance passed to his nephews and nieces. The property was divided, but one nephew, G.N., acquired most of it through legal manipulations and purchases from the other heirs. (G.N. became the sindaco of Montecastello in about 1915, when he succeeded N.F. in that office. After the Fascists came to power, he was appointed to head the commune as *podestà*, a position he held for over a decade.) G.N. suffered a series of personal tragedies, including the death of his wife and their only child, and in the 1940s he sold his property and retired. The purchaser was a man from his own town who had a brick factory that prospered during the war; today this individual owns ten farms in Montecastello. Three other farms originally owned by S.P. are now held by a nephew and grandnephew of N.F..

E.P. married a well-dowered woman from another hill town and they had two daughters. The first married a doctor from Rieti; she moved there with her husband and eventually sold her property in Montecastello. Their daughter and three sons were all born and raised outside of Montecastello. The second daughter of E.P. was married in 1888 to a landowner from the province of Terni. She moved to her husband's town, where their three sons and a daughter were born and raised. None of the sons has any of the Montecastello property, but the daughter today owns nine farms; she and her husband, an engineer, live in Perugia and rarely come to Montecastello.

Around the time of the unification, the eldest daughter of F.P., L.P., had married V.R., a member of a prominent local landowning family. When the law recognized the right of females to inherit an emphyteusis, V.R., supported by his brothers (one was the priest of Montecastello), and later his son S.R. (the sindaco for over three decades, until his death in 1908), claimed that the descendants of L.P were entitled to a share in the property of the abbey. As a result of this claim, which created a long-lasting feud between the P.'s and the R.'s, some of the property that had been under the emphyteusis passed to S.R., then to his only daughter, and finally was divided among her five children. Three of these children are today minor landowners in Montecastello; the other two have died and their property has been divided among their children, who live in Rome and Milan.

G.P. (F.P.'s cousin, who was listed on the 1826 tax roll) had a daughter who was dowered and one son, L.P. L.P. (who appeared as a minor landowner on the 1868 list) married in the 1850s and had four children who survived to adulthood. The eldest, a son, married and lived in Montecastello but left no descendants; his property passed to his widow and eventually her kin. The second child, a daughter, married a local landowner of moderate means but was legally separated from him after a few years. She returned to the parental household and subsequently had an illegitimate daughter, who now lives in the community as the wife of a minor landlord, a downwardly mobile descendant of a high-status local family. The third child of L.P. married a man of Todi and received some land as a dowry; her husband became indebted to a commercial family of Todi, who eventually took over the property. L.P.'s fourth child married the daughter of a Montecastellese artisan. Their daughter, the only descendant still bearing the family name, is a spinster who lives in Montecastello. Her only property is the family palazzo, in which she takes boarders—unmarried people from outside who have jobs in Montecastello.

While the property of the old landowning families was thus dispersed, the predominance of mezzadria tenure was not seriously threatened until the 1950s. After World War I some mezzadri were able to benefit from the new legislation (especially laws favoring the mezzadro in calculating credits on livestock sales) and to purchase land of their own. This area, however, played only a small part in the expansion of peasant proprietorship that occurred in Italy after World War I, particularly between 1918 and 1921.[5] In the nation as a whole the amount of arable land held by owner-cultivators increased by about 6 percent between 1919 and

1933 (by which time many of the new owners had already lost their land). In the hill region of Perugia province the increase was only 2 percent, and it was at the expense of medium-sized but not large properties (Lorenzoni 1938:10, 66). As has been seen, the number of mezzadri in fact grew during this period.

It has only been since World War II that many mezzadri have been able to purchase land. A series of laws passed since 1948 provided funds for credit and other limited measures to encourage peasant proprietorship (Corvisieri 1972:8–11). More important, some families were able to accumulate savings through the expansion of cash crops and livestock production, through work in the tobacco factory, or through temporary emigration. Not all of the new smallholders abandoned the mezzadria system: some became landlords themselves, while others remained mezzadri and at the same time cultivated their own land or let it to other peasants. In general, however, the amount of land in mezzadria tenure has decreased steadily as property has shifted to peasants and other smallholders.

The result of these processes of change is a wider distribution of property. This is indicated by an increase in the number of persons who own land (both mezzadria landowners and peasant proprietors) and by a decrease in the average size of holdings. Table 10 shows the distribution of land worked under the mezzadria system in the commune at the time of

Table 10   Distribution of Mezzadria Holdings by Area of Holding, 1960

Area of Holding (hectares)	No. of Owners	Total Land Area (hectares)	Percentage of Total Mezzadria Land
0.5– 1.9	9 ⎤	13.2	0.7 ⎤
2 – 4.9	22 ⎟ 64%	85.8	4.5 ⎟ 26.5
5 – 9.9	32 ⎟	240.8	12.5 ⎟
10 – 14.9	15 ⎦	168.5	8.8 ⎦
15 – 19.9	19	330.0	17.2
20 – 24.9	10	216.1	11.2
25 – 34.9	6	177.2	9.2
35 – 49.9	3	131.1	6.8
50 – 74.9	1 ⎤	55.0	2.7 ⎤
75 – 99.9	3 ⎬ 5%	277.6	14.4 ⎬ 29
100 –124.9	2 ⎦	231.2	12.0 ⎦
Total	122	1,926.5	100.0

the field study. The 2,000 hectares in mezzadria tenure were held by a total of 122 proprietors, with the largest holdings measuring about 100 hectares each and the median of all holdings of mezzadria landowners encompassing less than 10 hectares. However, 5 proprietors held over a fourth of the land, while almost half the mezzadria land was held by only 15 of the proprietors. A more meaningful view of the contemporary situation is the distribution of mezzadria property in terms of the number of farms owned by each proprietor (Table 11). (In comparing

Table 11   Distribution of Mezzadria Holdings by Number of Farms, 1960

Number of Farms	No. of Owners		Total No. of Farms		Average Size of Holdings (hectares)
1	86	70%	86	40%	8.3
2	20		40		16.5
3	6		18		28.7
4	2		8		63.0
5	2		10		36.6
6	1		6		55.0
7	1		7		34.0
8	0		—		—
9	2 } 3%		18 } 18%		97.3
10	2		20		115.6
Total	122		213		

these data with those for 1868, it should be remembered that the average size of mezzadria farms has been reduced from about 15–20 hectares to under 10 hectares.)[6] Only 16 proprietors in 1960 (13 percent of the mezzadria landowners, and 3 percent of the household heads in the community) had at least three farms, about the minimum needed by a landowning family today to support itself without other sources of income. These 16 range from moderately prosperous (by local standards) to substantial (i.e., the 4 with holdings of nine or ten farms). In sum, while the mezzadria property was less concentrated than a century before, there was still a landowning class. The composition of this class, and how its members differ from landowners of the past, will be described later in this chapter.

The 1,000 hectares of land in the commune held under forms of tenure other than the mezzadria are more difficult to account for. However, if the mezzadria data are combined with the results of a 1946 study of property distribution (INEA 1947) and allowance is made for changes during this time, a general picture may be obtained. It can be estimated that in 1960 some 600 hectares of non-mezzadria land were in 10–15 properties of 25 or more hectares each. A large part of this land consisted of woods, pasture, and unproductive land; much of it corresponds to the category "enterprises worked by salaried labor" in the agricultural census of 1961. About 150 hectares were in 20 properties of 5 to 25 hectares (primarily properties under 10 hectares); these were mainly owner-operated farms equivalent in size to the mezzadria farms. Approximately 250 hectares were in properties under 5 hectares: about 40 were between 2 and 5 hectares, and 130-odd were from ½ to 2 hectares. These small units were primarily scattered plots worked by their owners in combination with other means of subsistence. In addition, there were about 200 properties of less than ½ hectare.

These data must be understood in light of the fact that properties are not total holdings. Individual landowners may hold a number of different properties, both in mezzadria and non-mezzadria tenure, both within and outside the commune. Nevertheless, the data reveal the growing significance of peasant proprietorship and the increased possibilities for people of all classes to acquire a bit of land. Since the total amount of land included in these small properties was not great, however, and since the large non-mezzadria holdings were relatively unproductive, the non-mezzadria land was still only a minor factor in Montecastello as of 1960–61. Agricultural property was mainly in the hands of a group of mezzadria landlords—albeit a larger group, with rather different characteristics, than the nineteenth-century landowners. Moreover, this group existed alongside a large class of landless peasants, for the vast majority of the 213 mezzadria families owned little or no land. Thus, landholding at this time still showed the outlines of the traditional social-economic structure of the community.

The Traditional Elite

The landowners of the last century demonstrate a fairly recent version of the civil life; how it may be related to earlier versions will be considered in the next chapter. For convenience, I refer to the time from the beginning of the nineteenth century (when evidence on social relationships becomes ample) until World War II as the "traditional" period, in contrast to the "contemporary" period following the war. The traditional period, of course, covers major historical developments which had repercussions in Montecastello, as will be seen. Nevertheless, there is sufficient continuity in patterns of social interaction to permit discussion of the period as a whole.

In the various descriptions of traditional Montecastello, three main categories of social-economic differentiation are highly visible: (1) a group referred to as *signori*, the local upper class, or the major local landlords; (2) the artisans and small-merchant population of the town, including some who owned land; (3) the peasants, comprising (a) the peasant proprietors, usually living on as well as cultivating their own land (relatively few in number); and (b) the mezzadri and other landless people of the countryside.

Documents of the time, as well as older Montecastellesi remembering the old days, tend to refer to these categories as if they were clearly identifiable, enduring, and stable in membership. Certain family names are cited as examples of those who "have always been" landowners, artisans of a particular trade, or coloni, and instances of intermarriage are explained as exceptions. Such views undoubtedly underestimate the continuities between categories and their fluidity over time. Nevertheless, several factors did act to produce relatively discrete categories: the concentration of landed property; the distinction between townsmen and countrymen; the tendency for occupations to be passed on within family lines. Above all, the dominance of the mezzadria system exaggerated categorical differences. On one hand, it reduced variation within the agricultural population and lessened the possibility for families to combine different economic pursuits. On the other hand, the contrast in roles of landlord and peasant tended to widen the social gap between the less prosperous landowners and the better-off mezzadri.[7]

The category that is most vividly portrayed is the local upper class, the signori. This category included families who bore a few distinctive surnames that can be identified with landowners of the sixteenth and seventeenth centuries, but it also included some families who arrived in Montecastello only in the latter nineteenth century. The term "signori" was almost synonymous with "landowners," indeed implied "large landowners." Yet the data already discussed indicate that the holdings of the Montecastellese signori, for the most part, were of medium size, sometimes quite modest. Moreover, there was no clear distinction between landowners and professionals or bureaucrats. A landowner was often also a pharmacist, a doctor, a schoolteacher, a notary, a shopkeeper, or a government functionary, and a landowning family might include several of these occupations. The families who at any given time made up this rather mixed category also formed an interacting social group, crosscut by ties of kinship, friendship, and enmity. They were always the leading citizens of the community: owners of most of its land, occupants of the key political positions, and links to the power of the church (as officials and relatives of officials, and as lay leaders of the local church).

The ideology of civiltà incorporates an idealized view of the role of this elite group in the community. In many of the qualities that it values, civiltà celebrates the patron. Phrased in terms of the positive potentialities of interclass relationships, this ideology is obviously not a straightforward description of traditional Montecastellese society. Actual patron-client relationships were surely less common than the ideology would suggest, and in those that did occur the exploitative aspects are apparent. But the ideology is a statement about structural realities—the lines along which relationships were possible, the forms they could take, and the symbolic terms that were relevant to the patterns of social life. It is important to know that in practice, patronage in Montecastello differed from the ideal; but what is most significant is that a role of patron existed at all.

The role of the local elite was in part an extension of the mezzadria system. Both within and beyond the actual terms of the contract, the relationship of landlord and peasant involved far more than the agricultural enterprise. The landlord could control virtually all the activities of the peasant family, approve or disapprove marriages, and dictate behavior. He might or might not have been constrained by the ideal of the "good" landlord—one who provided benefits not strictly required, was concerned to improve the living conditions of his peasants, and offered aid in times of need. In any case, the institution acted to bring proprietor and mezzadro into direct and continuing contact, generally over a long period of time. Thus, not only were the contractors defined as "padrone" (patron-master) and dependent, but a more pervasive patron-client relationship than specified by the formal contract often developed.

Further commitments could be initiated by either landlord or peasant. The colono might approach his padrone to ask a favor, such as a loan of money, or the landlord might offer his aid with a particular problem. Or, the peasant might be the first to offer services, anticipating favors he might later ask of the landlord. Whether or not a broader patron-client tie developed depended primarily upon the landlord's inclination and accessibility. In any event, such a relationship encompassed not only the two contractors but their families as well. All members of the peasant family were automatically clients, while the wife of the landlord became *la padrona*, a role defined particularly in relation to the women and young children of the peasant family. To a lesser extent, other members of the landlord's family also were treated and acted as patrons.

The services that could be involved in patronage were many: lending money or guaranteeing loans; obtaining employment for members of the family not needed on the farm; helping to provide dowries for the daughters of client families; providing medicines and helping to obtain medical services; aiding with the schooling of talented youths; and in general, providing some defense against emergencies. In addition, a patron could perform important functions in helping the client deal with the world outside the community, as will be discussed in the next chapter. In turn, the peasant could send choice offerings from his share of the farm produce; perform personal and domestic services for the landlord's family; refrain from cheating the landlord; comply with his decisions and wishes; show him loyalty and deference; and provide publicity for his reputation and honor. In ways such as these, the peasant invested in the future of the relationship.

The two families linked by such ties interacted frequently, in an intimacy that imitated familial affection. The landlord's family visited the farm during the summer and participated in the festive harvest gatherings. The padroni were honored guests at every major event of the peasant family. This interaction served to reinforce rather than to nullify the rank difference inherent in the relationship. Landlord B. and his mezzadro M. are among those who still illustrate the pattern:

Following the baptism of the son of M., there was a dinner at the farm. The padrone and his wife attended and were seated in the places of honor. . . . At the end of the meal, *spumante* was served. The padrone stood up and offered a toast, saying that as one very close to the family, in fact one of the family, he offered fervent wishes for the boy whom M. was finally able to produce [all the guests laughed], and on this occasion he was thinking of M.'s dear father [now dead]. M. and his family all wiped tears from their eyes. . . .

Another example of the asymmetrical exchange of services between landowner and peasant families, and the affective forms that accompanied it, is provided by the D.'s and one of their mezzadri:

The teen-aged daughter of one of the D.'s mezzadri was living in the town with Signor and Signora D. She had been brought there by the D.'s to work as a dressmaker's apprentice and to help Signora D. with the household tasks. The girl told me that she had been very happy to come, for there was little work to do and she could enjoy the life of the town. . . . While I was visiting at the D. house one afternoon, the girl kept asking Signora D. to let her show me the pictures of the D.s' grandchildren. When Signora D. finally agreed, she ran to get the photos. She spread them out and continued to look through them for several minutes after I had finished. She picked up some pictures of the children and kissed them. . . . Later, Signora D. said sadly, "Of all our mezzadri this family is the only one that is still affectionate toward us, as in the old days. As for the others, *non si affezionano più* (they no longer become attached to us). . . ."

From the point of view of the landlord, a patron-client tie with his mezzadro provided concrete advantages. It facilitated contacts between landlord and peasant and contributed to the day-to-day efficiency of the enterprise. It was a source of free services and social honors. It was a check against petty stealing and a control on potentially disruptive influences, for the pervasive dependency of peasant on landowner meant that the risks of withdrawing from or challenging the mezzadria arrangement were very high indeed. These advantages were especially important for the kind of medium-scale local landlords who dominated Montecastello. Landowners with the power of vast holdings, and those who depend upon fattori to administer their properties, have less need of personal relationships with their peasants. Very small proprietors, on the other hand, have little to offer a potential client, unless they have other sources of income or influence.

From the point of view of the peasant, there was something to gain and little to lose in furthering a patron-client relationship. There was, moreover, reason to promote such relationships in ideology even when the reality was very different. The ideology of patronage at least made a claim on a landlord in a situation that offered the peasant few alternatives. Thus, it is not surprising that despite gross abuses, even small favors and occasional expressions of concern could reinforce the ideal—

could assure the landlord of his moral worth and give the peasant a slightly better edge on survival.

Patron-client relationships on the mezzadria model were also formed between lower-class persons other than mezzadri and members of the local upper class. A potential client might approach one of the signori with a request, or else make himself available to run errands or help out in various ways. Apart from those aspects that in the landlord-peasant relationships are specifically concerned with agriculture, the goods and services exchanged and the quality of interaction were similar. An example of such a relationship that survives into present times is the "friendship" between two women, S. and P., and their families.

S., the wife of a local landowner, and P., the wife of a laborer, are two women of about the same age. S. and P. both describe their relationship as that of old friends "who always ask each other for favors." P. does domestic work in S.'s house from time to time, and if they encounter each other by chance S. readily asks P. to run errands for her. S. does not pay P. for her services directly or at an agreed rate; rather she gives P. "gifts" of food (on various occasions) and of money (shortly after P. has performed some special service). These payments are defined as "generosity," because P. helps S. and because S. is "fond" of P. In addition, S.'s husband employs P.'s husband when he needs extra labor and uses his influence to help him in minor difficulties, and S.'s daughter has her clothes made by P.'s daughter, who is a dressmaker. . . . . I observed that interaction between the two women is close and affectionate, though the rank distinction in terms of address and behavior is always maintained. . . . . They often pass the evening together in S.'s house. Occasionally they play cards; the loser is supposed to buy beer, but in fact S. always pays for it and P. always goes out to buy it.

From the late nineteenth century on, various bureaucrats and professionals—people with little or no land, both Montecastellesi and outsiders—entered into such relationships, became padroni to dependents of their own, and in their general status and behavior were soon indistinguishable from the landowners.

The idiom of patronage was extended also to the role of the elite in relation to certain groups and to the community as a whole. I was first alerted to this pattern when I heard people use the expression *Paga Masci!* Someone asking for credit, or responding to the question, "Who will pay for it?" would say, jokingly, "Masci will pay!" Masci was a member of the nineteenth-century elite who was known for his readiness to support minor community projects and pay small bills for any member of the community who was deserving and needy.

The ideal role of the signori as a group was defined as that of public patrons, who bear responsibility for the material and spiritual well-being of the community, and who also have the right to active leadership and "command" of the community. In fact, this group did subsidize political administration, social benefits, and "cultural" life in Montecastello. There are many examples scattered throughout the history of the community. Buildings that housed the municipal offices were donated by members of the local upper class, and salaries of some clerks were provided for in the wills of certain landlords. Landowners helped pay for local roads and for the public gardens. Members of the elite sometimes left a part of their patrimony to the community. Such endowments at various times supported a local teacher and doctor, medicines for the poor, a fund to assist youths to study for the clergy, a subsidy to provide dowries for poor girls, and general charities. The ideal is also expressed in negative examples. An elderly informant described how the signori had urged one of their number who was childless to leave his property to found a local hospital; when he refused, he was criticized by public opinion. The phrasing of criticism is significant too, such as the comment about a landowner: "He is cordial, but thinks only of his own affairs."

Official records and acclamations glorify public patronage. When the administrative council voted in 1896 to name various streets after leading local families, it entered into the record the following description:

The Baldini, their cultivation coupled with a love for their native place second to none, consumed their considerable wealth for the good of the paese and for the public. . . . Their members served as public officials and delegates to Perugia and Rome. . . . To this family we owe projects for the community . . . for which they spent substantial sums. . . . Because of them we had academies and societies, for which illustrious persons would come to Montecastello. They were always jealous custodians of the glory of the paese and of the progress of the sciences and the arts.

Similarly, the inscriptions on tombs of the traditional elite emphasize their devotion to the public welfare, list their acts of charity, and attest to the community's collective gratitude. As in the ideology about personal patronage, the language exaggerates rather than describes the actual contributions involved in public patronage.

Members of the local elite also acted as patrons in initiating and helping to finance a variety of local associations and organized activity. In 1806 nine landowners financed the construction of the theater, baptizing it "il Teatro di Concordia," so named "for the community of sentiments that tied the founders together in one single thought and aspiration," to advance culture in the paese. In the years that followed, the theater was managed and maintained by an association with an elected council that generally consisted of descendants of the founding families. Local landlords supported Montecastello's band, whose existence is documented since the early nineteenth century; a photograph taken in the 1920s shows that it then consisted of over forty men. The band played regularly for local events and in nearby communities, the patrons contributing part of the cost of a maestro, instruments, uniforms, and rehearsal rooms. The local upper class were instrumental in a variety of other activities, including a dramatic society that presented plays and musical performances, a large church choir, a library, a hunting club, an insurance society, and an agricultural marketing cooperative.

The history of one association suggests some of the factors that might have been involved in public patronage. It is clear that the elite themselves were the main beneficiaries of most of the activities they sponsored. But beyond this, such patronage meant control of public life. Challenges to the power of the local upper class increased following the unification, particularly as waves of the Italian labor movement began to reach Montecastello. They came rather slowly. In 1894, a congress of Umbrian mutual aid societies was held in Perugia; 63 municipalities were represented. Montecastello was one of the few communes that did not yet have—or whose officials claimed did not have—a workers' society (Grohman 1968:158–60). Yet the year before, three men described as *operai* (laborers) had begun to organize a mutual aid society in Montecastello, the purpose being "to serve the working classes" (Silvi 1911). When the elite of the paese learned of this, they took it as a challenge to their authority and promptly founded a second society, one which promised the workers more benefits than its competitor. This elite-sponsored society succeeded in enrolling a large membership, apparently by pressures exerted through the mayor's office, the local bank, the tax collectors, and the priest. Finally, the first society was forced into a merger. The resulting "Workers' Society"—including members of different classes, and firmly under elite control—continued to identify itself as a brotherhood of working men. In 1911, when a report of the society was published, its president was a literate, lower-class man. (In a preface to the report, he begs indulgence for lacking "that purity of style possessed by those who

are accustomed to using the pen," for he is only "a humble worker.")
However, the names of landowners and other elite appear when critical
financial business of the society is discussed.

Throughout the history of Montecastello, the landowning elite were
also active in the church, even when their politics were anticlerical.
They formed commissions to raise money to build and maintain the
church, contributed sacred objects, and were leaders of the confraternities that practiced various cults, supported masses for the dead, and
provided aid for the sick and the poor. The charter of a women's confraternity specifically states that "all councilwomen should belong—as
much as possible—to the first families of the paese." In addition, the
local upper class sponsored much of the ceremonial life of the community, providing the economic wherewithal and playing prominent roles
in various events of the festival cycle.

The forms of interaction between the local signori and the rest of the
community also followed the patron-client model. An elderly carpenter
remembered the group in this way:

They were all persons who were authoritative, serious, who frightened one
with their physical presence. They were the seven or eight *caporioni* (big men) of
the paese. They always dressed irreproachably. . . . They wore boots without
laces. . . . They commanded respect. If someone was standing near the campanile and some one of these personages came by the arch, if one did not wait to
pay his respectful greeting, that house would be closed to the rebellious vassal!
At that house the person no longer entered. . . . They were all very wealthy. In
their houses the table was never cleared. Whoever entered there, spontaneously,
to pay an errand, or called there, was well received. And they said to them: *"Va
là, cocco mio; magna e bevi!"* ("Go, my dear, eat and drink!")

The comments about these signori point up the connection between
the patronage role and the values of civiltà. A prime measure of the signore who is truly civile is generosity, the readiness to *give* to his social inferiors. This notion assumes the possession of wealth. Most Montecastellesi are little impressed by political slogans condemning landlords for
enjoying unearned wealth and leisure, but they do not forgive the failure
to demonstrate generosity. At the same time, generosity in an inter-class
context carries the expectation that the giver (inevitably of higher status
than the recipient) is entitled to loyalty, obedience, and respect. One
who is generous but cannot impose his authority over others is only a
fool; a true signore has the capacity to win compliance. (These qualities

were mentioned by several townspeople during the 1960 elections, in discussions of the qualifications of candidates for sindaco. The *ideal* candidate—one truly fit to govern Montecastello—would be someone who had no need to work so that he could dedicate his time to the office, who was wealthy enough to give the community what it needed, and who was able to "command.")

If some values incorporated into the ideology of civiltà are based on a patron's relationship to his own clients, others express the traditional elite's role as public patrons: commitment to the community, a sense of social responsibility, and active identification with Montecastello. These values must be understood in terms of the political history of Montecastello, as will be seen in the next chapter. That they are essential to Montecastellese notions of civiltà is clear. This was expressed by one middle-aged upper-class man as he explained why wealth, good manners, and culture were not enough to give a signore real civiltà. Speaking of a contemporary landlord, who owns one of the largest holdings in the community and who has a villa in the Montecastellese countryside where he lives for several months a year, the informant said:

He is best considered as a guest of Montecastello. . . . He takes from Montecastello but has his home elsewhere. . . . He is fond of Montecastello but just as an artistic object, as a historical monument, not as his own paese. . . . True, he has wealth, and he also has an appreciation for art and fine things. But he is not a true signore because this requires generosity. The real signori must be protectors of others. Theirs must be an attitude of *contributing* to the paese. . . .

Just as the values of civiltà reflect the role of the traditional elite, so were the styles of the civil life *their* styles. In contact with larger centers but residing in the community, the signori attempted to reproduce all the attributes of city life on the local scene, giving an urbane aura to the local associations, the Montecastellese festivals, and informal social interaction in the community. They pursued "culture" and carried out a lively round of sociability. Their dances and festive occasions, and even their daily strolls and street encounters, punctiliously observed the correct forms. They engaged in public discussion and exchanged rhetoric, both in the context of local politics and in informal conversation. They received visitors from outside the community and traveled back and forth to towns and cities of the region.

Although the ideology of civiltà is based on the social roles and styles of an elite, it was extended to wider segments within the population. In fact, in contemporary Montecastello it serves as a marker of social distinctions at different levels; this point will be returned to later in this chapter. Certainly the most avid spokesmen for elite values are those Montecastellesi closest to the traditional elite, particularly their less successful descendants, who draw on these values to make invidious comparisons with the "new" signori. The new elite draw on the same values and reproduce the same styles, to contrast themselves with others of their own background who have not improved their lot. Furthermore, the town as a whole identifies itself as "civile" (claiming, in a general way, the elite values) in contrast to the countryside. In making this contrast, townsmen use the term "paese" as synonymous with "town."

The relation of the countrymen to these values, however, is ambivalent. As the main victims of patronage, their view of the civile elite is ironic and bitter. At the same time, they partake of the civiltà of the community—"paese" in this case being defined as "town plus dependent territory." When the peasants speak of themselves as distinct from peasants of neighboring communes, they too become "Montecastellesi," and the identity they refer to is permeated with elite values. A middle-aged woman who had been a peasant most of her life gave the following assessment of Montecastello in contrast to another paese:

I would never live in Fratta. I would never marry into Fratta. If I ever should get another husband, I'll get one from Montecastello. . . . Montecastello has a lot of good families, like the R.'s, the E.'s, and the T.'s, and Fratta hasn't. What families does Fratta have? Maybe the G.'s, but that's all. You see, Montecastello has better people.

Yet, on other occasions, this woman recounted many stories of abuses committed by these same families.

It has been suggested that the ideology about patronage served certain functions within the context of the mezzadria system. More generally, the idealization of the role of the elite may be seen as a useful myth (or half-truth) about the social structure. The myth rationalizes and justifies the marked stratification of local society, and it reconciles the realities of conflicting interests with notions of "the community." It serves to perpetuate the position of the wealthy and powerful, but calls for a degree of reciprocity. Moreover, it acts to draw new members of the elite— especially professional and political appointees from outside—into local obligations. Masci himself was a bureaucrat born in Todi; he was buried in Montecastello with public tributes, having left his civil service benefits to the community.

The patterns of patronage described for Montecastello are related in a general way to the mezzadria system, but not all mezzadria areas elaborated patronage in the same ways or to the same degree. A crucial factor would appear to be the presence of a local elite. The mezzadria is conducive to more wide-ranging patronage only if the landlords are accessible and have a stake in the local community. This means landlords who not only live there or come there often, but (as argued earlier) who also stand to benefit from personalized ties with peasants and other clients. For the most part, such landlords are those with moderate holdings, above all, those who make up the *borghesia* of the towns near their land. It is significant that Montecastello's land remained predominantly in the hands of relatively small, non-noble proprietors. This class seems to have established itself firmly enough by the seventeenth century to resist the expansion of larger holdings that occurred in some parts of Umbria. Communities that were dominated by such large holdings might well have developed rather different versions of the civil life. Moreover, such communities have generally taken quite a different course in the twentieth century. Large fattorie were the first to shift to more commercialized, mechanized production and consequently the first to lose traditional social patterns. The quality of civiltà that could be detected in Montecastello in 1960 may be largely related to the fact that it still had remnants of a local landowning elite. At that time, many communities in Umbria had only absentee landlords and an agricultural proletariat, while others had long since lost their traditional elites through impoverishment or emigration.

The Decline of the Local Elite

In contemporary Montecastello, major socioeconomic divisions can be recognized that parallel those of the traditional period: a group identified as signori, comprising the most prosperous landowners as well as the professionals and higher-level bureaucrats; other townspeople—primarily tradesmen, skilled artisans, and petty bureaucrats; and a large lower class of the countryside, including peasant proprietors, mezzadri, and laborers. On closer examination, however, there are significant differences between the two periods.

The signori of today comprise two rather different categories, which tend to be merged in social interaction because of their small numbers. One includes the landowners who still own enough land to enable them to live more or less in the style of signori; the other consists of the non-landowning signori, including the professionals and those white-collar workers whose positions carry substantial authority. Higher education and employment in the national bureaucracy have increasingly rivaled land ownership as a source of elite status. The local landlords have responded to this trend by emphasizing a long-accustomed practice—educating their children for professions in law, medicine, government, and business. As in the past, land ownership is combined with non-landed sources of income and power, but the importance of the latter now outweighs the former.

The second large division—the townspeople who are not signori—includes a core of families of artisans and tradesmen, who show direct continuity with the past. In addition, it contains other economic categories: semi-professionals and moderately educated white-collar workers, small-scale landowners (including former landed signori with diminished holdings), a few recently successful merchants, and "new" townsmen—ex-peasants who are now nonagricultural laborers. The third division also includes a greater variety of economic categories than formerly; along with peasant proprietors and mezzadri—and often within the same families—are nonagricultural workers, both skilled and unskilled. Thus, residence in town or country is no longer an adequate guide, in itself, to significant economic and social distinctions.

The general structural similarity to traditional stratification masks changes that have had an impact on the civil life in Montecastello. Most important are the changes in the upper stratum. The signori are no longer a local elite based primarily on the mezzadria system, nor can they fulfil the role of the traditional elite. One factor in this change has been the shift in land ownership, which has reduced the holdings of the old Montecastellese families and brought quite different groups into the ranks of the mezzadria landlords.

The largest of the contemporary landowners are the four who have nine or ten farms each (see Table 11). Three of these four are "new" names in Montecastello, owing their wealth to commercial or industrial success within the past generation or two. The fourth is a descendant of the Pettinelli, whose history was given earlier in this chapter. None of the four was born in Montecastello or ever lived there, although two have built summer villas in the countryside. For all these proprietors, land in Montecastello represents only an investment, one of many business interests. They have little contact with their land or with the community in general, and their peasants deal primarily with the fattore. These landlords are not personally involved in local politics or informal conflicts; they are regarded by most Montecastellesi as part of the anonymous group of the wealthy and powerful of the cities.

The next four landlords, with five to seven farms each, are all Montecastellesi by birth; none, however, is from a traditional landowning family. Two, who are brothers, are grandsons of a local peasant proprietor. Their father had been an enterprising young man who both adopted a nonagricultural occupation and expanded his holdings on the active land markets of the late nineteenth century. He then married the niece of a major local landowner, who inherited seven farms from her uncle. The other two landowners are sons of Montecastellesi; their grandfathers came from nearby towns and gradually accumulated property in Montecastello. All these individuals live on the proceeds of their land, which is their primary or only source of income; all administer their farms personally. In general, their style of living is modest (or from others' point of view, "stingy"). In Montecastello they are referred to as "great proprietors," and they more than the first four are the targets of political attacks on the mezzadria system.

All of the eight padroni who have three or four farms each are of Montecastellese families. One is a sister of the two brothers mentioned above. Another is a local merchant who acquired considerable wealth in recent years through wholesale commerce in grain. The other six are descendants of important nineteenth-century landowners. Three of these live in the community on the income from their farms and look after their property themselves. The other three live in cities where they practice professions, and they come to Montecastello occasionally for holidays.

Twenty landlords own two farms each. Four or five of them are descendants of local landowning families. Six or seven others are from families that were until recently, or still are, peasant proprietors. (One case is a man whose father had supplemented the income from a piece of land with commerce in poultry. The family eventually moved into town where they embarked upon a series of small-scale businesses, including a butcher shop and a dry-goods store, purchasing farms with the profits.) A few of the owners of two farms are of families that were formerly mezzadri, and one owner is still a mezzadro. His family, which has been on the same farm for generations, is very large, and in the years since the war accumulated savings by sending some members into wage labor. Two holdings are church properties. The rest belong to people outside of Montecastello, who have contact only with their own peasants.

The padroni of a single farm include persons of every category: descendants of the traditional landowners; merchants and artisans who recently purchased land; peasant proprietors who also work other land or who have let their own farms under mezzadria contracts because they were unable to work them; and ex-mezzadri and mezzadri who are still on the farms of other landlords.

In general, then, the property of the former landowning elite has been distributed more widely among different social categories in present times. Also, the significance of land ownership has itself changed, as ownership of mezzadria land has become steadily less profitable and as power in the larger society has shifted away from the landed classes. Today, the largest of the local landlords do not rank as high as other signori, while most of the lesser landlords clearly are not signori at all.

Along with the change in landholding, the landlords became less and less a local group. At the same time that the holdings of the old landowning families were being divided and moving into new hands, their descendants were increasingly pursuing business, professional, and government careers, and many moved away from Montecastello to larger centers. On the other hand, many of the purchasers of their property were outsiders who could exploit their land by leasing it or hiring fattori and had no reason to move into the community. As the signori departed, residence in Montecastello became less appealing to others of this class, accelerating the movement away.

The result of this change in residence patterns of landlords is shown in Table 12. While the majority (about 70 percent) of the small and medium contemporary landlords are local residents, the four largest are not. One of the major landowners lives in Rome and another in Milan; the two others live in provincial cities. Many of the descendants of the old landowning families who might still claim an attachment to their remaining land have left Montecastello permanently or return only for brief hol-

Table 12   Residence of Mezzadria
Landowners by Number of Farms in
Holding, 1960

	Landowners	
Number of Farms	Resident	Absentee
1	59	27
2	13	7
3	5	1
4	1	1
5	2	0
6	1	0
7	1	0
8	0	0
9	0	2
10	0	2
Total	82	40

idays; most of those who still live there are elderly people who support themselves on the income from one or two farms. The only contemporary proprietors who are close to the land in terms of both residence and involvement are either new padroni or owners of very small holdings.

The disappearance of the traditional elite provokes ambivalent responses among the townspeople. Whenever a member of one of the old landowning families leaves the community, the sentiment—both regretful and cynical—that "all the best people are going away" is repeated throughout the town. The remaining members of those families complain of how Montecastello has been spoiled by the new local landowners (especially the ones with five to seven farms each). As one middle-aged woman, a descendant of the old signori, lamented:

The paese has changed so much. There used to be signorile families who were cultured and well-bred, people with civic feeling, who made something of the paese. Now there are just a lot of contadini who have made some money. . . . They are all contadini who came into the paese in the past generation and proceeded to act like signori. . . . The paese is nothing anymore.

Contemporary Montecastello has no true heirs to the former landowner-patrons, for there is no group that combines the requisites of their role: wealth, local residence, and status consistent with a patronage role. Their patronage functions have not disappeared but have been dispersed among a variety of persons and agencies. The most important source of services is the state, which gives much of the economic assistance people formerly sought from a patron. The state provides family subsidies, a national health plan, old age pensions, disability benefits, special allotments during agricultural crises, credit institutions, official charities, and other forms of assistance.[8] In addition to the state, several national organizations have entered the community, vying for support by offering conspicuous services. Thus, there are political party groups, trade unions, labor organizations, and the church, all of which provide assistance on a limited scale. However, the most important patronage services rendered by these agencies concern intervention with the world outside the community, which will be discussed in the next chapter.

Nevertheless, the pattern of personal, informal patronage persists. It still describes the relationships of some landlords to their peasants and some employers to their employees. However, the range of functions carried out in such relationships is limited by the economic and political power of the patron, and by the narrowed social difference between patron and client.

The pattern also survives in a few individuals who have deliberately tried to take on patronage roles in the traditional form. One of these is the wife of a prosperous but low-status merchant who recently puchased some mezzadria farms. She holds court behind the counter of her husband's local food shop, dispensing small gifts, credit, and advice (generally gratuitous) as a counterpoint to selling groceries. In addition, she gives gifts of food to many families on various occasions, is unusually generous in paying for services, occasionally signs notes on behalf of her clients, and frequently sponsors semipublic excursions and festive gatherings. In turn, she is treated with considerable homage by all who accept her favors, is invited to their family celebrations, and is showered with remembrances on appropriate occasions. A second such individual, a descendant of an old landowning family who does not own any land, tries to perpetuate the pattern by advising and aiding persons who seek him out, giving them the benefit of his long career experience in bureaucracy. He also considers himself a patron of the community in his role as guardian of local traditions. A third would-be patron is a young man, a government clerk, the son of a former peasant proprietor who now owns two mezzadria farms. He expends great effort in maintaining community activity, organizing festivals, and carrying out various projects. Finally, there is the pharmacist, a woman who is often pointed to as an ideal among contemporary signori; significantly, she is not of a landowning family. This gracious lady is a constant source of advice (both medical and personal) for lower-class persons, who find her attitude more sympathetic than the local doctor's and her remedies less costly. Her benefactors regularly give her and her family gifts, mainly food delicacies.

Each of these individuals has taken on a patronage role because of personal inclination. Each is limited by his or her own position and can provide favors only within specific areas. While these contemporary patrons perform certain functions that are continuous with those of the landowning elite, and while the behavioral forms are similar, the bases of their roles are rather different, and more tenuous.

As the traditional elite's functions of personal patronage were taken over by others (or else simply ceased to be performed by anyone), the role of public patron was also eroded. Public services related to local administration, roads, education, health, and charity are now controlled mainly by the state. As for the local associations and organized "cultural" activity, there is no one with both the means and inclination to assume their sponsorship.

The result is that few of the local organizations and community projects are still functional. The theater has stood unused since 1950. The families that sponsored it have been unable to agree either to restore it or to give it to a public corporation for possible restoration. The band broke up after the war, and attempts by some of its former members to revive it have been unsuccessful. During its last few years a merchant acted as maestro, but he was ridiculed for his lack of musical training and accused of using the band for personal profit. The dramatic society has not existed since the early 1950s. The church choir has dwindled to a small group of adolescents; some former members say they left because of antipathy toward the priest, while others thought it politically inexpedient to participate. The library has long since disappeared; the space was taken over by the commune for grain storage, and documents and books were scattered or left to deteriorate. The few religious confraternities that remain function only to provide masses for deceased members. The charitable organizations and mutual-aid societies have been displaced by the government and by outside bodies. The formal associations that still exist in Montecastello are all branches of national organizations, at least in part dependent upon outside sources of leadership and support.

The contemporary signori do not reproduce the role of the traditional landowning elite; their sociability now also differs from that of the community-centered civil life of the past. Today's signori, particularly the nonlandowning professionals, have ties outside the community that, to an increasing extent, are more important than those within. Many are not Montecastellesi, and all operate in a more fluid employment system. These changes, along with the availability of automobiles, mean that the signori now spend much of their leisure time in larger towns and cities. To participate in the "culture," entertainment, or social activity of urban life they can go regularly to Perugia or Rome; there is no need to recreate urbanity in Montecastello. Dances, visiting, and other occasions are as frequent as ever among the signori, but as often as not they take place elsewhere, and the events that are local are regarded as poor substitutes for those of the city.

In the past as at present, the social activity of the upper class was inspired by urban models. However, much of it took place in the context of local associations, and incorporated Montecastellese traditions or modes defined as "our own way." Today, what is considered "signorile" sociability in Montecastello is deliberate, unmodified imitation of outside patterns. Furthermore, those patterns are now familiar and directly accessible to all via television and other means of communication, and they can be imitated by the lower classes as well as by the signori. No longer are a local elite the communicators of urban styles to the rest of the population. Today, all classes attempt to conform to a common national model dictated from Rome and Milan, bypassing the local reinterpretation that gave the civil life its particularistic accents.

Civiltà in Social Distinctions

While the ideology of civiltà is based on an elite way of life, it influences the social interaction of a much wider population. Despite the considerable change that had occurred since World War II, that influence was still evident in 1960. The values summed up by civiltà played a central part in the code used to allocate social honors in Montecastello.

My understanding of that code is based upon a sorting method I devised in an attempt to discover the principles guiding the distribution of prestige in Montecastello. By "prestige" I mean other people's evaluation of a person's social rank and capacity to receive deference. The

method was designed to elicit the criteria that enter into some Montecastellesi's judgment of the relative prestige of members of the community.
Informants were asked to compare different persons in terms of their
"general regard" in the community, using whatever criteria they thought
were meaningful. Through such comparisons each informant built up an
overall sorting of the population into categories that in his judgment
represented ranks of relative prestige. I recorded the comments of informants as they weighed various considerations, and the questions they
asked themselves. Though the sortings of actual persons varied somewhat from one infomant to anther, there were basic points of agreement
on the relevant criteria and on the defining characteristics of different
prestige ranks.[9]

The Montecastellese phrasing of prestige emerged as the concept of
rispetto. Each informant adopted that concept spontaneously and restated
the task in these terms: "Between X and Y, which one gets more rispetto?" (My own questions, then, were: "Why?—how does one de-
cide?") A judgment of rispetto is an overall evaluation of a person's right
to receive deference, which is manifested in certain rituals of behavior,
modes of speech, and an appropriate order of action between individuals.[10] Rispetto crosscuts other sources of deference, such as age, kinship
status, and situational power, and it approaches a general summation of
informal social rank. A claim to rispetto is regarded as a more or less permanent, inherent attribute of a person, in contrast to *considerazione*,
which describes the actual manifestations of deference. Thus, one may
find it politic to show considerazione (for example, to the carabinieri),
even when the person's right to rispetto is not great. Both these concepts
are clearly distinguished from *stima*, the evaluation of an individual's personal worth. For example:

   Roberto and his brothers have rispetto, as much as any of the others in the
first rank. But he is a rascal. Their father stole from everybody. People look out
for them because they are dangerous. But they "respect" them. . . . For a man
who is dishonest and rich, they show rispetto, while one who isn't rich but is
completely good doesn't get as much as the other. A woman who is good but
poor, so-so. A woman who isn't good but has something is *rispettata*. That's how
it is around here. . . . Dario—he is *rispettato* as much as these others, even
though he drinks too much. . . . Giorgio—he is rispettato, as a landowner, as a
bank clerk. He has committed I don't know what kind of crime in the bank, but
rispetto they show him all the same.

It was also made clear that rispetto refers to relative rank, not patterns of association or intimacy.

The prestige ranks may be represented by the following model, which shows three major categories and several subcategories in descending order of prestige. The solid and broken lines suggest the magnitude of difference between the categories.

A–1
A–2

– – – – – – – –

B
_____

C–1
C–2
C–3

Each category (and subcategory) can be defined by certain criteria that contrast it with adjacent categories. The criteria that enter into each contrast combine a number of considerations, including a person's occupation, education, family name, and financial position. However, these cannot be taken as simple indices of rank, for their significance and relative weight differ at each level of the system.

A fundamental consideration in evaluating prestige is an individual's (or more precisely, a family's) civiltà. Judgments about civiltà draw on the other elements mentioned above, but also involve certain ways of evaluating them. Civiltà is not a single attribute, nor is it quantifiable; rather, it covers a range of meanings and qualities. Though all refer in one way or another to participation in the civil life, different aspects of the concept are relevant to making distinctions at different levels.

The major line of cleavage, dividing categories A and B from category C, parallels the contrast between *paese* and *campagna*—town and countryside (expressed also in the contrasts *paesani/contadini* and *persone di dentro/persone di fuori*, or "people of inside"/"people of outside"). The issue here is not place of residence but legitimate association with either town or countryside, i.e., a person's recognized sphere of social interaction. The issue becomes critical in distinguishing among non-elite families living in town, which include many of campagna background. Thus, those families who have lived in the paese for generations and "belong" there (B) are contrasted with those who have come into town only in the present generation, who are considered the highest rank within category C. One informant expressed the contrast in this way:

Between these two [B and C–1] there is a great difference. It is a question of civiltà. . . . Both groups comprise the main part of the *popolo*, but [B] are families with a long history of belonging to the paese, while [C–1] have recently come from the campagna. . . . [B] are not so much wealthy, as good people, respected, gente civile in short. . . . These others are good people, but *così* (so-so).

Some families assigned to B were described as follows:

The Ciani, though contadini originally, are an old and respected family in the town. . . . The Pianelli, though they were contadini, are a very respected family. They were always part of the community. They were elected as representatives of the people. . . . I must put them ahead of the contadini.

On the other hand, these statements refer to families placed in C–1:

These are workers who have come from the campagna a short time ago, just after the war. It's only recently that they've come inside. If not for that, they are contadini. . . . You understand, here, as yet, the people don't give them much rispetto. . . . After a while, with time, the sons may acquire much more rispetto.

These are mostly from contadino families, even if today they are artisans. Monelli—this is a good family, in behavior and everything, but still they are from the campagna, even if it has been many years now that they've been in the town. . . . Enrico—he is an artisan. You might ask why I don't put him with the other artisans here [in B], but no. Because in Montecastello he isn't considered like, for instance, Alberto, even though they are both artisans, this one a shoemaker, that one a carpenter. Enrico is of another background. In men like that, nothing has changed.

In this distinction between B and C, "civiltà" means the extent to which people have incorporated town ways and left the mark of the countryside behind them. The concept of *incivilimento* was used to describe a "civilizing" process. This refers to a gradual change whereby new residents in the town learn the outward styles of town life—civile dress, housing and speech, the skills of discourse, the etiquette of public encounters, and the forms of town sociability. One informant explained it this way:

If a contadino [who has moved into town] dresses well, talks well, it is likely that he will make an advance as his economic condition improves. But it is only with *la cultura* that they advance. For these [C–1], to come into the paese was just a matter of a change of trade. It didn't bring about any incivilimento.

The second largest gap, that setting off category A from B and C, is the distinction between a select group and "il popolo" (the common people). The first includes persons who command a high level of informal authority and deference in the community as a whole.

In the eyes of the people, they are a category higher than the others, in the rispetto due them. . . . Whoever meets any of them on the street will not fail to greet them. . . . They form a group apart.

With few exceptions the persons assigned to A are considered "signori," a category that is quite clearly distinguished by linguistic usages. The signori are called, by nonintimates of all classes, "Sor Giovanni" or "Sora Rosa" (or simply "Signora"), rather than "Giovanni" or "Rosa," and the *voi* rather than the *tu* form is used in addressing them.

Distinction between A and B draws on a wider range of the features of civiltà. Persons in A are measured against the qualities related to the traditional elite. Though many fall far short, the point is that this standard of judgment is considered appropriate. The B townsmen, on the other hand, are assumed to be simple, more-or-less honest people who don't try to set themselves apart from the masses and are not particularly expected to be cultured or generous.

The difference between A–1 and A–2 is a matter of the legitimacy of position, as opposed to a reasonably successful but questionable claim. The criteria of legitimacy make reference to the full gamut of qualities associated with the elite role.

Mortini Osvaldo—I put him in the first category. He comes from a family with the blood of bishops and cardinals. They are in an excellent economic position. . . . It is a family surrounded by consideration. I remember as a boy, at the end of vacation, the evening before leaving for school, I went to the Mortini family to greet them. It was an act of deference one performed for the four or five best families. . . . Now, Osvaldo himself holds a position of importance, one that is entrusted only to very capable men. . . . He is not only part of the local environment but he takes part in the environment of Rome.

Thus, legitimacy may be inherited—provided that one bears the family name with some distinction of one's own. However, it may also be acquired by higher education. This is the case in most instances today; the professionals necessarily have advanced degrees, and the title of Dottore (a university graduate) alone bestows A–1 status. It is often said that persons of A–1 are entitled to their prestige because they are "signori in mentality and behavior"; this genuine signorilità is considered attainable either through growing up in an elite family or through advanced schooling. In contrast, A–2 consists primarily of the "signori of financial means" (the five or six most prosperous local landowners), who have neither distinguished ancestry nor education.

The contrast between A–1 and A–2 is pointed up when people talk about the failure of today's signori to carry out the traditional patronage role. Those in A–1 have the personal capacity—whether by inheritance or by acquisition—to act the patron, and signorilità "in mentality" describes, in part, the inclination to do so. However, most lack the means. A–2, in contrast, either do not want the role or cannot carry it off with the requisite flair. Individuals in A–1 are likely to be described as "gente civile" without further qualification, while A–2 includes the people most often criticized as "poco civile"—stingy, ill-mannered, overbearing, and uncultured. In other words, the latter persons are matched against what they *ought* to be as claimants of signorile status. In fact, the term "signori" when used to refer to them, often has an ironic, pejorative sense.

There might be added to the two categories of signori a third and highest level, that of "the complete signori." The concept exists for some people, though no one in Montecastello today fits the description. This category corresponds to civiltà in full measure. It combines the virtues of A–1 (family and personal qualities, as well as a position of authority) with the economic means of the A–2 landlords. Above all, it implies a real patronage role.

Category C is marked by contadino origin and identification. Though "contadino" in Montecastello is synonymous with "mezzadro," it is often extended (with derogatory intention) to everyone who "belongs" to the campagna. (A few people, like fattori, who live in the country for reasons of circumstance or preference are excluded, if they have long been detached from working the land.) The distinction between C–1 and the two lower subcategories is based on incivilimento. While persons in C–1 have not fully integrated town ways they are recognizably in the process of doing so, having already changed residence and/or occupation. One informant gave this summary of C–1:

These are people of contadino origin who have been in the town for some time. Their work is more civile than that of a contadino. I don't mean more

noble. Perhaps the contadino's is more noble, but theirs is more civile. . . .
They are a little *paesati* [i.e. they have acquired some town traits]. . . . They go
to the bar in the evening, while people in the campagna might visit for an
hour or two between neighbors, and then go to bed.

The contrast between C–2 and C–3 is the distinction between the self-
respecting peasant and the *bifolco*, the peasant who is oppressed or mis-
treated, lives "like a beast," and has no prospect of improving his position. Here, the minimal definition of civiltà is called into play. C–2 as-
signment means there is a shred of resemblance to civiltà: some
awareness of the larger world and ability to manage in it; some display of
effort to make one's house "decent;" elegant dress on some occasions; occasional mimicry of etiquette and social forms—always provided that
these efforts are carried off in a manner that is not outlandish.

Take the Bernardi and the Santi, for instance. These are ancient families of
Montecastello. It is a hundred years that they are on the same farm. It is almost
as if they are of the paese. They are very good families, genteel, perhaps with a
little money. . . . The greater part of these others [C–3] are poor. Until just now
they were really the slaves of the landowners . . . These [C–2] want everything. If they don't like something, they leave the padrone. . . . Most of them
have money. . . . They come to the town a lot to amuse themselves. They have
raised themselves in everything. They all have a motor scooter, and some even
have an automobile.

This discussion has emphasized the convergence in Montecastellese
views on the principles for making appropriate social distinctions. However, the disagreements among informants are also revealing. In particular, some of the differences between Gianni, age 43, and Rinaldo, 65 (of
roughly equivalent status) point up ongoing changes in the prestige code.
For example, while Rinaldo was elaborate in describing the differences
among the three subdivisions of category C, Gianni—who recognized
the same distinctions—considered them too minor to call for any subdivision. His position reflects the trends leading toward a diversified
lower class, in which peasants are indistinguishable from many nonagricultural townspeople.

Gianni's comments suggest, too, that the significance of civiltà in assigning prestige is also in the process of change. Gianni is a schoolteacher
with a reputation for being highly civile in personal attributes though
lacking wealth or any position of real influence. In his view the main distinction between A–1 and A–2 is that between "professionals of high

grade" as against "middle-cut professionals," and he minimized other aspects of signorilità. In judging all categories he weighed family history against present occupation/residence/behavior and consistently decided for the present. His answers to questions about how people change category emphasized formal education, occupational training, the acquisition of "culture" in the sense of learning to appreciate the finer things of life, and in general stressed the ease with which this can be done today. When he spoke of civiltà he referred to personal qualities and behavioral forms potentially available to all who could learn them, and there was little trace of the traditional elite role in the standards he applied to today's population. Thus, Gianni's responses may well be indicative of an emerging version of civiltà and of new criteria governing informal interaction.

CHAPTER 5

The Context of Power

THE CIVIL LIFE revealed in Montecastello's recent history was primarily that of a local elite. The patterns enacted in the community, however, were products of a larger constellation of forces. To seek the origin of these patterns, one must look at Montecastello's changing relations to the polities of which it was part. From this perspective, the antecedents of civiltà appear as a series of strategies adopted by the upper class of the community in their maneuvers within a wider political framework. This chapter traces the development of the civil life as part of the political history of Montecastello.[1]

The Legacy of the Commune

The documented history of Montecastello begins in about the eleventh century, but it is likely that the site was occupied long before this. Scattered archeological finds in the area suggest a pre-Roman settlement (Ceci 1897:136, Alvi 1910:214). Local tradition has it that the founders of Montecastello were the Vibi, possibly connected with the Perugian family that produced Vibius Trebonianus Gallus, emperor of Rome from A.D. 251 to 253. The name appears in Roman inscriptions found near Montecastello, and it forms part of the ancient name of the abbey, San Lorenzo Ubiata. It was in honor of this presumed ancestral family that local officials added *di Vibio* to the name of the commune in 1862, when it became necessary to differentiate it from other places called Montecastello in the province. However, virtually nothing is known about the Vibi of Montecastello, since Vibius was a very common name (Harris 1971:324).

Todi, ten kilometers away, must have been a dominant force over the area from early times. An important center since at least the fifth century B.C., first for the Umbrians and then the Etruscans, it became the Roman municipality of Tuder; under the Roman system, a city and its surrounding territory formed a unity. By the fifth century A.D. Todi was an episcopal seat (Ceci 1897:3), and in the eighth century the limits of the diocese were fixed, giving Todi ecclesiastical dominion over the territory of Montecastello (Desplanques 1969:103).

In the centuries after the breakdown of the empire, Todi was conquered by the Ostrogoths, became an object of the lengthy struggle between Byzantines and Lombards, and then came under Frankish rule. Throughout this time the bishops gained steadily in power within the city. Control of the countryside, however, was fragmented among feudal lords and monasteries, while *castella* emerged as small administrative centers disrupting the territorial domain of the city (see Jones 1966:343). Montecastello may have been one of these. All that is known of this period is that there was a church on the site of San Lorenzo Ubiata by the eighth or ninth century. The abbey was probably somewhat later. Built as a Benedictine monastery, it was at once an agricultural estate, a fortress for nobles at war or in exile from Todi, and the original parish seat of Montecastello.

In the first references to what is now the town of Montecastello—which tell of an attack by Orvieto cavalry in 1077—it is described as a castle controlled by the Commune of Todi.[2] The time of this account corresponds to the emergence of autonomous communes throughout Northern and Central Italy. Like all communes, Todi was engaged in submitting the nobles of the surrounding countryside; Montecastello was one place where this conflict was acted out. From then on, Montecastello's course was intimately tied to Todi's. In particular, the development of the civil life in Montecastello was related to the communal phenomenon in this area.

The commune was basically a consortium among the major families of a town, created through a sworn oath and sanctioned by grants of privileges from an overlord. The commune developed characteristic institutions of self-government, but its essence was the common association, the "community"—an identity separate from that of the individual members, and the source of authority over functions exercised in common. Little is known of the origin of the Commune of Todi, but by the middle of the twelfth century it had two institutions diagnostic of the commune: a consulate or elected official body, and a magistrate independent of the judicial authority of the bishop.

Like other communes, Todi was sought as an ally by both emperor and pope. Its independence was, in fact, born out of the conflict between them. For most of the twelfth century Todi remained loyal to the German emperor, who in turn conceded Todi's municipal liberties. But this territory was part of the Patrimony of St. Peter, which had been claimed by the popes since the eighth century, and in 1198 Innocent III began to reconstitute the temporal power of the church throughout the Patrimony. In that year he came to Todi, confirmed the legitimacy of the consulate, and accepted vows of fealty from the communal officials (Ceci 1897:74–76). The pope replaced the emperor as overlord, but he was no more able than his rival to intrude upon the internal affairs of the city. Thus, the commune flourished, although there was continual conflict with the pope over questions of autonomy.

The creation of the commune went hand in hand with a process of bringing the contado into its jurisdiction. The commune conquered castles that did not offer their submission, struck bargains with local powers, and established new settlements. The nobles were required to build houses in the city (though they kept their castles as well), and they became active participants in the official and informal life of the commune. Whether one views the process as the commune's triumph over the countryside or as the nobles' infiltration of the commune, its result was the urbanization of the nobility. The nobles of communal Italy became townsmen as familiar with commerce and officialdom as with warfare and chivalry, as much at ease in city piazzas as in castle retreats.

This process was accomplished in Todi well before 1200, when the city embarked upon a policy of expanding its territory (Ceci 1897:54–55). By this time, the internal organization of the commune was also changing. The consulate was replaced by a *podestà*, appointed by the commune as its highest administrative and judiciary official. Always an outsider, usually a noble educated in law, he served for a fixed term of no more than a year. By the middle of the century a parallel official, but one with primarily military functions, also appeared—the Captain of the People (Popolo). This figure indicates the growing importance of the non-noble population, especially the newly rich—landowners, merchants, master guildsmen, and others. Though the Todi area never engaged in large-scale manufacturing or long-distance trade, agricultural commerce within the region seems to have allowed considerable social mobility. Todi had several noble families who controlled large quantities of land, but it also had a population of notaries, shopkeepers, money-lenders, and artisans, many of whom also owned land, and all of whom participated in the politics of the commune. In fact, the fourteenth century saw a Popular government that reacted against the nobles and severely restricted their prerogatives.

The statutes of 1275 give a picture of how the commune was governed (Ceci and Pensi 1897; Scalvanti 1897). The General Council of 300 members, 50 from each quarter of the city, acted as a popular assembly and gave final approval on all matters. Sixty of the members were elected to the Special (or Secret) Council, the active decision-making body. The councils appointed the podestà, who was required to bring with him a staff of judicial assistants, civil police, and minor officials. A Council of the Guilds appeared around 1250; its members, elected by the various guilds, appointed the captain. A number of other officials were named. Some were salaried bureaucrats; others served only part time. The main positions tended to be held by nobles, but most citizens were in some way involved in public affairs. Offices rotated frequently and citizens were not supposed to refuse an election. The one exception to this rule applied to ambassadors, who were elected as needed from among those with the necessary qualities and financial means.

In addition to governing the city, the Commune of Todi maintained control over the contado of some 30,000 people, and it engaged in continuous warfare and negotiations with other communes and with pope and emperor. The degree and nature of control over the contado fluctuated. The villages on the slopes below the city were firmly held. In the case of large fortified towns near the contado borders, in contrast, submission merely meant a treaty of alliance and an agreement to choose a podestà approved by Todi. Montecastello's position was intermediate between these extremes. It was held as a castle of the commune, which kept a permanent official there (the *castellano*) along with several sergeants. However, Todi's dominion was challenged frequently: by other communes, who recognized Montecastello's strategic situation; by factions within Todi (in particular the Guelfs, who retreated to Montecastello when they were out of power); and, to an increasing extent, by the Montecastellesi themselves.

Nevertheless, Todi retained its hold through most of the communal period. In 1245 Todi tore down the walls of Montecastello to restore control. In 1292 Montecastello was recorded in the book of hearths, indicating that it was taxed by Todi. In 1323 it was included in a survey of the fortresses of Todi. In 1340 Montecastello was listed among the *accavallata*, those in the contado required to support the cavalry of Todi (Ceci 1888:4).

From this period on, Todi pursued a number of continuing interests in its relations with Montecastello. The smaller community was a considerable agricultural producer. Todi constantly strove to tax it and to lay claim—directly or indirectly—to its grain and other produce, both for the city's own consumption and for a profitable (though geographically limited) commerce. Until the sixteenth century, Montecastello also held military significance for Todi, as a source of men and supplies and as a tactically important location. To protect its interests, the city attempted to keep judiciary rights over Montecastello and to appoint its own officials to the major executive posts.

From early times, the Montecastellesi are characterized as rebellious against Todi, and they appear to have increasingly been in a position to assert their independence. In 1292 Montecastello consisted of 199 households, or a population of about 800 to 900. It was one of the largest castles in the contado; most others had fewer than 50 households (Ceci 1897:320–26). Furthermore, at this time the area in general was witnessing the development of a middle class in the small towns as well as in the cities. Even if much of Montecastello's land belonged to nobles and to the church, it is likely that there were also new landowners, as suggested in chapter 4. There were, surely, persons engaged in the administration of properties and in agricultural commerce, as well as notaries, bureaucrats, shopkeepers, and artisans. Thus, it may be that even quite early, Montecastello contained a group that could represent local interests. This group persisted through time, even as overlords were superimposed. It grew in size and influence, especially when Todi's power diminished and the interests of Montecastellese nobles became detached from those of Todi. Eventually, this group initiated the organization of Montecastello as a separate commune.

The commune was more than an urban phenomenon. Many small towns and villages won the right to be organized as communes, gained a degree of control over internal affairs, and possessed communal statutes. The range of variation among Central Italian medieval settlements with communal institutions, from city-states to peasant villages, means that one must be cautious about interpreting the fragmentary evidence on Montecastello. However, the efforts of historians to identify types of settlements in medieval Italy provide some clues (e.g., Jones 1966:348–52; Volpe 1961:162–65). Montecastello falls into the general category of *castra* or *castella*, walled settlements that were intermediate (in terms of size, social complexity, and functional importance) between cities (*civitates*) and villages that were essentially aggregations of peasants. Although the differences among such types are matters of degree and are far from clearcut, according to Volpe there are grounds for regarding the castra as qualitatively closer to the urban than to the rural communes. Most significant for Volpe is the fact that the *castrum* often functioned as the head of a territorial circumscription, as the administrative, economic, military, and religious center for a rural zone. Except for the religious function (which was held by the abbey located close to the town), Montecastello was clearly such a center. It should be remembered, too, that the cities (whose defining feature was that they were episcopal seats) were with few exceptions very small; Todi, for instance, must never have had more than its contemporary population of about 4,000 living within the town. From this perspective, the indications that a small town like Montecastello attempted to become autonomous and to model itself after a neighboring city-state become more understandable.

In the fourteenth century the free communes gave way to *signorie* (lordships). The framework of communal institutions was retained but real power was taken over by despots. This was a century of intensified warfare between the cities, of plague, and of famine. The papacy, now controlled by the kings of France, withdrew to Avignon. Todi was at the height of its military power, and it kept Montecastello within its contado for most of the century. With the return of the papacy to Rome in 1377, however, the balance of power shifted. The popes once again attempted to subject the territories of the Patrimony. Now their means was to place their own clients in the signorie of the cities and castles. Thus, in 1392

Boniface IX ceded Montecastello in fief to Catalano degli Atti, a member of the noble family that headed the papal faction of Todi.

The Atti are popularly regarded as the lords of medieval Montecastello. They and their enemies are the main protagonists of the history that recent generations of Montecastellesi have glorified as a distinctive local tradition. For instance, a nineteenth-century local history talks of how in 1396 the Atti lost Montecastello to a relative of Biordo Michelotti, signore of Perugia, who had conquered a vast region of the pope's Umbrian domain. The Atti moved to retake the castle and laid siege to it, choosing a time when the lord was absent. His wife, Michelotta, commanded the soldiers and held out for several days; for this act she would become a heroine in local history. Finally, she had to surrender and the Atti regained their fief.

In 1405 Montecastello passed into the hands of a nephew of Pope Innocent VII. According to one account, the nephew had imprisoned one of the Atti (who were then in conflict with the pope) and won the castle in payment for his release. Innocent died the following year, however, and in 1409 the new pope lost control of the Papal States to Ladislaus, King of Naples, who returned Montecastello to the Atti. The family kept their hold until 1464, when Pope Paul II recalled the castle into the direct domain of the Church. The next pope conceded it to the signore of Urbino and then, in 1475, to the city of Todi. This subjection to Todi apparently involved more painful measures than the feudal lordships, for it was followed by "homicide, fires, and finally open rebellion" (Ceci 1888:7). In 1486, Pope Innocent VIII acknowledged this dissension and freed Montecastello from Todi, making it directly subject to the Holy See.

At this point, various documents refer to Montecastello as a "comune," and the evidence suggests that it was, in fact, organized as a commune (A.C.M., 4). For instance, in 1466 Montecastello was described as having a podestà and local officials, who represented the community in a dispute with Todi. It appears that while Montecastello was being passed back and forth among different overlords, it was also developing a local political structure and forms of public life that were a miniature of Todi's. This process became evident as Todi's ability to hold Montecastello weakened. By this time the popes were establishing their direct authority over the Papal States; their attempt to suppress the cities coincided with Montecastello's efforts at independence. In 1513

Pope Leo X confirmed all "privileges and exemptions" of the Commune
of Montecastello, and in 1516 he validated the communal statutes. Montecastello's independence was only temporary, for in 1547 it was once
again in the contado of Todi. Nevertheless, Montecastello was by then a
political entity in its own right. Its population was growing again; by
1571 it was well beyond the thirteenth-century level (see Table 13). It
had a landowning elite who were clearly Montecastellesi and who saw
their interests as distinct from those of Todi. By all accounts, it was a

Table 13   Population over Time

Year	Montecastello Parish	Total Commune [a]	Sources
1292	900 [b]	(1,200)	A.C.T., 1
1656	1,250 [c]	(1,400)	Corridore 1906
1701–8	1,110 [d]	(1,277)	Corridore 1906
1736	854	(1,045)	Corridore 1906
1769	917	(1,093)	Ferrantini 1948
1804	1,202		A.C.M., 6
1814	1,300		A.C.M., 7
1827	1,220		Calindri 1829
1855	1,588 [e]		A.C.M., 10
1861		1,923 [f]	ISTAT 1960
1871		2,041	ISTAT 1960
1881		1,986	ISTAT 1960
1901		2,209	ISTAT 1960
1911		2,276	ISTAT 1960
1921		2,415	ISTAT 1960
1931		2,697	ISTAT 1960
1951		2,751	ISTAT 1960
1960–61	1,885	2,388	ISTAT 1965 and commune registers
1971	1,508	1,881	ISTAT 1973 and commune registers
1973		1,862	Commune registers, as of December 31, 1973

[a] Figures in parentheses are sums of estimated populations of Montecastello
and Doglio parishes.
[b] 199 hearths (population estimate based on 4.5 persons per hearth).
[c] Population estimated by adjusting for omission of children under 3 (after
Beloch 1959).
[d] Average of figures for 1701 and 1708.
[e] 271 in town, 1,317 in countryside.
[f] Figures for 1861 through 1973 pertain to resident population.

thriving, small-town version of the communal life. Thus, the patterns that arose out of the autonomy of city republics were most clearly manifested in Montecastello only when the territorial state emerged—when the possibility of real autonomy was past.

Yet like other communes large and small, Montecastello continued to be concerned with issues of autonomy within the state. For Montecastello, autonomy meant avoiding Todi's control. Its main tactic was to submit itself to Todi's enemies. At times this meant the pope; at times it meant the city-states whose territories bordered on Todi—for neighbors were always potential enemies, and neighbors of neighbors potential allies. Such submissions, or alliances, lasted only as long as circumstances warranted. For instance, in 1563 Montecastello offered its submission to Perugia but revoked it little more than a year later, when it found the taxes imposed by the city to be too oppressive (A.S.P., 1).

The political maneuvers that Montecastello engaged in in defense of its autonomy are illustrated by a series of events in 1565. In that year Todi purchased Montecastello from the Ecclesiastical State. The price was 20,000 gold florins, plus 3,000 florins for the right to receive two-thirds of the income from fines and to operate the civil notariate. A few weeks later, the General Council of Todi elected two proxies to take possession of the town and to implement the terms. The Montecastellesi thereupon sent ambassadors to the pope offering to match the price and place themselves under the domain of the Church, in return for nullification of Todi's purchase. The pope agreed, and Todi was forced to revoke its claim. However, soon afterwards the Todi Council sent its own ambassadors to the pope to ask that the original contracts be upheld, with the condition that Todi would maintain the castle in the name of the Apostolic Seat. (As the nineteenth-century local history comments, "By doing so, Todi thought to equal the ability of those of Montecastello, but their efforts did not succeed.") At this point, the Montecastellesi began to negotiate with Orvieto for a voluntary submission to that city. Todi sent new ambassadors to the pope to argue that "both for reason of distance and of tradition" Montecastello's submission to Orvieto rather than Todi was unjust (Ceci 1888:8–9).

In the end Montecastello paid its price and remained under papal dominion. It regained "its communal privileges, the full and free possession of its lands and of both banks of the Tiber"; the right to elect and to remove its own governor, who was to be subject "in all affairs criminal as well as administrative" directly to Rome; and the right to elect all the officials required for public services. Thus, within the territorial state Montecastello had come to resemble the free communes in form and spirit, though not in real power.

If one stands in the main piazza of Todi on a Saturday morning today, or mingles with the crowd in front of the church in Montecastello after Sunday mass, it is not hard to imagine what the towns of the communal period were like. Many of the patterns shaped by the commune persist in the civil life of present-day Central Italy, even within vastly different political realities. The town is a hub of social activity and power in the midst of the rural territory it claims. Each town appears as a world unto itself. It contains remnants of the institutions through which it once managed its own affairs, and it still conserves the spirit of autonomy. It also has its own reference points for identity and value; it is the focus of civic pride and campanilismo. The town piazza is a forum, a place for sifting information, for plotting intrigue, for personal presentation and public spectacle. All "full" citizens (i.e., townsmen possessing property or a trade) have the right to be passionately interested in politics, to have an opinion, and to concoct schemes of their own. All can speak their views in public—to be judged not only by what they say but, even more, by how they say it. The piazza is a marketplace too, and all citizens, from landed aristocrat to humble shoemaker, are caught up in commerce. Their talk is about a piece of land for sale, about a deal someone has made, about an irregularity in the public accounts. And while the church looms large in the piazza, the values expressed are predominantly secular: respect for formal education and "culture," faith in written law and bureaucracy, an appreciation of quality and quantity in material things.

The commune was not a democracy. In Montecastello as elsewhere, it was sponsored by an elite, who used it in defense of their own interests and who always held effective power in it. Others in the population participated to a degree, but it is likely that most of the peasantry had only a marginal connection with political affairs. The precise makeup of the communal elite in sixteenth-century Montecastello is not clear, but some general inferences can be made from the documents. First, they were local men, not necessarily by birth or even by permanent residence, but in the sense that they identified themselves as Montecastellesi and

regarded their interests as located there. Certainly they expressed civic
spirit in their references to Montecastello. Furthermore, this elite included men other than nobles and owners of large holdings. More important, there was no sharp distinction between aristocratic and bourgeois
members of the elite. The nobles who appear in the accounts of Todi
and Montecastello were often soldiers and horsemen, but they were also
lawyers and petty officials. One reads of nobles whose military escapades
consisted of making banking arrangements to pay off mercenaries, and
who each month carefully balanced the books of the communal accounts.
This elite, in short, seems much like that of nineteenth-century Montecastello.

The commune looks like a self-contained entity, and its own battle cry
was autonomy, but it was in fact an adaptation to forces outside it. It
reflects a political context characterized by many centers, none of them
able to permanently dominate or absorb the others, and by the constant
intrusion of external powers (such as popes and foreign invaders). The
commune's survival was predicated on its ability to maneuver within that
context. To defend its interests, Montecastello had to deal with city-
states and would-be empires. Larger communes engaged in military ven-
tures as well as statesmanship, but since Montecastello's military force
was limited, its moves were made mainly through negotiation. This activity began in the time of the early communes, but it was increasingly
emphasized as the Papal States brought an end to internecine warfare.
Such diplomacy, enacted by the local elite, played an important part in
the formation of the civil life.

For much of Montecastello's history, its relations with outside powers
were conducted through representatives who argued on the community's
behalf. Ambassadors presented Montecastello's grievances before the officials of Todi and carried out missions to other city-states and to Rome.
In early periods the community's major strategy was to play off greater
powers against each other; mainly, as we have seen, this was a strategy
to increase its effective independence of Todi through nominal submission to more distant overlords. Negotiations involved both written communications and oral discourse, and along with the actual argumentation
they required various embellishments that served to reveal more about
the arguers than about the case itself. The success of a mission seems to
have depended in large part on an envoy's appearance, manner, learning,
and eloquence. An ambassador who cut a poor figure or spoke badly was

likely to be ridiculed in the courts he visited. It is significant that the provisions for choosing ambassadors imply that they were elected from among the upper class.

The manner in which proxies presented the community's case may be suggested by the survival of such diplomacy into recent times. Again, there is apparent concern with the self-presentation of the spokesmen, and their ability to convey personal cultivation along with just a hint of potential power. Some examples from the nineteenth century record the proxies' arguments in detail. They follow a standard form. The language is eloquent and elaborate in its etiquette ("I am afraid I have too much abused your courteous hospitality . . . and so I get to the point. . . ."). Literary and historical citations are presented to justify the case. The representative explains his own interest in terms of attachment to his paese ("I will consider myself repaid by the inner satisfaction that I feel for having fulfilled my duty toward the town where I was born and for which I have nourished and will always nourish the most fervid affection.") Personal connections, lines of influence, and unpaid political debts are just barely suggested. Finally, the virtues of Montecastello are lauded, while its modesty of power and ambition is declared.

The qualities involved in the exercise of statecraft are reflected in several of the patterns that today are defined as "civile": mastery of discourse and argument; facility with formal language, spoken and written; familiarity with the instruments of government and bureaucracy; ease with etiquette and the formalities of social interaction; cultura, or acquaintance with the historic and artistic glories of Italian civilization.

If some of these qualities are clearly necessary to conducting affairs of state, the functions of others are not so obvious. Why should there be such an emphasis upon etiquette, drawing-room formality, and "culture," and why should practical political skills be exaggerated into virtual art forms? The answer may lie in what these forms expressed about those who enacted them. Unlike the skills of politics, which might be readily learned, the embellishments built upon them were complicated and required careful socialization. As such, they implied long-term control of economic resources and powerful connections. They indicated to adversary and ally alike that such men could operate in a world of statehood. In this way, the forms served to stake out claims to power. At the same time, the elaborateness of the forms tended to keep them the exclusive property of an elite. Thus, while they were instruments of external political relations, they also contributed to the perpetuation of power differentials within the community.

Many of the elements of civiltà may thus be traced to the political action of the communal period. If the styles of the civil life—such as the verbal contests in public and the mannered interplay of polite society—sometimes resemble games, they were never idle games. They were played for real stakes in an arena much larger than the town piazza.

Within the Papal States

From the middle of the sixteenth century until 1860, the papal state was in effective control of Umbria. The communes continued to be the units of organization, but they lost their municipal liberties and were progressively converted into administrative organs of the state. For Montecastello, the main political aim continued to be avoiding Todi's dominance by remaining under the direct rule of the Church. For the most part it seems to have succeeded, though at various times the community was returned to Todi. In many documents of the period Montecastello appears as a separate entity, arguing with Todi over boundaries and regulations concerning the sale and transport of crops and livestock (A.C.T., 2). Until the late eighteenth century Montecastello used certain weights and measures, including the units for measuring land, that were different from those of Todi (A.C.M., 3). Especially revealing evidence comes out of a long-lasting dispute that the commune carried on with Todi, concerning Montecastello's claim to exclusive control of the tract of river bordering its territory. The commune operated a boat that carried traffic across the river at a strategic point, connecting Todi with parts of its own territory and with the road to Perugia. Several times the bishops of Todi challenged Montecastello's claim by setting up their own boats, but each time the community won out. Montecastello's success was based on support from the papacy; once the bishop's own brother, a cardinal, intervened on Montecastello's behalf. The community seems to have cultivated its standing with the pope; for instance, it demonstrated its "fidelity" repeatedly with financial contributions to support "holy wars."

Montecastello's concern with political autonomy did not mean that it was economically independent of Todi. On the contrary, economic relations between them were always important. In fact, when in 1596 the city ordered that all commerce between them be suspended, the smaller town was forced into temporary submission. Montecastello's prosperity was based on selling agricultural products to Todi and other urban centers of the province. Grain production in Montecastello generally exceeded local consumption; even with a limited surplus there were possibilities for profit, for prices fluctuated a great deal and varied from place to place. In this context it is understandable that Montecastello strove for political independence of Todi, for this would allow its landowners greater flexibility to operate within the markets of the area.

The vigor of the civil life in Montecastello seems to have depended upon the degree of prosperity of the landowning class. Landlord prosperity, in turn, was related to the size of the local population, since the limiting factor in profits from agriculture was labor. (On the other hand, the peasants' situation probably worsened whenever population increased, since the contractual terms depended upon the availability of labor.) The second half of the sixteenth century was a time of rising population, when mezzadria farms began to be created and peasants settled on the land.[3] In Montecastello, the landowning elite appears to have been growing both in size and in wealth, despite the heavy state taxation. Thus, it may not be entirely due to accidents of preservation that the documents of this time contain expressions of civic pride by the local elite. The same combination—population increase, landlord prosperity, and public spirit—recurs at the end of the eighteenth century. The intervening period, however, was rather different. The population of Montecastello decreased, gradually but more or less steadily, from the early seventeenth century until the census of 1769, after which it began to grow again (see Table 13). There was no apparent structural change within the community during this time, but various references to epidemics, poor harvests, and low agricultural prices suggest a picture of economic and social stagnation.

The general economic revival of the late eighteenth century involved neither agricultural innovations nor social reforms in Montecastello, as it did in Tuscany. But the landowners prospered, and in a general way reflected the new energies of the period. They invested in making Montecastello a more civile town. They talked a good deal about Montecastellese glories and its ancient privileges (A.C.M., 4). They were aware of new ideas spreading into the area and considered themselves men of their time. With the Napoleonic conquest of Central Italy in 1798, the Montecastellese elite declared themselves avid supporters of Republican ideals and promptly adopted the rhetoric of "Liberty, Fraternity, and Equality." At the same time, they mounted a campaign to demonstrate to their new French rulers their historical autonomy and capacity for administration. Their political skills are attested to in the fact that they managed to have Montecastello designated a *cantone* of the Roman Republic. It became the administrative head of a zone comprising 24 communities, including Fratta, which had been detached from the territories of Orvieto and Todi. When the French were ousted two years later Montecastello lost this favored status, but its citizens continued to point to this brief period of glory as evidence of their special civiltà.

A picture of Montecastello at the beginning of the nineteenth century is available from two revealing documents: a report of a visit in 1803 by a papal representative, and a citizen's description written about the same time (A.C.M., 6, 7). The population in 1803 was about 1,200, in 243 families. The agriculture is described as prosperous, with considerable surplus production of grain, grapes, and olives. The territory had several grain mills and six olive mills. There was commerce in elm timber, which was transported down the Tiber to Rome, and domestically produced linen cloth and silkworm cocoons.

The town contained several grocers' shops, a slaughterhouse, and a bakery and public oven; the artisans included six smiths, four tailors, six carpenters, three shoemakers, and a leather-tanner. There were teachers "employed in public instruction," a physician, and a surgeon. Three notaries were supported by the community's business and administrative activities. The civiltà of public life was attested to by a café, a billiards hall, and by the "modern theater constructed with the finest elegance." The Montecastellese writer also comments on the "quality and culture of the inhabitants":

> Although the paese does not demonstrate modern elegance in its buildings nor ampleness in its road, due to its antiquity, still the major landowners—who are not restricted in finances due to the property which they have in abundance even outside of the territory—do not lack that coltura, civiltà, and *educazione* which one sees in a city (A.C.M., 7).

The community had nine resident priests, half the number that existed before 1798. Four churches within the parish held daily services, and seven confraternities were active.

The political organization that is documented suggests the survival of the communal institutions. The citizens elected a governor, who had to request renewal of his contract twice a year. The formal governing body was the General Council, with forty members. Since the size of the council was close to the total number of households in the town, it must have functioned as a popular assembly. The community also had a magistrate's court, consisting of four judges. These judges were supposed to rotate every four months, though in fact, the same persons served continually, "since those who are capable of holding such office are quite few." (Judicial independence of Todi dated from the 1565 purchase, and since then it had been repeatedly challenged and reaffirmed.) In addition, there was a *segretario-computista*. The governor and secretary received salaries; other official positions were filled by unpaid citizens. In other documents, the citizens proudly assert that public works, buildings, jails, and "all other public services have always been the responsibility of the community itself" rather than of the state (A.C.M., 4).

Montecastello's "autonomy" was, of course, a function of the state within which it existed. The official business of the community always had formal papal validation, but the state appears to have operated mainly through a local and secular bureaucracy, tax-farming, and periodic official visits. The 1803 investigation seems to have been more thorough than most, since it was ordered by Rome to determine the status of public properties and accounts following the Napoleonic upheaval. The representative's report describes at length how the Montecastellesi ignored their debts to the state and perpetrated frauds against it. He complains that Montecastello was indifferent to its obligations to the state:

> [The request for permission to assume a legacy] has been the one and only act with which the public representatives of Montecastello have demonstrated their dependence on Rome . . . they being firm in the determination to make themselves independent of the government . . . One should not be surprised at the plots, the private agreements, the secret intrigues, the independence, and the egoism that have had free reign, since this community has never had any visit from Rome. There is no doubt about the malicious acts and frauds, especially in public concerns; only the strictest measures will serve. . . . (A.C.M., 6).

However, the representative concedes that the Montecastellesi had always been faithful to the pope and compliments them on the fact that "they did not innovate anything, in matters of religion, during those turbulent times" (of the Roman Republic).

A second French occupation began in 1808. Though it lasted only six years, French rule had profound effects. It introduced new institutions, such as the Napoleonic code of law and an administrative system based on the principle of uniform law. It also brought a first experience with the idea of nationhood. Thus, when the papal regime was restored in 1814, communities like Montecastello were already caught up in the incipient movement toward nationhood. The 1814 change of government saw another campaign by the Montecastellese elite to win favorable administrative status and a last bitter conflict with Todi over the issue of formal control. The Montecastellesi were successful once again, for the town was made the seat of a *comune*, the same status granted to Todi.

After the restoration, a series of insurrections in the Papal States soon led to repressive measures. These events are reflected in Montecastello in an increasingly overt anticlericalism. In fact, this became the dominant theme sounded in this area during the Risorgimento, the movement for national unity. The rhetoric of progress and social reform was directed against the privileges of the church; the rights of the landowning class were hardly questioned. This is, of course, the same development *all'italiana* which was already under way in more advanced areas, like Tuscany: "progress" there meant abolishing ecclesiastical abuses, feudal ties, and all other impediments to the growth of capitalism—but within the traditional social structure (Sereni 1972:291–92).

As the Risorgimento gained momentum, several members of the Montecastellese elite actively associated themselves with it. Most notable were the two Pettinelli brothers, landowners and descendants of the Atti. They were in regular contact with the Liberals of the region and communicated news of the movement to Montecastello. The brothers protected and aided supporters of the cause, but at the same time they maintained their connections with the church. (One story has it that when the Garibaldini came through Montecastello, the local priests hid in the attic of the Pettinelli house while the brothers festively entertained the troops in the sala below.) Some Montecastellesi joined the Garibaldini and were rewarded with favors and glory on their return.

The brothers (so their descendants claim) participated in the insurrection in Perugia in June, 1859. A year later, the army of Piedmont marched through Umbria. In a plebiscite held on November 14, 1860, the citizens of Montecastello voted on the question: "Do you want to become part of the Constitutional Monarchy of King Victor Emanuel

II?" The vote was 410 Yes and 3 No, with 89 eligible voters not casting ballots (Ciaurro 1963:198). The elder Pettinelli brother was elected sindaco of the commune. He promptly detached the papal coat of arms from the town hall and sent it to the parish priest with the message, "Put it away carefully, because it will never be displayed again." The local *papalini*, those loyal to the pope, reported instead that he had desecrated the coat of arms (one version claimed he had urinated on it). A warrant was sent out against him; when he later went to Rome on business, he was arrested and imprisoned. Within 48 hours, his family obtained his release through the intervention of a high-ranking functionary in the Vatican. Evidently, the elite kept personal ties with the clergy, despite their opposition to the temporal power of the church. This incident is, in fact, symptomatic of how this class would adapt to the new nation.

These three hundred years of papal dominion affected the development of the civil life and the ideology of civiltà in a number of ways. It is clear that many of the patterns of public life that appeared in the commune continued within the framework of the Papal States. But during this period, when the countryside was being settled, the "civile" must increasingly have defined town in contrast to country. The idea that an urban center claims dominance over its surrounding territory was, of course, present during the communal period. However, now that Montecastello was more independent of Todi, the smaller town became a center for its own countryside, dominant over its own dependent population. The life-style of that center was distinctly different from that of the rural area, and townsmen accentuated that difference in ideology.

At the same time, townsmen were still close to the country. This was especially true of those who were involved in the mezzadria system. This period saw the main development of the landlord-peasant relationships, and probably also of the more general patronage roles. The townsman's attitude toward the country combined two different elements: deprecation of peasant life—the attitude particularly of those who had escaped it more recently; and a romanticized view of it—the view of those who enjoy the benefits of the land but do not work it. For their part, the countrymen remained close to the civil life.

During this period the term "civiltà" appears in local documents. The earliest uses have a clearly local referent: a seventeenth-century chronicler of Todi used it almost as a synonym for "citizenship" in the town

(A.C.T., 3). When the term occurs in the Montecastellesi's own self-descriptions, it refers to the patterns of town life that had been developing there since the communal period, yet it also points in a new direction. At the beginning of the nineteenth century, a local writer could say of Montecastello that it possessed that civiltà "which one sees in a city." This suggests that the standard of comparison was a larger world than that of Montecastello's own hinterland and of neighboring communes.

Soon the frame of reference would expand even more: "civiltà" would come to denote the degree to which places like Montecastello were open to the influences of the modern world. But civiltà also remained a way of talking about the glories of the past and the value of local distinctiveness. The different levels of meaning are made explicit in Getulio Ceci's preface to his history of Todi. Commenting on the rash of local histories in the first half of the nineteenth century, he says that Italians living under the imperious papal government used this means to educate people to the "civili virtues," namely the liberty of the medieval communes. Yet in the same discussion, Ceci compares the backwardness of the Todi area at that time with Tuscany, "one of the few Italian states on the road to progress and civiltà" (1897:xxx–xxxi). Thus, the concept of civiltà could cover seemingly contradictory values: both local autonomy and identification with a larger universe; both a cherishing of the past and a commitment to change.

Nationhood

Once unity was won, the new nation began the long and painful task of tying together previously separated and diverse regions. "Modernization" was the official goal—one that was echoed by the Montecastellese elite. Several processes of change were set into motion, but they did not significantly alter the social structure of Montecastello until well into the twentieth century.

On the political level, nationhood brought little discontinuity in the local distribution of power. Since few people were literate, and official jobs depended upon connections, the bureaucracy remained in the hands of a restricted local elite. Some functionaries were drawn from the landowning families. Others were outsiders, but they tended to be absorbed into the local upper class. Their appointments were often of long duration, and like other high-status newcomers they readily married into landowning families, allowed themselves to be drawn into patronage ties, and were soon defined as "Montecastellesi." For instance, the first segretario after the unification stayed in the post for 36 years, running his office like a benevolent local patron.

The elite also controlled elective positions, for literacy was required to serve in office, and only men with property could vote. In the period from 1860 to 1880, eligible voters in Umbria included little more than 1.5 percent of the total population, even less than the national average of about 2 percent (MAIC 1883:vi). In the 1880s, more liberal criteria for voting increased the Umbrian electorate to 6–7 percent, still slightly lower than the national average (MAIC 1885:vi, xviii). The situation changed substantially only in 1912, when the introduction of universal male suffrage brought the electorate to 25–30 percent (ISTAT 1958:105). The first communal council elected in Montecastello after the unification was made up almost entirely of men from the major landowning families; their sons comprised over half the membership of the council thirty years later (A.C.M., 11, 12). In the six decades from 1860 until the Fascist takeover, except for brief interims Montecastello had only four mayors, all landowners (see chapter 4). National unity did not change the structure of authority within the community but rather the source of its legitimacy.

Nevertheless, the nation began to expand the range of experience for Montecastellesi. An important factor was the requirement for military service; young men who had never before left the immediate area learned at first hand about the diversity of Italy. Another factor was the improvement in transportation. A major effort went into building railroads, and by 1870 the city of Perugia was connected with Rome, Florence, and the Adriatic coast. However, the railway network followed the perimeter of the province, bypassing the central area until the Umbrian Central Railroad was built in 1915. The old highway between Todi and Perugia was improved (although a carriage trip still took at least six hours), and in the 1870s a new road connected it with the plain of Montecastello.

The industrialization of Italy began in the 1880s, but the nascent industries were mostly concentrated in the North. The one major industry in Umbria was the steel works of Terni, in operation by 1886. In the province of Perugia industrialization was limited to a number of small factories, most dating from the early twentieth century.[4] These were located in Foligno, on the outskirts of Perugia, and in various towns of the plain. Hilltop strongholds like Montecastello and Todi would have little direct part in industrial development, and their traditional agriculture would become increasingly backward in the context of a national economy.

By the end of the century, there was little apparent change in the social order of Montecastello, but the unification had affected agricultural markets, the mezzadria system, and patterns of landholding. The processes under way posed real threats to the position of the Montecastellese elite. On the one hand, the local landowners' economic status began to suffer from the breakup of patrimonies. On the other hand, the peasants' situation had not been improved by the oratory of modernization, and Montecastello offered fertile ground for the emerging labor movements. The continued dominance of the local upper class, despite these threats, may be due partly to the fact that they had widened the system of patronage. Specifically, the local elite had assumed the role of mediating contacts between the community and the nation. In so doing, not only could they increase their clients' dependence upon them, but they could to some extent also control influences coming into the community and thus keep "progress" within the bounds of the traditional order.

The new nation-state had presented both problems and opportunities for Montecastellesi of all classes: it encroached upon the lives of all individuals and had to be coped with, yet it offered benefits to those who knew how to manipulate it. The local elite was the one group able to meet the challenge. They possessed the skills and contacts required, and they had moved into the critical positions in local government. Moreover, their patron-client ties within the commnity had always involved a degree of mediation with the world outside. Patronage relationships could be extended by landlords attempting to shore up wavering control, or they could be adopted by bureaucrats and local politicians trying to build a personal following. Toward both ends, various members of the elite took on roles as buffers between lower-class Montecastellesi and the external world.

These persons could fill out the papers required at every significant step in a citizen's life and speak to officials on a client's behalf. They might interpret the law, offer advice, and intervene with the authorities in case of trouble. As government benefits were introduced, they could help their clients through the complicated process of claiming them. Their personal connections outside the community were especially valuable, for anyone who had to leave Montecastello—for instance, to report for military service, to seek temporary work, or to make purchases for a marriage—found it prudent to go with a recommendation from a respected signore. To an increasing extent, even the local patronage functions described earlier (such as guaranteeing loans or helping clients find jobs) required dealing with national institutions.

A few examples will illustrate:

S. G. was always protected by R. C., who arranged a job for him as a street-cleaner and bell-ringer. S. G.'s wife once had an argument with a neighbor and attacked her with a pruning-knife. She was denounced and arrested by the carabinieri, but the patron intervened and won her release.

M. S., a blacksmith, hoped to get the local concession for the sale of salt and tobacco. He obtained it through the intervention of T. R., who considered the award due him because M. S. had served briefly with Garibaldi.

F. L. wanted to take his deaf sister to Rome to be treated by specialists. He was given a loan from the bank countersigned by B. E., providing him with sufficient funds to spend forty days in Rome and to pay for the medical services. B. E.'s wife gave him a letter of presentation to the specialists.

During World War I, M. A.'s soldier husband fell seriously ill. She had to go to the town hall to fill out papers requesting that he be sent home and certifying that she was able to support him; B. E. handled the papers for her. After her husband died, she tried for months to collect the pension for war widows but did not succeed, in part because she had already claimed she could support herself. B. E. spoke of her case to the appropriate officials and managed to obtain the pension for her.

C. S. described a local signore (notorious for his unscrupulous business practices and immoral personal life) as "a real gentleman" (un signor uomo), recalling that he had handled the financial arrangements for C. S. to buy a cow and that he always gave advice on the law ("his advice was better than a lawyer's").

Several of the nineteenth-century local elite had relatives and friends in influential posts in the government and the Vatican. Through these contacts, sovereign grace was obtained on various occasions for Montecastellesi who met trouble with the law: for instance, for P. F., arrested for throwing a placenta into a peasant's well; for C. L., who shot a man for stealing hay from him; and for C. F., who stabbed and killed a man during an argument at a dance in the theater and ended up with only one year in prison.

By the early twentieth century, job opportunities in national institutions had expanded, and they began to be assigned on the basis of the *concorso* system. Theoretically, this was an open competition among qualified applicants for all the available positions in a given category, but in fact, success in a concorso depended upon recommendations. The role of the local elite in providing such recommendations became especially important, particularly as the number of formally qualified candidates grew more rapidly than the jobs available. The significance of the *raccomandazione* continues to the present time, although the channels have changed. Now, as then, a raccomandazione consists of a request to someone that he give help or protection to one's client. It is a request for a personal favor which appeals to the relationship between recommender and the person addressed; it is only marginally concerned with the qualifications of the applicant. (For example, a recommendation addressed to an army psychiatrist, on behalf of a Montecastellese youth applying to a military technical school, asked that the psychiatric examination be lenient.)

The mediating role of the local upper class represents its response to challenges of its position, but it grew out of the fact that this group controlled the main links between the community and the larger society. Peasants and lower-class townsmen were never isolated from outside contacts, but the nature of their contacts differed from those of the upper class. The elite managed external political affairs, even after nationhood defined all Montecastellesi as citizens. For centuries, Montecastellesi had participated in markets and fairs, including a regular Thursday market and four or five annual fairs in Montecastello itself.[5] However, the major commerce in agricultural commodities was always handled by the landowners, assisted by fattori and professional middlemen (the *sensali*, who still travel the circuit of fairs and help negotiate deals for a percentage). Similarly, only the upper class could maintain kinship and informal social connections beyond the area. It was common for these families to contract marriages in other towns, and they had the mobility to keep up contacts with kin, friends, and their own patrons. Furthermore, so long as literacy was restricted and communications difficult, the elite constituted the main channel for the diffusion of national styles to the community.

In the context of the nation-state, facility in the world of statehood and bureaucracy took on greater importance. More than ever, the civil life of the town involved dealings with the larger society; more than ever, attributes that showed familiarity with the larger society became marks of a civile person. Signs of personal connections with the centers of power took on special value—movement back and forth to the cities, the visits of friends and relatives to Montecastello, knowledge about urban life. Though these patterns were as yet limited to the elite, the politics of mediation may help explain why they could become more widely held values. To the extent that mediators were adept in the ways of the larger society and well connected with it, others in the community might benefit indirectly.

The ideology of civiltà reflects the politics of this early period of nationhood in other ways. An idiom of patriotism appeared at this time, alongside the expressions of civic pride. The local upper class had identified with the new nation from the beginning; their attempts to manipulate the national system meant becoming part of it, and they declared their nationalism in extravagant terms. This patriotism did not replace their identification with community, but rather complemented it. For instance, the names conferred on the town streets in 1896 gave places of honor, side by side, to national heroes of the Risorgimento and to illustrious local citizens of the past.[6]

In this period, too, when national development raised issues of change for Montecastello, the term "civiltà" was used to talk about the benefits of the modern world. For example, the community leaders in the 1880s argued the need for improvements in transportation on the grounds that they were necessary for the "incivilimento" of the population. However, the openness to outside influences was always qualified by an emphasis on conserving the values of the past. Thus, the rhetoric of civiltà could serve a highly selective program of change.

By the end of World War I, the lower classes of Montecastello were being drawn more directly into the life of the larger society, and the local elite met new threats to its control. Men of all classes had fought in the war and had come into close contact with persons from distant regions and ideas that challenged the social order of the community. In the years following the war, the Montecastello area itself was caught up in waves of renewed labor militancy. As the Fascist movement grew in response, Montecastello saw several incidents of violence. The threat to traditional

authority is reflected in the fact that for a brief time, in 1921–22, landowners were in the minority on the communal council, though the same
sindaco continued in office (A.S.P., 5). The local elite welcomed Fascism
as a stabilizing force, although at the same time, some of their educated
sons professed socialist ideals.

The general effect of the Fascist regime was to sustain the traditional
social structure of the community. The mezzadria system was solidified.
The landlords' position was further reinforced by laws preventing
changes of residence or occupation. Moreover, Mussolini's "battle of the
grain" discouraged innovations in the pattern of production. The personnel and structure of formal authority was modified somewhat. A podestà
was appointed instead of an elected sindaco, though the individual appointed was the incumbent sindaco. Party officials and representatives of
the "corporations" held considerable power. There was also an expansion
of the bureaucracy. While these changes opened up opportunities for a
few townsmen of modest background, landowners dominated the local
officialdom.

The Fascist period left its mark on many areas of life. The church
once again became allied with the political system—a result of the Con-
cordat of 1929, the official reconciliation between the pope and the Fascist state. In Montecastello, this meant that on the surface at least, the
long conflict between secular and clerical authority was resolved; it also
signaled the active re-entry of the church into politics. Much leisure activity in the community centered around the Dopolavoro, the party-
sponsored recreational society, while young people were assigned to a
series of age-graded organizations. The propagation of local "culture"
became an official goal, and the government subsidized the band and the
theater (A.S.P., 8). The state intruded into informal life to a greater
degree than ever before. For example, family subsidies were introduced
to encourage the birth rate, and certain styles of speech and address were
promulgated. Though neither of these programs met with great success
in Montecastello, they fostered the idea of a more intimate relationship
between individuals and the state.

The specific events of this twenty-year Fascist period in Montecastello
are difficult to uncover, but clearly the regime forestalled any fundamental social change. Indeed, its appeal for many Montecastellesi seems to
have been its promise that values of the past would be revitalized. Order
would be maintained—by means of the *bastone* (the cudgel). Interclass

collaboration would be assured—under the enlightened control of the upper class. Italy would realize its destiny as a world center of civilization, and a civil life would be perpetuated.

During the Fascist years many local men had fought in Ethiopia and in Spain, but World War II was an immediate experience for the community as a whole. Although the town itself saw no fighting, German troops were stationed there and a prisoner-of-war camp was located nearby. Montecastellesi, both civilians and soldiers, came into contact with other nationalities and formed ideas of other ways of life. For instance, a number of lower-class men describing their experience as prisoners of the British remember their surprise at being treated with respect by social superiors.

After the Mussolini government fell in 1943, soldiers began to come home, partisan activity in the area intensified, and the response of the Germans and die-hard Fascists grew more brutal. A plaque in Montecastello commemorates a day when ten citizens were shot in reprisal for a German officer killed by a partisan. The Allied front passed through in the summer of 1944, and a British detachment was quartered in a landowner's villa. The period that followed the Allied advance remains the most bitter part of the war for Montecastello, as people sought retaliation against local Fascists. The strife of those days foreshadowed the political conflict of the postwar years: Montecastellesi would be polarized around two dominant parties—the Communists, who had grown strong in the course of the partisan struggle, and the DC (Democrazia Cristiana), the Democratic party backed by the church.

In the years following the war and the decade of the 1950s, major changes were effected in Montecastello's internal structure and relationship with the larger society. Some of the processes involved have already been discussed; others are well-known phenomena of modern Italy. The establishment of free elections widened political participation, brought national parties and interest groups into the heart of community life, and changed the distribution of formal authority. At the same time, the community was left as only a minor administrative unit within a centralized national government. Italy went through the economic boom of the 1950s, and though this area was again excluded it sent large numbers of temporary laborers to the northern industries. Others in the population left permanently, especially peasants abandoning the mezzadria system, while those who remained in Montecastello were drawn increasingly into contact with the world outside. The changes of the postwar years completed the process begun with unification a hundred years earlier: the Montecastellesi, individually and as a community, became integral parts of the national society.

The Present

The civil life of contemporary Montecastello shows the traces of its past. The community still has a corporate identity. Public sociability still calls upon forms of behavior that once served in self-government and in dealings with outside powers. There is still a high value on knowledge of the larger society, effective contacts with it, and ability to manipulate within it. These elite patterns are now much more widely disseminated but they still serve as a measure of social rank, and there is still a place for power brokers who negotiate relations with the nation-state. Nevertheless, the political significance of this civil life has changed in the postwar period, for it exists within a different structure of relationship between community and nation. The description that follows refers to Montecastello in 1960–61, but the general processes under way at the time are still at work today.

Even the semblance of local autonomy is impossible in contemporary Montecastello. Not only is the community part of a highly centralized state, but it is now also marked by a disjunction in authority between representatives of the state, elected administrators, and wielders of informal influence. Moreover, the links with the national society, which were once controlled by a single group, have multiplied and dispersed. Official positions, as well as the unofficial functions of mediation, are distributed among a variety of groups and organizations.

Theoretically, the community is governed by an elected mayor and a communal council. The council is elected from two lists of fifteen candidates each; it is made up of twelve members from the list that wins a majority, and three who are the leading candidates of the minority slate. A newly elected council at its first meeting chooses a sindaco and two other officials from among its members. The lists in local elections are actually coalitions of national parties, but in Montecastello they correspond to the basic line of political opposition: the Left and the Center-Right (mainly the DC). When Montecastellesi vote in provincial and na-

tional elections, they must indicate specific party preferences. The results of such elections in the 1958–60 period indicate that the vote of the
Left was divided between the Communists (PCI), who received 30–35
percent of the total vote, and the Socialists (PSI)—20–25 percent of the
total. Supporters of the Center-Right gave most of their votes to the DC
(30–35 percent of the total vote), with the remainder split among several
parties, most going to the neo-fascist MSI (6–8 percent).

The Left won control of the local administration in the first postwar
election, and until the 1960s there was never any question about the outcome of local electoral contests. The mezzadri have been the major support of the Left. As of 1960, they made up the majority of the membership of the council and held the positions of leadership in it. While
this might seem to be a reversal of the traditional power structure, in fact
few real functions remain in the hands of the communal council. Even
within its limited sphere of authority, it is dependent upon unpredictable
financing by the national government. Furthermore, many of its decisions are subject to approval by the provincial Prefect, an appointee of
the national bureaucracy (see Fried 1963). At the local level, too, the bureaucrats are in effective control, though the elected sindaco is dominant
in principle. In contrast to the personal rule exercised by mayors of
traditional Montecastello, in the contemporary period the office has been
practiced on a part-time basis. The elected leaders (most of whom live in
the country) come to the town hall a few times a week, while the bureaucrats are there daily.

The local bureaucracy is appointed through the Prefect and is directly
responsible to him; it forms a sphere of operation largely separate from
the elected administration. The personnel of this bureaucracy are distinct from the local leadership, both elected officials and local signori.
Many are outsiders, for the national bureaucracy tends to distribute personnel over an ever-expanding geographic range. Unlike the situation in
the past, there appears to be little incentive for new arrivals to build local
support; many appointments are short-term, and advancement depends
upon gaining merit and connections within the national system. The
segretario comunale, the senior bureaucrat, is a case in point. In the contemporary period this position has been held by a series of appointees,
all outsiders; none remained for more than two years. The segretario at
the time of the field study was an austere man who kept a careful routine
of "house and office." The Montecastellesi regarded him as antipatico and

criticized his thorough detachment from the life of the community. Yet such solitary behavior seems to have been usual among contemporary segretari. It appears to be due less to individual disposition than to the fact that local involvements represent hazards for a bureaucratic career.

Few of the other *autorità* have a local status analogous to the traditional elite. The civil police officer is an ex-carabiniere from the South, while the town-hall clerks, the postal employees, and the tax-office functionaries are either outsiders or Montecastellesi of non-signorile origin. The professionals, who are also government employees, are signori by definition, but most are recent arrivals in Montecastello. Only a few have any connection, by descent or marriage, with the traditional landowning families.

The carabinieri stationed in Montecastello, as everywhere in Italy, are outsiders who must keep free of personal ties in the community. As paramilitary national police, they form still another, separate structure of local authority. Despite the fact that they are independent of other officials and avoid informal socializing, they are an integral part of the local political scene. The fragmention of power in Montecastello has enabled the *maresciallo* (the commanding officer) to become actively involved in the affairs of the commune; some Montecastellesi claim that he sees himself as the padrone of the community. At the same time, the population use the carabinieri as a medium for interpersonal conflicts. People with grievances often find reason to denounce their offender before the maresciallo. This has the effect of announcing the grievance publicly and confirming its seriousness, while allowing the parties to avoid face-to-face confrontation. The maresciallo is not actually an arbitrator. The conflict itself must be resolved by other means, either informally or by resort to lawsuit; in many instances (such as an accusation of sexual misconduct with one's spouse) the accuser clearly does not intend the maresciallo to settle the conflict.[7]

Contemporary Montecastello thus shows a contrast to the traditional situation in which a restricted elite claimed the whole range of political positions, in addition to their unofficial authority based on economic and social rank. The contrast is just as great in the extent to which officials are now removed from informal community leadership. The individuals holding the main positions in local government—the sindaco and the majority of the council, the segretario and most other bureaucrats, and the maresciallo—have little to do with social and ceremonial events in the community. During the field study, on several occasions that gave ritual expression to local identity, these figures were conspicuous for their absence. Part of the explanation lies in the conflict between the Communist administration and the church; part lies in the nonlocal origin of many officials. In a more general sense, however, the contemporary autorità derive their power from organizations that crosscut communities; their success depends upon identification with these extra-local interests. Community involvement may not be inconsistent with outside connections; it most certainly was not for the traditional elite. But in the present political context it suggests the possibility of commitments that are inimical to crosscutting interest groups.

The main proponents of community identity today are the signori of local origin and the popolo of the town. However, the communal political institutions can no longer be the vehicles of that identity; instead it is now expressed largely through ceremonial. Most of the signori have little role in official administration and avoid any active part in party politics. The resident landowners may attempt to manipulate decisions quietly, with a word here and there to officials, but landlords are vulnerable figures in any public political role. Some signori, especially those closest to the traditional elite, avoid involvement with the DC because of conflict with the priest. In general, the signori profess support for the DC, but the party activists are mainly minor professionals, artisans, and merchants.

The political conflict in contemporary Montecastello follows the lines of long-standing social divisions within the community, but it also represents a contest between national organizations and interest groups. The polarity between Center-Right and Left draws on the oppositions between padrone and mezzadro, and between "people-of-inside" and "people-of-outside." The language of political conflict in the community emphasizes these identifications, and national issues are readily translated into the terms of local divisions.[8] These alignments, however, are becoming less and less fixed. The competition between national parties in Montecastello is thus increasingly open. Much of it is played out through the mediating functions once monopolized by the local elite.

The Montecastellesi still need aid and intervention in dealing with the national government, both to gain its benefits and to protect themselves against its demands. Even more, those who hope to improve their status need connections in the world beyond the community. Both party coalitions in Montecastello try to meet these needs, but they do so in different ways. The differences are expressed in their explicit appeals to the voters. The Left emphasizes class solidarity and asserts that only peasants and workers can be genuine intermediaries for others of their class. On the other hand, the Center-Right argues that it has access to the intervention powers of higher-level functionaries. These contrasting ideologies reflect a more fundamental difference. Since the war the Christian Democrats have controlled the national government, the civil service, and most importantly, the *sottogoverno*—a vast network of patronage through which favors and political spoils are distributed and through which the maze of officialdom can be penetrated (e.g., LaPalombara 1964). The parties of the Left dominate local and provincial governments in much of Central Italy, but at the national level they form a minority. Moreover, even the Center-Left coalitions of the 1960s did not bring major inroads into the DC hold on the sottogoverno. The way political intermediaries function in Montecastello is a consequence of this national structure of power.

While control of the communal administration by the Left does not mean that the peasants have gained real power in the community, it does give them sympathetic intermediaries in official positions. The elected administrators try to offer guidance through the bureaucratic maze, as social equals rather than as officials. For example, the sindaco would explain national welfare services to illiterate peasants, reading the relevant document aloud, restating it in simple terms, and giving specific advice on how to collect benefits. Similarly, during the visit of a government representative distributing grain to peasants who had suffered crop damage from heavy rains, the vice-sindaco bustled about the town hall answering peasants' questions, attesting to the legitimacy of their claims, and generally helping and making a show of helping.

The political parties of the Left also act as intermediaries for the lower classes.[9] Various provincial functionaries visit the Camera del Lavoro (the local party center of the Left) and provide information and advice for peasants and laborers. In addition, a number of labor organizations affiliated with the Left represent the interests of their members. For instance, the union of mezzadri pressures for improvements in the official contract, advocates reform of the system, and organizes public demonstrations of its power.

In contrast to the class-based action of the Left, the DC emphasizes its vertical connections at the national level. The party secretary in Montecastello continually tries to get recommendations from higher-ranking DC officials on behalf of supporters who are competing for jobs, applying to schools, or seeking some other favor. The concorso is more than ever an important field for this kind of mediation, for in competitions today there may be as many as twenty qualified applicants for each available position. The local DC efforts in this area have had only limited success, perhaps because until the 1960s the party showed little prospect of electoral victory in Montecastello; still, a sympathetic message from an *Onorevole* (member of Parliament) encourages further requests.

The church is an integral part of this vertical mediation of the DC. The local priest is himself a useful source of recommendations, and many a concorso candidate has scrambled for that most valuable of recommendations—a bishop's. At the same time, the priest in Montecastello has engaged in a vigorous effort to offer organizational services as alternatives to those of the Left. In 1960 he set up a local chapter of ACLI, the Catholic Association of Italian Workers. He converted a section of the parish house into a bar and clubhouse, offering television, billiards and other games, and special events; later, a weekend cinema was added. In the first few months, 130 members were inscribed; while both mezzadri and large landowners are scarce in the membership, it includes men of every other category. Its success is due as much to the mediating services it offers as to its recreational facilities. A provincial official comes to Montecastello once a week to give legal advice, help in filing claims for pensions or health benefits, and assistance of all kinds in dealing with the bureaucracy. The provincial office also publishes informational material, such as a pamphlet for migrant workers. The counterpart association for women is CIF (the Italian Women's Center).

Intermediary roles may be taken on by individuals as well as organizations. The retired bureaucrat mentioned in chapter 4 often has people waiting to ask his aid and advice. He sometimes intervenes with local authorities and has personal contacts in Rome whom he can enlist on someone's behalf. Other signori may be asked for the benefit of their contacts in the larger society, and they occasionally oblige. However, such roles are uncommon, for unlike the traditional elite who used this means to maintain their own positions, individuals today have little to gain from offering such favors.

Bureaucrats may offer informal intermediary "services" of a different kind. One Montecastellese official illustrates the local version of a familiar pattern. His tactic is to compound the bureaucratic confusion and thereby enhance the value of his own favors. Peasants who appear in his office for some necessary paper are apt to be greeted affectionately and then told sorrowfully of the complexities of the request. Proper obeisance, perhaps a chicken delivered surreptitiously, may expedite the matter. The official then explains the successful result as a personal favor, for he has set aside his other pressing work, labored overtime, or pulled strings. The applicant's alternative to going through this intermediary is to enlist the aid of some other intermediary.

It is clear that although mediation is as vital today as in the early period of nationhood, the contemporary situation involves a qualitatively different kind of community-nation relationship. Instead of a small group that controls all connections with the national society and allocates them through ties of patronage, today there are diverse, competing intermediaries. At the same time, there has been a great increase in unmediated participation in the national system. The expansion in the means of transportation and communication since World War II has made it possible for individuals to have their own ties and sources of information beyond the community. The situation in 1961 shows the process under way. The advances occurring in the nation as a whole were all reflected in Montecastello, though on most measures it lagged behind the national averages. The improvements in communications were spreading rapidly among all classes, but there was still a marked difference between town and country.

By 1961 about a fourth of the town families owned small automobiles, and many families of both town and country had motorcycles or scooters. (Townsmen would sometimes point to the row of cycles parked outside the gate and talk about it as a symbol of the changing times—never before could peasants come into town on a weekday just for recreation.) The *postale* bus provided at least minimal public transport; it took children to schools in the town and in Todi, transported groups on excursions, and connected Montecastello with the railroad. The local road was unpaved, but dozens of vehicles moved in and out of the town in the course of a day.

Elementary education had widely extended literacy, though higher education was still limited to a minority of the town. As of the 1961 census, 85 percent of the commune population over six years of age were classified as literate. Included in this 85 percent are 20 percent who had less than five years of schooling (some less than three years), and another 60 percent who had an elementary school certificate (which can represent anything from three to seven years of schooling). The remaining 5 percent had completed at least a middle school; of the 98 individuals in this category, 32 had advanced high school or professional diplomas, and 6 others had university degrees. (These figures are taken from ISTAT 1965:42–43.) The average level is rapidly being raised, however. Until 1959 Montecastello's schools only went to the fifth grade; today, eight years of school are compulsory. At the time of the study, many lower-class families of both town and country were sending their children on to higher schools in Todi or Perugia, a practice long common among the signori.

By far the most important medium of communication available in contemporary Montecastello is television. In 1960 there were 27 sets in the commune, four in public places (ISTAT 1961a:139). Probably a large majority of the town population watched television regularly, in evening visits to a bar or to friends' houses. Radios are more widespread, though their overall impact is less than that of television; almost half the families in the commune owned a radio in 1960 (ISTAT 1961a:139). The movies now shown at ACLI are well attended, and many people occasionally go to the movies in Todi. The written media are less widely distributed. The spaccio sold twenty-odd copies of newspapers daily during 1960–61: in addition, the political organizations made the party newspapers available, and perhaps a dozen people had mail subscriptions to newspapers and magazines.

This expansion in the means of communication implies a structural change. Montecastello has always been in contact with the world outside, but it is only in the contemporary period that such contact has been directly accessible to all classes. This change has been accelerated by the increased population movements, which give even the nonmobile viable social connections with other places. As a result, new ideas are no longer filtered through an elite, but are directly accessible to many.

The processes by which Montecastello has been incorporated into a national polity have modified the significance of the civil life, but they have not obliterated it. In some ways, the transformations of modernization are familiar and congenial to Montecastello. It has long been open to outside influences, ready to imitate urban models, and accustomed to governments and the ways of manipulating them. Electoral politics and improved communications have drawn many more people into public affairs. Though the basis of their participation is different from that of elites of the past, many of the forms of the civil life can be enacted, particularly the patterns of public debate and sociability. At the same time, this broadened participation is changing the definition of civiltà. Increasingly, to be "civile" is coming to mean the ability to take one's place as a citizen in national life and to subscribe to acceptable standards of behavior. Increasingly, those standards are external ones, the national models projected via television and magazines. Thus, it seems likely that both elite and local connotations will be eliminated.

Like the patterns of the civil life, the idea of civiltà may continue to play a part in modern politics. The specific values that were associated with the civiltà of the traditional elite still influence the ideology of the Center-Right in Montecastello. Its standards for evaluating candidates continue to lay stress on elite demeanor. Woven into its formal statements and the comments of its supporters are the themes of civic pride, local commitment, and the benefits of patronage. The Left, in contrast, refers to the community mainly in the context of exploitation by landlords, and it emphasizes the opposition of interests within Montecastello. It judges candidates in terms of their class identifications, and its appeal is to class solidarity on a national and international level. Thus, while the DC denounces the incompetence of the local administration, the Communist orators speak of the lot of peasants throughout Italy and of the Cuban revolution. Each side, of course, also includes a diversity of views. For example, some descendants of the traditional elite were enthusiastic about the DC candidate for sindaco because of his education, eloquence, and local attachments—his civiltà. Yet he himself was scornful of localism, elitism, and patronage politics, and his own assumptions about what constitutes civiltà were universalistic.

The term "civiltà," however, is not limited to a particular set of values. Indeed, its adaptability to different political contexts lies in the fact that it is not precisely defined. In the nineteenth century, it served as an ideology of selective modernization, and it still lends itself to a great variety of attitudes toward the modern world. Two incidents of a recent visit to Montecastello illustrate the point. A young Montecastellese was describing his great distaste for the now-popular practice of taking summer holidays at the crowded seashore resorts. A middle-aged landowner, listening and thoroughly agreeing with the young man's judgement, turned to me and said: "Now *that* is civiltà!" At this time, legislation to permit divorce in Italy had just been passed. While all the forces of Church, Family, and Tradition were mobilized against it, graffiti appeared announcing, "Divorce is civiltà." "Civiltà" means both progress and continuity with the past, and it can be invoked in either cause.

CHAPTER 6

Festivals

THROUGHOUT ITS HISTORY Montecastello seems to have followed a strategy of welcoming incorporation into larger polities within which it could further its local interests. This political action had symbolic counterparts: the Montecastellesi readily identified with the encompassing unit (such as Papal States and Italian nation) but at the same time maintained a sense of local distinctiveness. Neither identity was precisely specified; the larger universe was represented by grandiose but general symbols, while there was considerable flexibility in what could be thought of as "Montecastellese."

The way in which local identity could coexist with membership in a wider sphere is seen most clearly in ceremonial. To be civilized in Montecastello has always assumed being part of the universal church and conforming to its formal precepts, but it also meant "a Montecastellese way" of being Catholic. Local and universal elements come together within traditional Montecastellese festivals, both complementing each other and occasionally coming into conflict. The contemporary period has minimized the local dimension of religious as well as secular life. Nevertheless, public ritual remains the primary means for expressing community identity.

Church Festivals

The traditional ceremonial round was still enacted during the period of the fieldwork, but the emphases of the rituals and the nature of participation in them were undergoing change. This section describes the festivals of the church calendar as they were celebrated during 1960–61, pointing up the "traditional" aspects. The changes that have taken place since World War II will be considered later in this chapter.

The period of most intense ceremonial in Montecastello is Holy Week. Preparations begin about ten days before Palm Sunday, when the priest starts the blessing of the houses. Every house is cleaned to perfection, for all parts of the home will be blessed. Over the course of several days the priest makes the round of the community, always followed by the sexton, who carries a basket for the eggs that each family offers. Beginning on the Friday before Palm Sunday, religious activity centers on the little church in the Piazza of the Market, which contains the statue of the Dead Christ. On that day a procession of women (the Confraternity of the Addolorata) carries the statue of the Sorrowing Madonna from the parish church to join her Son in the chiesina. The statue of the Madonna used until the 1950s was a local creation that was a source of great pride to the community. It had been made during the mid-nineteenth century at the initiative of the prioresses of the confraternity; a local carpenter carved it, one member cut off her hair for the wig, and other women made the black silk and brocade clothing.

Holy Week is spent in a public reenactment of the death of Christ. Each day's development in the story is followed intensely, and people speak of the events in the present tense, as if they were taking place anew every year. From Palm Sunday until Wednesday, women representing each family of the community spend a designated hour, in rotation, sitting with the Mother and Son in the chiesina "so that they are never left alone." On Wednesday the statues are taken in procession to the parish church; the women dressed in mourning carry the Madonna and the men carry the Dead Christ. From Thursday night until Easter the bells are silent, and the boys of the town go about with noisemakers, calling out the messages that the bells would ordinarily impart.

Good Friday is the climax of the week. The day is spent in preparation for the procession of the Dead Christ, which people describe as the *accompagno* (funeral procession) of the Lord. Every house along the route is decorated and strung with lanterns, and in the church a crucifixion scene is prepared. (In the past, the dramatic society sometimes organized a passion play, which was presented in the theater.) In the evening, the populace goes to the church to hear the sermon of the "seven words." The procession follows—the men carry torches and the women lighted candles, all chanting mournfully. When the band was in existence, it would play funeral marches. The procession ends with a reentry into the church, where each person kisses the Dead Christ and takes a leaf from the garland representing the crown of thorns.

On Holy Saturday, every family prepares a decorated basket containing the cheese, bread, eggs, lamb, and wine for the Easter meal, and brings it to the church to be blessed. At midnight there is a mass, which most of the community attends; even the most casual of Montecastellese Catholics take communion on Easter. Then, on Sunday afternoon the community carries the Risen Christ in procession around the town and through the campagna. The atmosphere is festive and the songs spirited, and the brilliant banners that will be used in all the spring processions are brought out for the first time. Each of the *contrade*, the fourteen segments of the parish, has its own banner picturing its holy places or patrons.

To Montecastellesi, Easter Monday is especially important. It is the day of a community pilgrimage to the monastery of Spineta, about five kilometers to the north. Other communities in the vicinity make the pilgrimage on their own days, and there is concern that "our" procession should make a better showing than others. The procession takes about two hours, following paths through the countryside; several priors act as guides and help people cross the streams. Near the destination the ranks are straightened, and the young women change from their walking slippers into high-heeled shoes. Finally the procession arrives in full glory at the church, which is crowded with people from the surrounding area. After the mass, which is sung by the Montecastello choir, groups of families and friends share elaborate picnic dinners, and there is a carnival set up by traveling gypsies. Toward evening, the procession regroups for the return.

The spring season continues the pace of ceremonial activity. Much of it is concerned with the well-being of the growing crops. Several holidays contribute to making crosses that are placed in the wheat fields, where they are believed to ward off hail. The cane arms of the cross are interlaced with a candle blessed during Candlemas (February 2), an olive twig blessed on Palm Sunday, and the *giglio* leaf blessed during the St. Peter the Martyr festa (April 29). The crosses are then blessed on the Holy Cross holiday early in May. In the early morning of the three days preceding the Ascension, there are processions around the town walls for the blessing of the fields. On the eve of the Ascension, as on several other holiday eves, peasants light fires all through the countryside, and call from house to house with a formula that is intended to forestall the dangerous storms of the season.[1] The festa of the Ascension itself centers on the blessing of the children, who walk in procession carrying flowers for the Virgin's altar and singing songs in her honor.

The spring ceremonial involves the community as a whole and emphasizes common concerns; some of it specifically affirms community identity. The patron saints of the parish church are celebrated on the first of May. Throughout the season, processions to churches and shrines in the region are carried out in a spirit of rivalry with other communities. Both community and internal divisions find ceremonial recognition in the festival of the End of May. Every evening during May, the month of the Madonna, people of each contrada say rosaries in the neighborhood chapels.[2] On the last Sunday, a festa "closes" the month. In the afternoon residents of each contrada gather at their chapel and form a procession, carrying their banner and singing their favorite songs in praise of the Madonna. All the processions (including one from the town) meet at the cemetery crossroads, where they form one long procession into the town. With each section still singing its songs and trying to drown out the others, the procession comes to its final destination—the parish church. Thus, both the distinctiveness of the contrade and their ultimate unity are expressed.

The origin of this festa illustrates a common feature of Montecastellese ceremonial life: the practice of taking patterns from a wider cultural sphere, usually through the medium of some elite individual, and redefining them as community property and part of a distinctive local tradition. The festa was initiated during the 1930s by the priest of Montecastello, a man of nonlocal origin. The contrade were areas designated by traditional names, but they had possessed little functional significance in the recent past. When a contrada had a Madonna or saint of local significance the priest had it displayed on a banner; when there was no local "patron," he assigned one. In addition, he had two other saints depicted on each banner, apparently for educational purposes. Despite the clearly invented origin of the festa, the populace regards it as a unique Montecastellese tradition; those who remember its origin explain that the innovator was "our own" priest.

On the morning of Corpus Christi, the neighbors within each section of the town work together to beautify their area. They create designs of wildflowers in the street, construct an outdoor altar, and arrange decorative linens or rugs at the windows. Later in the morning there is a procession in which the community follows the priest carrying *il Signore* (the host). The procession stops at each altar, and each section of town is blessed. After the procession returns to the church, people watch eagerly for signs of rain, for if the flowers are washed away a good harvest is foretold.

The day of St. Anthony of Padua (June 13) traditionally included an important procession in which the spinsters of the town asked the saint's aid in getting husbands (loudly singing "Pray for me, Sant'Antonio!"). St. Anthony is also the patron saint of Doglio, which holds an elaborate festa on that day. Montecastellesi attend in large numbers but they go as spectators. The festival of St. John the Baptist (June 24) in Montecastello is organized by the older children; people refer to it as the *Festa dei Potti*. Boys make the round of the community for contributions of foodstuffs and money, and they plan games, races, and fireworks. The festival also features a procession to the San Giovanni shrine just outside the walls. In mid-July an important festa honors a miraculous crucifix, supposed to have belonged to the beatified ancestor of a local landowning family. On this day, too, the motor vehicles of the community are blessed, as in times past carriages and oxcarts would have been.

The public rituals of summer guide the grain harvests. St. John's is the signal to begin the reaping, and the day of St. Peter (June 29) means it must not be delayed any longer.[3] The crosses that stood in the fields of growing wheat accompany the round of harvest activities. They are placed on the bundles of cut wheat set in the fields to dry, and are put atop the haystacks after the wheat is threshed. On the day of St. Anne (July 26) all threshing is halted, although the harvest season is in full swing. The story is told that some peasants once defied the tradition, and the threshing floor collapsed, killing them.

In mid-August, when the grain harvest is over and the vendemmia not yet begun, many holidays coincide: the church festival of the Assumption (August 15), the nationwide holiday week of Ferragosto, and the festa of Montecastello's patroness, the Madonna dei Portenti. The development of this festival shows several ways in which universalism and localism have been interrelated in Montecastellese ceremonial.

According to local tradition, in 1732 the image of a Madonna painted on a farmhouse talked to a ten-year-old boy who was passing by. She asked the boy to have his mother light a lamp for her. The boy told his mother what had happened, but she scoffed and responded that anyway, they had no oil. The boy reported this to the Madonna, who told him to look for the oil in a certain place. When the boy carried the message to his mother, she was much annoyed with his foolishness, but she looked in the place indicated and found the oil. People readily accepted this as a miracle, and the local priest requested permission of Pope Clement XII to erect an altar at the spot. Later, the municipal council voted to move the image to the church, and workmen were engaged to remove a portion of the wall. Legend has it that the men marked out the area in charcoal and then stopped to eat; when they returned the picture had completely detached itself from the wall along the lines of the charcoal. In November 1732 the community moved the image to the parish church in a procession led by the local priest, with the bishop of Todi and many other high-ranking personages in attendance. The bishop fixed the official name of the Madonna and the date of the annual festa. Thereafter the image was said to have performed miracles on several occasions and to have granted numerous graces.

Each year, an elaborate festival was held in honor of the Madonna, climaxed with a procession in which the image was carried to the place of the original miracle. On the centennials in 1832 and 1932 lavish celebrations were held, which involved extensive preparation and substantial expenditure. Plans for the second centennial began in 1928 with the formation of an organizing committee of local landowners and autorità.[4] The festival lasted five days and included masses, processions, fireworks, band concerts, lotteries, and other events. Some 10,000 people were present on the final day, including distinguished outsiders and organized community delegations.

Throughout these events in celebration of the Madonna dei Portenti, formal church and local community interact. The origin of the festa was local, but it was sanctioned and sponsored by the official church. The institutions of church (and of nation) were represented at the festivities, but they were linked to local leadership. Formal church ideology was incorporated but translated into community symbols: local history, traditions, and persons were referred to, and the rhetoric was marked by expressions like "the affection that all we Montecastellesi feel toward our wondrous Madonna. . . ."

The larger society is manifested in the ceremonial round of Montecastello not only by the official church, but also by symbols of nationhood. Indeed, Church and Nation are not clearly distinguished. The processions that are part of so many holidays always stop at the Monument to the Fallen, where some demonstration of patriotism usually takes place. For instance, during the intensely religious Corpus Christi procession, a speaker elaborated on the closeness of Church and State. He spoke of the similarity between Christ and the patriot soldiers, the responsibility of true followers of the faith to uphold the patria, and the equal obligations to be faithful to God, devoted to family, and respectful toward those in authority. On the other hand, secular national holidays are incorporated into the ceremonial cycle and treated as religious occasions. The Festa of the Fallen on November 4, the national holiday in honor of the war dead, is an example. In 1960, the festa was observed with a mass honoring the heroes, symbolized by a coffin in the center aisle of the church. A procession to the monument followed. An honor guard placed flags, while the crowd listened to a recording of the national anthem, after which there were speeches by a DC party representative from Perugia and the local priest.

Fall and early winter witness several church festas: the Nativity of the Virgin on September 8, All Saints' Day on November 1, the Immaculate Conception on December 8, the "Sabatina" festival on the evening of December 9, Christmas (which is celebrated for three days), the New Year, and Epiphany. The predominant tone of the season, however, is familial. In early October there is a festa for the Confirmation of children, a mass *rite de passage* which is followed by private family festivities. The Day of the Dead (November 2) the community spends in the cemetery. As masses are said all day long, families visit among their dead, in a mood more convivial than solemn. The Christmas season is a time for family dinners and visiting between neighbors and relatives. The main focus of Christmas is *il Bambino* (the Baby). At midnight mass people "watch the Baby's birth," and at the mass on Christmas afternoon they "kiss the Baby." Christmas decorations consist of creche scenes; children find gifts from "the Baby"; and family rituals talk of the goodness of children and their obligations to their parents. There is another midnight mass on New Year's Eve, but many people go to dances instead or visit among friends, marking midnight by smashing bottles or crockery.

Later in the winter the festivals again feature processions and other community-wide activity. The festa of St. Antony the Abbot is celebrated on the Wednesday following the saint's day (January 17), to coincide with the cattle fair in Montecastello. On this day, the animals of the community are blessed. The statue of the saint is carried in procession to the fairgrounds, where he blesses cattle, pigs, and family pets—many bedecked with red tassels to ward off the evil eye. Another fair and animal blessing is held on February 3 for the festival of the patron saint of the little church in Madonna del Piano. Church ceremonial is subdued with the advent of Lent, interrupted only by St. Joseph's day (March 19). This holiday is celebrated as a generalized name day, honoring not only the many men named Giuseppe, but also the carpenters and, by extension, all other artisans.

In addition to the regularly recurring festivals, there are also special community rituals from time to time. In the past, a prolonged weather crisis or other disaster would be met with a festa to supplicate the Madonna dei Portenti. Sometimes individuals would initiate a ritual in response to a personal crisis. Particularly when members of the elite were involved, the private matter was likely to become a community event. For example, in the 1930s a landowner's wife, still childless after eight years of marriage, made a pilgrimage to the shrine of St. Rita in Cascia and soon after became pregnant (it was to be her only pregnancy). In gratitude, she sponsored a celebration for the saint's day, which has thus become part of the Montecastellese ritual calendar.

The traditional festival cycle of Montecastello was fully within formal church dogma and organization. The townspeople always took pride in being "civilized" Catholics, in contrast to those they regarded as ignorant and crude practitioners of folk Catholicism in backward places. Yet in several senses this ceremonial had a distinctly local quality as well.

Much of this activity was defined as "our" way. In some instances, there seems actually to have been a local origin; in others, what was viewed as a local pattern was in fact a more general practice. But if the particularity of their own ways was emphasized, this was never seen to be in contradiction with the formal church. Rather, local customs were considered as creative variations within the church and the best expression of its spirit. What is more, much of the ceremonial focused on common local concerns. The major emphases of the festivals (regardless of their official significance) were the highly valued objects of the community: its crops and animals, its children, its homes, its dead, its motor vehicles, even the marriageability of its old maids. In addition, leadership and material support for this activity to a large extent derived from the local upper class. This class encouraged localisms in ritual, while at the same time maintaining extensive personal ties in the hierarchy of the church. Finally, these festivals provided many occasions in which the community participated as a whole, while several events underlined the community as an entity in itself and in rivalry with others.

Counter-Church Ceremonials

Although universalism and localism were complementary within the traditional festival round, there was always some tension between them. The church defended itself against the possibility that localism might intrude upon its own authority, while the community strove to maintain its identity. This tension is most overt in the period between Carnival and Holy Week, when various events take place that express the subtle conflict between community and formal church. Ceremonials outside the church play with church themes but develop local interpretations and assert local initiative in implicit opposition to the church.[5] These celebrations of Carnival and mid-Lent are versions of widespread European customs (e.g., Toschi 1955; Caro Baroja 1965). The Montecastellesi, however, regard them as their own distinctive community traditions and as genuine creations of "the people."

Carnival is celebrated in Montecastello for about four weeks. It is welcomed with parties on the first day, and throughout the period there are organized dances several times a week, as well as frequent visiting. The pace of activity intensifies during the final week until the climactic last day, Martedi Grasso (Shrove Tuesday). In the afternoon, children (and some of their more exuberant elders) don masks and costumes and go about to all the houses, singing and collecting offerings of *strufoli*, the Carnival sweet. That evening the dances are more festive than usual and the attire more elegant. Almost everyone goes somewhere to dance, to organize some hilarity, or to watch others doing so; many stay up all night and share a dawn breakfast of *pasta'sciutta*.[6]

At the time that Carnival is officially over and the church calls its flock to the solemnity of Lent, sociability, flirtation, and merriment are at a peak. At this point, on Ash Wednesday, the community under the leadership of several men of the town stages a festival commemorating the "death of Carnival." This festa has taken place for as long as anyone in Montecastello can remember. It always occurs over the objection of the church, which tolerates the excesses of Carnival but condemns gaiety and dancing on the first day of Lent. The events of 1961 illustrate the patterns of the festival.

On Tuesday, "Carnival," a straw dummy masked and dressed in men's clothing, was set out in a conspicuous place in the Piazza of the Market, holding a sign saying it would be put to death the following evening. Although Wednesday was a regular work day, in the afternoon several men appeared around town in fragments of costumes—some dressed as women, in standard Carnival inversion—and small groups formed to concoct pranks or tease women passing by. Soon word spread that it was time for the funeral accompagno. Men gathered in the piazza and placed the dummy atop a truck; about twenty men climbed on, including two carrying accordions. Several motorcycles were arranged in front of the truck, and a number of cars followed. The procession made a round of the town, with much singing, waving, and shouting to people in the streets. Then it set out along the country roads, orderly at first, the singing spirited and, for the moment, in tunc.

At various places along the way the procession would stop, the men would scramble down, and they would sing out to the people at the place:

> Siamo venuti per salutarti
> Se ci vuoi bene, dacci da bè.
>
> (We have come to greet you,
> If you like us, give us something to drink.)

The host would pour wine for all. Then the accordionists would begin to play, some men would form couples and dance, and everyone would cavort about, singing:

> È morto Carnevale,
> Chi lo sotterrà?

> La compagnì di zoppi
> Farà la carita.

> (Carnival has died,
> Who will bury him?
> The company of cripples
> Will do the charity.) [7]

and to the tune of "Dacci da Bè":

> Papa non vuole, mamma nemmeno,
> Come faremo, fare l'amor?

> (Father doesn't want it, nor mother either,
> How will we manage it, to court?)

At each stop the singing would grow more drunken, the dancing would develop more sexual suggestions, and more men would venture out among the crowd to chase girls. Then, the procession would re-form, in increasing disorder. Much of the Montecastellese countryside was covered; stops were made at each hamlet and fattoria, and at a few farmhouses where lights indicated they were prepared with wine and strufoli. Doglio and Fratta were also visited, with much boasting about the *matterìa* (craziness) that only Montecastello is capable of. Long past dark, after the truck had broken down repeatedly and various revelers passed out, what was left of the procession roared back into town to the cheering of the waiting crowd.

At this point in the festa, some humorous presentation is staged in the piazza showing how Carnival meets his death. At times it depicts a surgical operation. Carnival is stretched out under bloodied sheets, and the participants, dressed in robes and masks, "operate" on him, extracting from his interior animal intestines, scissors, hammers, even a screeching cat, and throwing them to the crowd. Carnival always dies in surgery, but sometimes he simultaneously gives birth to next year's Carnival (a chicken). Often a "priest" mourns Carnival's sinfulness and blesses him before he dies. In 1961, a mock trial was held. Carnival was the accused; the charge causing the citizens to sin. A local clerk and a few other young townsmen organized the general proceedings, assigning roles and distributing the makings of costumes and props. The honored roles as judges and attorneys were for the most part given to signori, and all those who were invited to participate accepted. These arrangements

were made shortly before the trial was to begin, and the performance itself was entirely spontaneous.

The presiding judge (played by the clerk-organizer) opened the trial
by announcing the purpose of the assembly: to judge the gravity of Carnival's offense. Each attorney then argued his case and called upon people in the crowd to give testimony—namely, to tell how they or others
had been led to sin by Carnival. All of this was accompanied by constant
commentary and heckling from the crowd, and there were many references to current scandals and to incidents of the recent Carnival, both
real and fictitious. The "witnesses" called on most often were old
women, while the more likely sinners were approached more cautiously.
Finally, the judges retired to reach their verdict—"guilty," with the
penalty to be death at the stake. Some men placed the dummy on a pyre
and set it on fire. As Carnival burned, the men formed a circle and
danced around the pyre.

After the ceremony, the men who had participated and several others
assembled at the bakery. There they were served a supper of spaghetti in
tuna sauce (for Lent had already begun); expenses were covered by the
merchant's wife who has become a kind of community patroness. The
wine flowed freely, and until late at night there was singing, dancing,
and exchanges of *stornelli*. (Stornelli are brief verses—some much-
repeated and others spontaneously composed to describe people and
events of the day—whose humor is based on insult, sex, or both.) [8] The
participants in the day's events included townsmen of all classes, as well
as a few peasants, but the predominant group appeared to be the popolo—artisans and workers of the town.

The next day, there was much discussion about how the festival had
gone and how it compared with past Carnivals. Those who had participated more actively recounted the adventures of the day. The descendants of the traditional elite talked appreciatively of this evidence of
Montecastello's uniqueness, but they complained that the performance
was not as well-planned or as smooth as in their day, when certain signori had organized it. The clerk who had acted as leader took credit for
the idea of the trial, though he acknowledged that others had picked it
up and made it a spontaneous community event; most likely, his inspiration was the product of Carnivals he had heard of or remembered. Older
people agreed that the funeral procession was shorter than in years past
and less festive than it had been when the town band would accompany

it. Everyone wondered how the priest had taken it, and there was much amusement and general satisfaction at reports of his disapproval and discomfort. At the same time, many admitted that they had been cautious about provoking overt conflict with him and had therefore omitted the burlesques of priests that were formerly a standard part of the festivities.

The Death of Carnival dramatizes the collision between community and organized church. It develops the contrasts between abandon and restraint, between sin and repentance. The masquerades, the pranks, and the procession give vent to abandon, the final breath of Carnival. Then, the performance in the piazza confronts the theme of sin, toying with it, celebrating it, but finally yielding to the inevitable: Carnival must be put to death. Though it is Carnival who is punished and not the mortals he "caused" to sin, the people repent by killing him and then accepting Lent.

This festival also reflects the specific influence of a civic history (see Toschi 1955:228 ff.). Carnival cannot simply be put to death; he must be properly tried, condemned with the sanction of the municipal statutes, disposed of with a full panoply of bureaucratic procedure. The trial employs a large number of official roles, the main ones—judges and attorneys—played by the educated elite. The popolo, however, is more than an audience; it actively participates in the judicial process. Elements that commonly occur in Carnival festivities, such as sexual license, social satire, and collective confession, are here incorporated into a parody of communal government. The whole event, moreover, is acted out in a spirit of civic self-consciousness and rivalry with other towns.

Thus, the Montecastellesi bring Carnival to an end, as the church demands, but in their own time and in their own way. The resolution, however, is only temporary. What people talk of as "the urge to dance" surfaces repeatedly throughout Lent. The more defiant actually hold or attend dances. The church mobilizes against this with one of its harshest sanctions—the threat to withhold the blessing of the houses during Holy Week; this in turn increases people's resentment. The tension comes to a head at Mid-Lent, an unofficial holiday that is popularly regarded as a permissible break in the Lenten prohibitions. Despite condemnation by the church, parties and even dances are held on that day. The conflict, which today turns on the issue of dancing, seems to be long-standing. Until recently it found expression in the performance of the Segavecchia.

The Segavecchia, or "the sawing of the old woman," is a masqueraded comical dramatization played by groups of six to ten men. It was enacted both by peasants, who circulated from farm to farm repeating the performance in each place, and by townsmen who gave performances in the piazza. During the last years that it was performed, the groups consisted mainly of lower-class townsmen, who were coached by the upper-class local historian. Such a role by a member of the elite was not new. Older informants remembered that a version of the Segavecchia had once been written down by a local man, and this written version served as a standard point of reference, though not actually as a script. The ceremonial continued through the 1950s. In 1961 a group was formed and began rehearsing, but it broke up before any performance was given.

The Segavecchia acts out the story of an old woman who insists on dancing, although it is Mid-Lent. Her old husband and her sons try to stop her and call her to the appropriate Lenten activity—prayer. In response, she only gets wilder, calling for more music and forcing her husband to dance with her. The husband goes into a soliloquy: he recalls their youth when he loved her and she wore beautiful clothing, laments her ugly old age and scandalous behavior, and concludes with the wish that she might die. At this, the sons join in; one tells of the sorrow and pain she has always caused them, not even allowing them to take wives. The old woman realizes that they intend to kill her, and she curses her assassin husband and sons. The sons than attack her. One holds her fast, while the other proceeds to saw her across the middle, saying that if the sawing doesn't do the job they will take a hatchet to her. Finally she falls dead.

After some moments of awed silence, the men become alarmed at what they have done, beg pardon of the Lord, and try to call their mother and wife back to life. The old man thinks of calling the doctor and sends a son to fetch him. While the woman is lying on the ground, presumably sawed in half, the son is reporting to the doctor that mama is very sick and in danger of death, and he asks the doctor for help. The doctor arrives on "horseback" looking serious and important. He examines the body, and then announces that this is no natural illness but someone's evil deed. Everyone denies this, but the doctor threatens to denounce them to the authorities and have them sent to jail for forty years. The sons beg him not to, saying they will pay him whatever he asks. The doctor suggests that he might be able to set things right, in return for the basket of eggs they are carrying. When they protest that this is asking too much—the fruit of all their labor—the doctor begins to write out the denunciation with great flourishes. Father and sons see that he is serious and plead with him to stop, offering him their basket of eggs plus a large sum of money. The doctor is skeptical that they have the money to pay, but they assure him they will borrow or beg for it. When the doctor is satisfied, he gives the old woman an injection. She begins to stir, whereupon her husband curses her revival! The performance ends as all give thanks to the doctor and to the audience.

Afterwards, the performers take off their masks. The accordionist plays and the young people dance, while the people acting as hosts pass around drink and refreshment. The troupe is then presented with a quantity of eggs, and they move on to another place. The performances continue over several days, and at the end the group divides its collection of eggs.

The Segavecchia is a version of an old Mediterranean festival held at mid-Lent, in which an old woman represents Lent and sawing her in half depicts the halfway point in the Lenten period. However, the specific themes vary in place and time. In the Montecastellese Segavecchia, the themes of abandon versus restraint and sin versus repentance are explicit, the same themes that marked the Death of Carnival. The *vecchia* defies the church in her abandon (the uncontrollable urge to dance), and husband and sons try to restrain her in the name of the church; finally they punish her for her sin. In doing so, however, they reveal that they are not acting on behalf of Religion but in response to their own secret impulses and resentments; then the sin becomes theirs. They quickly repent their deed, less in guilt or sorrow than in fear for the conquences, but it is repentance nevertheless. They do what they can to undo the damage; namely, they call a representative of Learning and Authority, bribe him to cover up their guilt, and mechanically set things right. The sequence is similar to that of Carnival: the pleasures of sin and defiance are indulged; the consequences are confronted; and finally there is the resolution—yielding to authority and the restraints of Lent.

Apart from these themes, the Segavecchia involves a dramatic inversion of values. The revered symbol of church and family life within the church, the Mother-wife, is overturned and exposed for all her faults. She is shown as the reverse of the ideal: ugly, self-serving, uncontrolled, sexual, troublesome, subversive of those who would be virtuous. Those who denounce her are the men who are supposed to idolize and protect her, the men ordinarily regarded as sinners who must be retrieved by her purity. Finally they commit the unthinkable, the contrast in the extreme with the behavior expected of sons. It is significant that this portrayal occurs precisely at the beginning of the church festival period that will center upon the Mother in her most idealized form, the sorrowing Madonna. The dramatization explores the negatives of all virtues of the Mother-Madonna. Then it yields: the vecchia is restored to life, and husband and son welcome her, reluctant but chastened.

The Segavecchia thus ends with the symbol of the Mother accepted once again. Soon after, another popular tradition expresses restoration of the Mother to her rightful place of honor. Throughout the second half of Lent, especially as Holy Week approaches, groups of two or three people (men or mixed groups), perhaps accompanied by an accordionist, circulate around the farms and centers of the community singing the *Passione*. After each performance, the singers are given eggs that, like those collected during the Segavecchia, are used for the *pizze* (cheese bread) of the Easter season. The custom was still practiced by a few people in 1961, although the songs were then mainly standardized texts taken from published books.

The traditional Passione consists of lengthy songs, in dialect, that retell the Holy Week story.[9] Though several versions are known in Montecastello, they invariably focus on the Mother, and they depict a mother's torment over the suffering of a loved son.[10] At the time that the church is organizing its presentation of the official Easter story, the Passione tells the people's version, with different emphases and modes of expression. While it is not in opposition to the church, it might be seen as the people's claim to make the story their own. At the same time, it reintegrates the Mother into the order of values. The way is thus paved for the Holy Week events and for the ceremonial reconciliation of church and community.

Events similar to what I have called counter-church ceremonials have sometimes been described as survivals of peasant traditions. The material from Montecastello suggests, however, that they may be as much the specific products of town life. Whatever their origin, these ceremonials were readily taken over by townspeople and incorporated into the town's view of its civiltà; it was also in town that they continued longest. The town offers stage and audience, while the close proximity of potential participants encourages the organization of such events. Moreover, as the traditions become entwined with the self-image of the town, it exerts deliberate efforts to maintain them.

The elite and other literate people also play a significant role. The written versions of the Segavecchia, as well as the guidance of individuals like the historian, certainly helped to preserve it. Similarly, the Carnival festivities have generally been influenced by sophisticated men who drew upon ideas from the outside and self-consciously tried to perpetuate local traditions. In both events, the signori as a group have a supportive part, furnishing costumes, providing festive meals for the participants, and lending their prestige. It may well be that elites such as the one in Montecastello often play an important role in innovating or sustaining folklore in rural communities.

To the extent that these ceremonials express conflict with the church, they undoubtedly owe some of their vigor to anticlerical attitudes in this region, which were especially pronounced during the nineteenth century. Such attitudes still color much of the folklore of Montecastello. Popular humor—sayings, jokes, and tales—mocks priests and other *religiosi*, quietly subverting church officialdom while avoiding any open challenge to it and any questioning of its spiritual authority. Not surprisingly, in view of the vigorous anticlericalism of the Liberals, the local elite have had an important part in encouraging this folklore. Members of this class also figure prominently in the stories. One anecdote, for instance, is about a nineteenth-century Montecastellese notable, a man who considered himself extremely religious. Once when he was away for some time on a trip, he was brought news that seven priests had died at Montecastello. "Excellent," he said. The bearer of the news continued: "And three others have sent for the doctor." "Excellent, excellent," he rejoiced.

The lore of the non-elite tends to be more indirect in its criticism of the church. The following story, which was told by the grandson of the hero, is an example. While taking Catholic ideology for granted, it subtly ridicules church practices and practitioners.

Pietro was a carpenter of an old Montecastellese town family who lived during the nineteenth century. In addition to practicing his trade he played the violin, and he would often play at festas for a fee. One evening he confided to his *compare* that since no one had called him to play, he thought he would go to play at the house of the devil, and he set off into the country with his violin.

Once on his way, he met a tall, handsome young man who asked where he was going. He answered that he was looking for a place to play his violin. The young man asked him to come with him. Soon they arrived at a great house. When Pietro entered he saw many people of Montecastello, all long since dead: there were priests, monks, nuns, and all the greatest landowners of the paese. Among them was his own *comare*, who said to him:

"*Compare mio*, do you know where you've come?"

"Where?" asked Pietro.

"To hell! Have you made an agreement about how much you will be paid?" Pietro said he had, five *paoli*. The comàre warned him not to take one *centesimo* more.

Then Pietro was shown into a grand ballroom, full of couples all dancing like madmen. He played, but the violin seemed to be playing by itself. Pietro had agreed to play until midnight, and he watched the great clock in the ballroom carefully. Precisely at midnight, he stopped. The young man took him into another room heaped with money and precious metals, and he began to fill Pietro's pockets with coins. Pietro refused them all, except for five paoli. Finally, the young man took him back to the exact place where they had met, and Pietro returned home and went to bed.

The next morning, he said to his compare: "You see, compare mio, what it means to joke! Last night I really did play at the house of the devil!" And he told the whole story. The rumors spread quickly and reached the local priest. He called Pietro to him and asked whether all that had actually happened. Pietro would not answer yes or no, but said: "I don't know if it is true or not, I can't assure you."

The families whose dead were supposed to have been among the dancers urged him to tell what the truth really was, but he was always ambiguous. Everyone was left in doubt. And (concludes the narrator), many masses were ordered and many funeral services were said!

The discussion thus far has focused on traditional elements in the ceremonial cycle, on continuities with the past. Yet what appears as traditional to an observer or to the people themselves at any given time is not the enduring product of an undifferentiated past, but rather the outcome of social processes rooted in the specific conditions of time and place. An understanding of these processes would require more historical data. Nevertheless, even the observation of ceremonial during the course of one year can offer clues to the factors involved.

The festival round is structured by the church, but it is not rigidly prescribed. Thus, it affords a wealth of symbolic material that can be manipulated by different groups to different ends. The symbolic emphasis upon the community in Montecastello is a case in point. Localism in traditional ceremonial is not simply the consequence of limited contact with the larger world; it has also been deliberately fostered. Its main proponents have been members of the local upper class. That their concern with localisms went along with a commitment to official Catholicism is reminiscent of the way in which Montecastellese elites have long operated politically. In their relations with the church as with states, they declared themselves faithful subjects, capitalized on their personal connections in the hierarchy, and in general, actively identified with the wider sphere. At the same time, they asserted the ritual identity of the community. It was in the name of that identity that they pressed their claims to political autonomy.

The "community" that the local upper class strove to preserve—one symbolized by localisms in ritual—was a social order under their own control. Though the church in many ways helped sustain that control, it was also a source of challenge to it. Repeatedly over the course of recent centuries, opposition to the landowning elite has been voiced by the local priest. Several times the documents tell of a sindaco deploying his legalistic skills and maneuvering his contacts in an effort to have the priest removed. In 1901, for instance, the sindaco accused the priest of agitating against the peace of the community, hinting that he was spreading socialist ideas (A.S.P., 6).

It may well be that in the past, at times of such conflict between church and local elite, there was more contention between universalism and localism in ceremonial than I could reconstruct from fieldwork in 1960–61. For most of my informants, the remembered past extended back no more than forty or fifty years. Many of the "traditions" that they referred to and that I observed date from the years 1920 to 1940. This coincides with the Fascist period, a time of alliance between the church and the landowning class. It may not be accidental that the priest during this time was a vigorous defender—what is more, an innovator—of local traditions. Contemporary landowners still speak of him as a "true Montecastellese priest" (though he was not from Montecastello) and commend him for the harmony that he brought to community life. If one could illuminate the "traditional" past of Montecastello beyond the range of an ethnographic study, it would undoubtedly appear that the symbols accented in ceremonial have varied over time in relation to the shifting balance of forces within the community and within the larger society.

Community and Church Today

Since World War II, the interplay between universal church and local community revealed in the festival cycle has undergone renewed change. As a result, localism has lost much of its previous importance in Montecastellese ceremonial. The church has followed an energetic policy of encouraging universalism as part of its efforts to adapt to the changing conditions of the modern world. At the same time, the processes that have brought people into more direct participation in national life have also affected religious activity.

Although as of 1961 most of the ceremonial cycle persisted in outward form, the patterns of participation had altered. Increasingly, people participate in festivals as individuals and as Catholics rather than as members of a community. Ceremonial events that used to include the whole community are attended according to personal conviction, inclination, or convenience. Only "the more religious" follow all the details of the Holy Week reenactment or walk in the less important processions. Easter Monday is becoming more an outing than a community manifestation, and many people ride to the monastery in private vehicles or the postale bus to meet the procession. The daily rosaries during May are attended by a handful of old women, and on the day of the festa for the closing of the month, many country people ride motorcycles up to the town to watch the now dwindled procession. Some ceremonies have disappeared, while others are maintained by a few individuals who exert great effort to keep local traditions alive. For the most part, the holidays lose the special features that had local referents and are now simply observed in the standard patterns of Italian Catholicism.

While attendance at local ritual events diminishes, visits to festivals and holy places elsewhere are becoming more frequent. People go with friends, or as members of voluntary associations that sponsor these excursions, but they no longer go as a religious community. A striking example is provided by an important diocese gathering that was held in Todi during 1961. Traditionally on such occasions, the population of each parish would go in procession led by its priest and carrying its banners; at Todi, all the parish groups would join into a great diocese procession. In 1961 the priest hired a bus, but only about a dozen people went with him to form the Montecastello procession. Many other Montecastellesi went separately, but only to watch the spectacle.

Several persons go to other priests for rites as a matter of preference. The postwar factionalism within the community has contributed to this practice, but it is part of the general trend toward individualization and universalization of religious activity. Instead of community cults centered about local holy figures, individuals more often have personal devotion to universal saints. Saints mentioned on radio or television may strike someone's fancy and become the object of a private cult. Similarly, private needs motivate most participation in ritual events, local or otherwise. For instance, several girls who walked in the 1961 procession to the monastery did so as vows to the Virgin, requesting personal favors like success in a concorso for a teaching job or the happy conclusion of a courtship.

The counter-church ceremonials have suffered the same fate as local events within the church. The Segavecchia did not survive the abortive efforts of 1961, and that year's Death of Carnival proved to be one of the last. According to some Montecastellesi, there was no one left to organize these festivals: the old people who cared about the traditions were dying out, and the young people with spirit and initiative were moving away. Moreover, the new signori and would-be signori, sharply aware of the distinctions of social class on the national level, had found out that it was not signorile to actively participate in such local customs. Even for persons who rarely leave Montecastello, the truly important events had become—by definition—those that happen outside. Thus Carnival, which traditionally had brought Montecastellesi together in its round of dances and visiting, had become a time when all who had the means went out of town as much as possible (while the local dances were crowded with people from the country and from surrounding villages). Carnival activity was being carved up between commercial entrepreneurs and the church. The former, finding profit in the restless mood, were organizing dances with entrance fees. Their ambitions increased visibly during the course of the 1961 Carnival. The events began to be advertised as "signorile": local musicians were replaced by combos bearing the names of other towns, vocalists were added, and lotteries were held to elect a queen.[11] The church, meanwhile, took over the daytime events of Shrove Tuesday. In 1961, two nuns led the masqueraded children about, then organized a party for the children and adolescent girls. The nuns encouraged the girls to dance together to phonograph music, and they exerted valiant efforts to produce Carnival merriment.

In general, ceremonial activity corresponds less and less to the community: it no longer takes in the populace as a whole, and it no longer emphasizes specifically local concerns. This change is analogous to the loss of local autonomy in the political sphere. However, ritual life, unlike politics, still provides symbols around which community identity can be mobilized. Furthermore, in contrast to the anonymous sources of political change, there is a figure who can personify the changes in ceremonial—the priest. Thus, he becomes the focus of resentment over the loss of localism. The Montecastellesi continue to declare themselves faithful subjects of the church; their resentment is directed against the priest as an individual, not against the universal church or its current policies.

There are many issues wherein this conflict between community and priest has been manifested in recent years. Some emerge during Holy Week. There is much concern over the priest's refusal to bless the houses of those who, in his view, have sinned during Lent. Most people believe that such blessing is a right of all Catholics; that it should be withheld from that most fundamental value, the home, is especially resented. The priest is accused of omitting the procession to take the Sorrowing Madonna to her Son and of changing the timing of other Holy Week events. People would complain that they had gathered for a procession, only to learn that it had been postponed or that the priest had hurriedly accomplished its formal purpose. The old statue of the Madonna was itself the object of much bitterness, for it had mysteriously disappeared in the early 1950s. One man said that the priest claimed it had fallen and broken, so he had it thrown away. The man raged as he spoke of this, calling it an act of calculated destruction, a crime, evidence that there is a curse over Montecastello: "That Madonna was made here, by *us*, with all *our own things*. . . . Why did "they" destroy her, why did "they" kill her? . . . At least if she had been sold, she could still have been gotten back. But no. She was destroyed."

Other objects of the church that had been associated with Montecastellese history have also been lost; with or without justification the priest is blamed, on the grounds that he is indifferent if not actively opposed to local tradition. One example is that of a life-sized carved wooden statue of the Risen Christ. A story circulated to the effect that the priest thought it worthless and had called in a carpenter to cut it up for firewood; though the carpenter was fearful of doing so, the priest insisted.

Another story developed over the bell which used to announce the meetings of the communal council. During World War II, when all extra bells were requisitioned for smelting, the priest secreted it in the church, providing another bell in its place for the requisition. After the war he had it mounted on the roof of the church. Some time after the present priest had come to Montecastello, the local historian noticed it was gone. Upon inquiring, he learned that the priest had sent it to the foundry, claiming it was old and cracked. He went to the priest, paid him for the value of the metal and rescued the bell, placing it among the local archives.

Whenever there is some modification in the ceremonial round, the priest is personally blamed by many people ("that —— priest, he wants to change everything!"). When the children were preparing candles to present to the Madonna as part of the traditions of the Ascension, the priest announced that candles would be omitted, because they are troublesome and mess up the church as they melt. He instructed anyone who wanted to make the offering to make it in cash. Some people criticized this as a mercenary act; others were angered at the priest for not understanding that both the candles and the children's special role were essential parts of a *local* custom. When word spread that the St. Anthony of Padua procession would not be held, the priest was accused of sabotage; actually, it seems that he had been unable to recruit enough men to carry the heavy statue. Similarly, when he assured the peasants that it was all right to thresh on St. Anne's day but forbade them to thresh on Sundays, several people complained of his disdain for this local custom; in fact, no one did thresh on St. Anne's, though many did on Sundays. Again, when the day for the First Communion of the children was changed, it was talked about as a destruction of fine local ways because of the priest's newfangled ideas and political purposes; he had changed the day so the festa would coincide with an ecclesiastical congress. Resentment over this issue provoked some people to ask one of the local signori to complain to the bishop on behalf of the community.

The festival for the Madonna dei Portenti evoked particular bitterness. People accused the priest of indifference to their patroness: he failed to instruct the children in the local traditions; he made no mention of the special significance of the Madonna when announcing the festa; and on the day of the festa itself he scheduled a football game, so that the procession to the place of the miracle could not be held. On the Sunday following, when another procession to the spot was supposed to be held to close the festa, the priest went there in his car, recited the service quickly, and disappeared to supervise another football game.

Some of this antagonism can be related to the persistence of anticlericalism, especially among descendants of the landowning elite. They, however, phrase the issue in terms of this particular priest. In contrast to "our own" priests of the past (especially the one who served during the Fascist years), the present *arciprete* is seen as in league with those elements of the church that would destroy localism. His own stance has encouraged this view, for he has aggressively pursued the policy of universalization. He condemns the campanilismo of the Montecastellesi as detrimental to true religion, and he places most of the blame— quite correctly—on the "leading families." In his modernizing efforts he has not limited himself to religious activity as such but has initiated various social programs. Because of these efforts, many Montecastellesi commend him as a force for progress.

The role of the priest in contemporary Montecastello must be seen against the background of the national political conflict in which the church has been engaged since World War II. Like the other organizations which seek electoral support, it must appeal to interests that crosscut localities. The church in Montecastello has had as its major target the peasants and workers, the strength of the Left. They were never alienated from the church and, in fact, have remained the staunchest participants in its rituals. If the effect of discouraging localism has been to antagonize some potential supporters, particularly among the tradition-oriented elite, the overall political cost to the church and its ally, the DC party, is slight.

In its battle against Communism, the church in Montecastello frequently enters into direct opposition with the Left, as well as opposing it indirectly with religious sanctions. Most Montecastellesi of the Center-Right do not welcome these political efforts of the priest. They accuse him of fueling dissension by acting the politician, and they join the Left in the cry, *il prete deve fare il prete* (the priest should be a priest). Both factions attribute the loss of the community's ritual unity to the political activity of the church. Indeed, much of the ceremonial round has become a staging ground for the political conflict within the community.

Several festivals are used by the church for political purposes. The St. Joseph's festa was chosen as the day for the ACLI inauguration, with the rationale that the day of the patron saint of artisans symbolizes all workers. The bishop attended the event, giving a sermon in church and a speech at the recreation hall, and his visit became a strictly political occasion. Using terms indistinguishable from those of the two regional politicians who also spoke, he talked about the need to bring Christ to the unbelievers, the struggle against the heretic Communists, and the terrible state of affairs created by the Red administration. The important visitors added excitement to the festa; for most people, however, the main interest was the movie shown later in the evening.

The day of the official patron saints of the parish coincides with the May 1 labor holiday, for which the Camera del Lavoro organizes festivities every year. The priest of Montecastello treats the coincidence as an explicit challenge, planning attractions to compete with the Leftist festa. In 1961 he arranged a football game, *porchetta* sandwiches and wine at minimal cost, loudspeakers blaring music, and a choice movie—"Don Camillo," which tells the adventures of a priest in a Communist-dominated Italian town. After the festa, the priest expressed satisfaction that many of the peasants who usually go to the Communist celebration came to the church this time. Throughout the holiday there was no explicit reference to the patron saints. The extent to which this festa had become the priest's own program, devoid of local initiative or custom, is reflected in themes written by sixth-grade schoolboys on the topic, "The Festival of the Patron Saint in my Paese." The following theme is typical:

At nine o'clock there is a sung mass, and when the mass is over there is the display of relics of the saints. . . . After the mass il signor arciprete offers refreshments in the asilo. During the refreshments he plays records. And the morning passes very gaily between talking of this and that. Before the evening mass there is the football game; last year we played against the Fratta team. Il signor arciprete has said that this year we would play against Doglio. After the evening mass we have fireworks, and thus the day passes with great pleasure. After the fireworks il signor arciprete takes us boys to watch television in his house.

Another coincidence of Communist and church festas occurred in 1961, when the PCI's Festival of Unity held at Madonna del Piano and the diocese gathering at Todi fell on the same day—whether by chance or calculation I could not determine.[12] However, the local priest clearly took the coincidence in a spirit of competition. It also created some confusion. One old ex-peasant, who was an outspoken Socialist, boarded the bus hired by the priest thinking it was going to Madonna del Piano. Only after the bus went some distance did he and the priest discover each other, much to the amusement of the other passengers.

In addition to the religious festivals, the church makes political use of some national ceremonies. Thus, the festa honoring the war dead, occurring a few days before the election, was controlled by the local church and the DC party. Following the mass and procession to the monument, a DC official spoke of the link between the war heroes, the guidance of the church, and politics. (To paraphrase him: No one can accuse me of partisanism if I compare our heroes' struggle with that of the election day coming. It would be the lowest thing to talk politics here, but I feel I must say this, spontaneously. . . .) The priest then took the microphone and responded to remarks made by a Communist speaker at a rally the evening before.

Perhaps the most controversial political activity of the church concerns its conduct not of public ceremonials but of private ones. The most important example is the priest's refusal to baptize an infant if one of the godparents is an avowed Communist. Prospective godparents from other communities must bring a certificate from their parish priest stating that they have sworn not to profess heretical theories nor to belong to parties condemned by the church. Parents who are refused the sacrament must either find some other priest to perform the rite or choose other, acceptable godparents. The priest defends the policy on ecclesiastical grounds, but almost everyone who talks of it considers it morally wrong and politically unwise.

The program of the church in contemporary Montecastello has more than specifically political ends. It is engaged in a vigorous effort to influence local life in the direction of church values, and its objects include private as well as public activities. It pursues campaigns against birth control, against "sinful" forms of dancing, and even againt undesirable fantasies (for instance, condemning the photo-romance magazines popular among adolescents). However, the priest knows well that preaching from the pulpit has little effect. The Montecastellesi—well practiced in skepticism and compartmentalization—listen, accept the spiritual leadership of the church, and reject its interference in other areas of their lives. Thus, the priest has attempted more subtle approaches, bringing modern forms of persuasion to bear upon the traditional purposes of the church.

His establishment of the ACLI chapter was the most conspicuous step, but he has also brought two innovations to Montecastello: football (association football, or soccer) and movies.

The priest exerted considerable effort to raise funds for a football field, drawing mainly on church and party sources in Rome. He thus succeeded in establishing one of the major recreational activities of the community. He organized the Montecastellese team (which is made up of boys from about 14 to 20) and he continues to control the sport. Games are played in Montecastello approximately every second Sunday and holiday from April until mid-autumn, and it has become a standard festive-day pastime for people to stroll down the passeggiata in the late afternoon to go to the *calcio* game. For the priest, football is a quite explicit way to gain influence over the adolescent boys and to take the population away from attractions of the Left. For instance, on May 1, the football game was scheduled for the same hour as the main speech at the Communist festa, and then rescheduled when the speech was rescheduled. Moreover, the team that the priest arranged for the Montecastellesi to play that day was from Madonna del Piano, an area with heavy Communist support. The priest's involvement in the games throughout the football season annoyed many people, who described it as "playing politics" at the expense of the festival traditions.

Apart from the purely recreational function that football serves, it seems to be the contemporary approximation of ceremonials that traditionally marked Montecastellese identity vis-à-vis other communities. Although there is little overt partisan enthusiasm (it is often difficult to learn from the spectators who has won and what the score was), the games become occasions to express contrasts between Montecastello and the opposing community. The match itself is viewed in terms of the images of the communities. When the competitor is a more powerful or sophisticated town, such as Todi, the Montecastellesi assume that "we can't possibly beat them", while teams from less important and less civile places are deprecated. The most equally matched town is Fratta, and in games with this opponent the spirit of rivalry becomes most overt. (In contrast, in matches with Madonna del Piano, which is not considered a separate community, the razzing was friendly and directed at individuals rather than the hamlet.)

Movies, as passive entertainment, play a rather different role in local life. They constitute a kind of modern morality play, developing some of the same themes that appear in the Carnival and mid-Lent dramatizations, though in a very different spirit. Since all movies in Montecastello are shown at the Cinema Parrocchiale, it is not surprising that their points of view are always consistent with church values. Still, the degree of thematic similarity among the several films featured during the first six months of ACLI's existence was striking. The film *Disperato Addio* (Desperate Good-bye) is typical; it was one of the best received movies shown in Montecastello during that period.

The story is about two young doctors, best friends, who are in love with the same nurse. One is a handsome playboy, the other plain, pure, and devoted to his saintly mother. The playboy wins the nurse and enjoys a brilliant career. As his success increases he takes up with flashy women, while the nurse-wife remains angelic. Eventually, she leaves him and turns to the friend, who urges her to go back to her husband (whom she loves as he himself loves her—only once, and for life). The next day she has an appendicitis attack. Misled by her murmurings while she is under anaesthesia, the husband accuses her of infidelity and, worse, of disgracing him before the hospital staff.

The heroine goes away, pregnant but fearing to tell her husband. She bears the child and cares for it alone, submitting to humiliating work and going blind from a brain tumor. Finally, she leaves the beloved boy at her husband's office, a note pinned to his clothing, and throws herself under a train.

Meanwhile, the husband discovers the baby and is immediately won over by him. The friend finds the injured heroine and reunites her with her husband. At the urging of the friend, the husband tries the one-chance-in-a-thousand surgery, and it succeeds. The self-sacrificing friend says "addio" and walks off into the mist of a lonely piazza. The now-remorseful husband has been saved from his wanton life, and the couple's happiness is crowned by their son—the perfect child.

As in the traditional popular dramas, there are the contrasts between good and evil (the devoted friend and the playboy; wife-mother-nurse and flashy women), abandon and restraint, sin and redemption. Sins are depicted in great detail, then their rectification is accomplished in a few moments. Finally, the resolution: cleansing and perfection are achieved through acceptance of the values of religion.

From the perspective of the present, it is evident that many ceremonial patterns that marked out local identity have given way to universalistic practices. Participation in religion, as in politics, continues to be essential to the civil life, but the Montecastellesi now enact their roles less in terms of the local community and more in terms of wider memberships—in the universal church and the Italian nation. The ideology of civiltà serves as an idiom for talking about these changes—in welcome or regret, in the name of either progress or tradition.

Carnival on the eve of his death, 1961.

Landlord and peasant carrying the Easter meal to church.

Good Friday: announcing midday.

The End of May festival.

Football. In the rear, the civic tower (left), the new school (center), the public gardens (right).

Outside a café. At right, the carpenter whose grandfather played for the devil.

A bride and her father: procession to the church.

Corpus Christi.

CHAPTER 7

———— ◆◆ ————

The Life Cycle

SO FAR we have looked at civiltà in relation to structural characteristics of the community. Now our point of view shifts to the family and
the individual: what it is like to grow up within and to live the civil life
of Montecastello.

The Family

Both officially and informally, Montecastellesi are identified as members
of a family first and as individuals only second. The unit used by the
government for registering the population is the *famiglia*, whose
members are described by their relation to the legal head of the family
(*capofamiglia*). The family forms a unit in informal social life too. Thus, a
whole family is considered to participate in events (such as the funeral of
a neighbor, a community procession, or a public fund-raising occasion) if
it sends one member as representative, and for such purposes the
members are essentially interchangeable. Similarly, in casual interaction
individuals are referred to in terms of their family or its head; for instance, Maria, the wife or daughter of Giovanni Tebaldo, is "Maria di
Giovanni" or "Maria la Tebalda."

The term "famiglia" in the popular sense is approximately equivalent
to the "household." It consists of all members of the household who are

related by blood, marriage, or adoption; domestics, hired hands, and other unrelated persons who have lived in the household for many years may occasionally be incuded as well.[1] On the other hand, the famiglia is distinguished from the *parenti* (relatives), the circle of kinsmen beyond the household. In defining the boundaries of a household, the most meaningful criterion seems to be a common budget. Physical boundaries do not necessarily correspond, since kinsmen living in adjacent apartments or houses may or may not form an economic unit. Moreover, the family listed in official records may be rather different from the social reality. As a tactic to collect maximum government benefits, a large group that functions as a unit may report itself as two families, or an employed son may be designated the legal capo though he is not the real head.

When people talk about the ideal family, they generally describe a three-generation family in which the sons all bring their brides into the paternal household. The family in Montecastello that was most often pointed to as an example included an elderly couple, their two sons, and their wives and children. The success of this family was attributed to the fact that the old people were "good" (the father not excessively stingy, the mother not overly domineering) and the young women even-tempered. However, such harmony is considered unusual, and the version of the ideal regarded as more workable and modern is the family in which only one son remains after marriage. At the same time, the nuclear family is supported by an ideology of its own, which recognizes that it is necessary or wise to "go alone" under certain circumstances.

The ideal multi-generation family is, in fact, relatively infrequent. Table 14 shows the distribution of different types of families in Montecastello. The two major categories comprise, in the main, nuclear families (Category II) and stem and extended families (Category III). Of the family groupings in the commune in 1960, the most common type was the nuclear family, consisting of about 60 percent of the total; only about one-third comprised some form of extended family. However, a count of actual groupings does not adequately reflect cultural patterning. Many of the nuclear families are consistent with the "ideal"—those whose capo has no living parent, has parents living with another son, or holds a job that required a long-distance move. Moreover, a large number of the nuclear families (over 40 percent of them) had at some earlier time formed part of extended groupings. Thus, the family types existing at any given time are best regarded not as "regular" or "deviant" in relation to an ideal, but rather as alternative outcomes of certain principles that guide residence decisions (see Goodenough 1956).

At marriage, decisions are made about where the couple will live, and several considerations enter. If father and son work together in an enterprise that can support a large group, it is likely that the young couple will remain in the boy's parental household. When the boy is an only son or the only one left at home, there is great pressure on the couple to live there. On the other hand, in a family without sons that has a prosperous farm or business, a daughter's husband may enter the household. In all cases, the physical possibilities of the house are also a factor. As for the young people themselves, those of today generally prefer to live by themselves. They are supported by the increasingly common belief that once the old people's security and the family's continuity are provided for (preferably by one son remaining at home), the other children ought to go wherever they can best improve their position in life.

The variation in family organization is related in part to socioeconomic differences within the community. If family type is an outcome of residence choices, this variation might be accounted for by the hypothesis that all Montecastellesi share the same principles for making decisions about residence, but that these lead to different residence arrangements under different economic conditions. The effect of economic factors is especially clear among the mezzadri, who have a relatively high proportion of extended families (see Table 14). Until recently, a large family was an advantage for mezzadri, for it gave them a better choice of farms. Since the amount of land under cultivation increased until about 1930, a growing family could usually find a large enough farm to support itself. Thus, families of twenty or more members were not uncommon before the contemporary period. Large families were the result of a combination of factors: all sons were encouraged to bring brides into the household; high fecundity was the rule; and it was common for families to take in extra hands—peripheral patrilineal relatives and adopted children. Since World War II, labor-saving technological advances, as well as the overall decrease in the mezzadria population and the reduced size of many farms, have considerably lessened the pressures toward large families. Now a family of six to eight members can bid for and work the most desirable farms, but even this number usually requires a stem rather than a nuclear family.[2]

Landowning families are a diverse group—in their family structure as

Table 14 Distribution of Types of Families

Type of Family [a]	1960 Total Commune		Mezzadri (1960)		Resident Landlords (1960)		Town Population (1960)						1900 Total Commune	
							Professionals & White-Collar Workers		Merchants		Artisans & Laborers			
	No.	Percent	No.	Percent	No.	Percent	No.	Percent	No.	Percent	No.	Percent	No.	Percent
Category I														
Single and unrelated persons														
Total	40	6.9	0	—	7	10.9	7	21.2	0	—	3	5.5	17	4.0
Category II														
Nuclear	210	36.1	75	35.2	16	25.0	11	33.3	2	18.2	24	44.4	166	39.0
Nuclear (incomplete)														
husband-wife	65		7		13								34	
widow-offspring	19		3		3								29	
widower-offspring	6		1										8	
unmarried siblings	7		1										8	
total	(97)	16.7	(12)	5.6	(16)	25.0	8	24.2	1	9.1	14	25.9	(79)	18.5
Expanded nuclear	41	7.0	14	6.6	5	7.8	3	9.1	1	9.1	3	5.5	31	7.3
Total	348	59.8	101	47.4	37	57.8	22	66.7	4	36.4	41	75.9	276	64.8
Category III														
Stem	75		49		5								33	
Stem (incomplete)	68		28		7								48	
total	(143)	24.6	(77)	36.1	(12)	18.7	4	12.1	5	45.4	10	18.5	(81)	19.0

Town Population (1960)

Type of Family [a]	1960 Total Commune		Mezzadri (1960)		Resident Landlords (1960)		Professionals & White-Collar Workers		Merchants		Artisans & Laborers		1900 Total Commune	
	No.	Percent	No.	Percent	No.	Percent	No.	Percent	No.	Percent	No.	Percent	No.	Percent
Extended	17		11		1		0				0		20	
Extended (incomplete)	17		10		1		0				0		6	
total	(34)	5.8	(21)	9.9	(2)	3.2	—	—	1	9.1	0	—	(26)	6.1
Joint	17	2.9	14	6.6	6	9.4	0	—	1	9.1	0	—	26	6.1
Total	194	33.3	112	52.6	20	31.3	4	12.1	7	63.6	10	18.5	133	31.2
GRAND TOTAL	582	100.0	213	100.0	64	100.0	33	100.0	11	100.0	54	99.9	426	100.0

[a] The categories follow, in general, the family types used by Pitkin in his study of land tenure and family organization in Latina province (1954). However, the data on Montecastello required a distinction between families referred to here as "stem" and as "extended": the stem families have only one married offspring, while the extended families include two or more. (The text uses the term "extended family" in the more general sense, to describe all families of Category III.) "Joint" families consist of two or more married siblings (almost always brothers) and their spouses and children. "Incomplete" families in Category III refer to situations in which the older-generation member is a widower or widow; in such cases the married children have remained in the parental household—in contrast to the "expanded" families (in Category II) in which a widowed parent has joined the married offspring's household (see Fei 1939:28).

in their economic status. Peasant proprietors occupying farms like the ones worked by mezzadri seem to have a distribution of family types similar to the mezzadri. On the other hand, mezzadria landlords resemble the community as a whole in the frequency of different family types, reflecting the contemporary diversity of the landlords (see Table 14). If one considers only those who own three or more farms (the number of which is too small to permit quantitative analysis), it appears that these are mainly couples, nuclear families, and single elderly individuals. Their children are educated for professions or for "good" marriages which frequently take them away to larger communities, while the older generation remains in Montecastello to manage their land and enjoy their local status. Among the traditional landowning families who had larger properties than those of today, there was a real advantage to maintaining their holdings intact and under direct control of the owners and their heirs. Thus, a greater tendency toward extended families seems likely. Several family histories suggest that this was, in fact, the case.

If one looks at the town population in terms of major occupational categories, striking differences in the frequency of various family types appear.[3] The professionals and white-collar workers include few extended families. These families generally lack resources that are best conserved as a unit (their "resources," skills and connections, are not enhanced by large households), and they must be geographically mobile. The merchants, in contrast, have the largest proportion of extended families of any occupational category (though unfortunately their total number is too small to allow firm conclusions). A shop or business (other than those of minute scale) can often use the labor and talents of several adults, and it represents an investment in which all members of the family have an interest. Informal observation suggests another possible factor. The most common source of conflict between generations in a household is the father's control of the family's money. Among merchants, however, adult sons necessarily handle cash and they can claim small sums for their personal use—a minor part of the total family budget but perhaps enough to avoid a major cause of tension in the family.

The category "artisans and laborers" actually covers a wide range of economic and social differences. In the group as a whole, the nuclear family is most common (about three-fourths of the total). However, the minority that are stem families (ten cases, or 18 percent) seem to be affected by the same factors as the merchants, for most of these families actually operate businesses, i.e., employ nonfamilial labor or handle substantial amounts of cash.[4]

The family types present at any given time reflect not only initial residence decisions but also the phases of domestic cycles. Extended families go through cycles of expansion and breakup. These groups are built up as inmarrying spouses are added and children are born. The household may continue to expand until its size creates problems: it may become too large for its economic base of support or for the physical arrangements of the house; or the multiplication of divergent interests and personalities may increase interpersonal conflict. At this point, one couple and their children usually move out. Such a move may also occur before the critical size has been reached—when a son finds an independent livelihood. Furthermore, families with more than one married couple in the dominant generation seem to have built-in instability apart from their size.

In the normal course of events, a household with two or more married sons would divide when the father dies. Most property is transmitted to the next generation at death; sometimes, however, an old man will "make over" his property before he dies, retaining the usufruct for his lifetime. Occasionally, the sons agree to keep both the household and the patrimony intact as long as the widowed mother is alive (partly because she has usufruct rights to a large part of her husband's property). In rare cases, generally where the family resources are the sole source of income, brothers remain together even after the death of both parents (forming the "joint" families in Table 14).

There is some evidence that as wage-earning opportunities have increased, intergenerational conflict has become more overt and the division of extended families more frequent. However, major changes in family structure are not yet apparent. A comparison of the distribution of types of families in 1960 with that for 1900 (see Table 14, last column) shows the most significant change to be a small increase in stem families, at the expense of both nuclear and joint families. At the same time, the total size of families has decreased—from an average of 5.5 in 1900 to 4.4 in 1960.[5] Thus, contemporary households contain essentially the same combinations of kin as at the turn of the century, but have fewer members. The nuclear family continues to be the most frequent type. That their number is not increasing is probably due to the fact that many of these families are drawn off by out-migration.

Learning Civiltà

Beginning with the earliest periods of life, the lessons of civiltà are woven into the socialization process.[6] The birth of an infant takes place in an intensely social context, and he is involved in a public life almost immediately. The world the newborn first encounters is made up of bustling, chattering women, for the birth draws together a network of female kin, neighbors, and friends who will hover over him during the first months of his life. One middle-class mother recalled that seven women were present when she gave birth a few years ago; older women counted more. The main topic at the birth gathering is the women's common bond—opposition to men; the talk, sometimes punctuated with bawdy language and stories, is of woman's lot and man's irresponsible sexuality. A midwife is in charge of the birth, for the doctor is called only if complications arise. Occasionally, a woman who expects a difficult birth arranges to go to a clinic in the city. Her mother accompanies her and remains with her for the duration of the stay, helping her to care for the infant. Since other new mothers, infants, and helpers share the clinic room, even the baby born away from home experiences a highly social reception into the world.

The mother's screams (she is given nothing to ease the pain) are followed by neighbors outside, and the progress of the birth is publicly noted. As soon as it is over, news of the sex and general condition is circulated, and people begin to come in to see the baby, in almost a procession of callers that continues for several days. The baby is freely picked up and handed about, and his cries are never ignored. The visitors watch his feedings, and in more modern families he is publicly weighed before and after each one. The women fuss over dressing him, first wrapping a swaddling bandage around his abdomen "to make him straight and firm." [7]

The different courses of socialization for boys and girls begin at birth. News of a boy is greeted with jubilation, for it is validation of the father's virility, and adults begin to address the baby with references to his own potential virility. A girl's birth brings a more subdued response (people may offer the parents words of consolation about some future son), and her appeal is defined as charm and grace.

For forty days the infant is kept indoors and protected, for this first period of life is tentative and precarious. It is assumed that until the forty days are over even a healthy infant may not live. He sleeps in a crib near the mother's bed, but he is never long out of contact with other people. During this period the mother too is in a dangerous condition: she is cautious about her diet and activity, and she rarely goes out. Toward the end of the period, the baby is baptized; earlier, if the parents are seriously worried about his survival. The day chosen is a Sunday or holiday.

The baptism is, of course, an infant's entrance into the religious community, but it is also his official introduction to formal social life. As such, attention focuses on the bella figura that he presents in public. He is carefully dressed in an elaborate outfit and adorned with jewelry, including the neck chain and medallion that are the customary gifts of godparents, and the coral pin—horn-shaped or of odd-numbered beads—that protects from the evil eye. He is placed on a luxurious pillow and thus carried by a young female relative. The baptismal party of infant, godparents, father, and various relatives (but rarely the mother) goes to the church in a procession, observed by people along the streets who admire the baby and say words of blessing to him.

When the party brings the baby home after the ceremony, the first questions asked by the mother, and repeated by others throughout the day, are: "Did he cry in church? How much did he cry? Did he behave well?" A lavish dinner or reception follows, to which the family's circle of kin, neighbors, and friends is invited, as well as all the high-status families with whom they have personal relationships. The event is similar to the festivities following a wedding, and the family observes as many formalities of civile sociability as they can. Guests are ushered into the sala, to see the display of gifts to the baby, and then are served dinner. After dinner there are champagne toasts, and the mother offers *confetti* (bouquets of three or five candied almonds) to each guest with various pleasantries. At some point, the baby is brought in and formally presented, and the guests remark on its good behavior, alertness (if a boy), beauty (if a girl), and other evident qualities.

After the fortieth day the infant begins to be taken out of doors and displayed in the streets. Until he is three or four months old, he is usually taken out in his crib to where the women are sitting, or walked around in a carriage. He is looked at and talked to by all who pass him, and occasionally picked up. During this time he is cared for by all the women of the household; the men talk to him but rarely handle him.

When the baby can support his upper body and he can be carried about comfortably, a subtle change occurs. In this stage, which lasts until he learns to walk, he spends much of his waking time being carried around by any woman of the household who is free. He is taken along on errands and to the women's gossip groups, and he is paraded around the town as a recreational activity in itself. Wherever the baby goes, people greet and talk to him, sometimes without exchanging a word with the adult carrying him. It is bad manners to fail to greet a baby or small child in public, and almost tantamount to denial of a relationship with the family.

On the surface, Montecastello seems a baby-centered society. Babies are often the center of attention in street gatherings, and they are the main topic of women's conversation. If the mother appears on the street without the baby, everyone asks where he is and how he is. A baby who is awake is held, publicly displayed, or talked to almost constantly. His presence is a link through which adults make contact: recognition of the baby often precedes and may substitute for interaction between adults. Nevertheless, babies have little fundamental influence on the course of adults' lives. I know of no instance in which important adult decisions, such as choices about residence or work, were made primarily on the basis of the presumed needs of young children.

All babies are breast fed, at least initially, and most mothers nurse on demand. Some modern young mothers switch to bottles after the first weeks or months, which evokes much criticism and prophesies of trouble. It is common, however, for professional women, like teachers, to go home during their work day to nurse. Contemporary young mothers also talk of four-hour schedules, though a baby's cries generally win out over the theory. Most mothers take inordinate pride in weight gains, particularly for boy babies: a greedy appetite is interpreted as a sign of masculine vigor. (I once showed a woman a magazine photo of an enormously fat year-old baby, featured as a curiosity. Her comment: "What a fine boy!") At four to six months the baby is given some table foods—soup or soaked bread to begin. Weaning takes place gradually and is generally completed by the end of the first year.

Toilet training begins at the time the baby begins to be carried about regularly. A woman holding a three- or four-month-old baby, sensing his need to urinate, will turn away from the people they are with and hold him in a sitting position, making a hissing sound. Babies are put onto a potty as soon as they can sit firmly. Some mothers claim their babies were completely trained by six months, and by a year many babies are indeed fully trained. When the woman in charge smells feces on a baby, she immediately hurries him off to be changed, and children are never seen excreting feces. The explicit message conveyed with this training is that a brutta figura must be avoided. There is no connotation that excretion is "bad" but rather the idea that one shows a clean, elegant, controlled self to public eyes.

Training in walking is almost as determined. Early walking is a great source of pride for parents, and even very young babies are jokingly held under the arms and their feet placed, alternately, in a walking position. Beginning at six or seven months, babies are systematically placed into position to stand and then "walked" about. When a baby succeeds in standing alone, he is urged to walk. A common technique is to place an appealing object out of his reach and point him toward it; if he tries to crawl he is put on his feet again and the routine is repeated.

When the baby begins to walk, he enters a period that lasts about two years. Now led about by the hand, his sphere of action expands and more people take turns at leading him. At this time, the father begins to walk his baby about, often taking him along to the bar or clubhouse. If the baby interferes with activities or if the father gets involved with his friends, he will immediately send the baby home. In this way, fathers introduce their children to the recreational life of the community and teach them that they will be welcome there as long as they are socially acceptable—that is, well behaved and amusing. Babies of this age are also the favorite play object of preadolescent girls, who go into ecstacies over them and beg for permission to take them for walks around the town. From this period on, the baby shares not only the whole spatial range of the community but also its time schedule. It is considered cruel to put small children to sleep while there is still public social activity to be enjoyed.

As the baby learns to talk he also learns the high value attached to talking "well." There is little specific baby language; adults address him in adult style and often in an exaggeratedly grave manner. Small children (boys in particular) are rewarded with special attention when they express themselves cleverly, and when they use sophisticated turns of phrase they are responded to in kind. The linguistic pleasantries of social life are part of the early vocabulary, and the formalities of etiquette begin to be learned at this time as well. For instance, small children can sometimes be observed struggling between the desire to accept some treat and the knowledge that they are expected to refuse it at first. Here again, the concern with bella figura is underlined. A two- or three-year-old who refuses to offer his candy to others or who has a tantrum in public will be chastised for "making a brutta figura."

Most of all, a bella figura requires cleanliness and tidy clothes. Very young children learn to play without getting themselves or their clothes dirty, and they somehow manage to stay clean during long periods of outdoor play. Some small boys are virtual dandies, demanding that their clothes be changed whenever they are slightly dirty and presenting an impeccable public appearance at all times. The parents' message on this matter is unmistakable. For example, one father of a boy about three doted on him and tolerated all kinds of mischief, but the one time I observed him hit the child in genuine anger was when the boy, completely by accident, tore his father's coat slightly.

The small child is regularly subjected to a favorite adult amusement: teasing the child affectionately so as to provoke anxiety or rage, then creating a happy ending. A typical scene is that of a mother telling the child that she is leaving him or that someone (person or fantasy figure) is going to take him away, after which she hides from his sight watching happily as the child shows anxiety at first, then real fear or anger. When his emotion is at a high pitch, she reappears and engulfs him in affectionate reunion. An adult greeting a small child on the street often proceeds to tell him that some terrible thing will happen (his grandfather will beat him, an animal will eat him, the butcher will cut him up). The person in charge of the child may join in or simply stand by beaming, and after the child is sufficiently distressed all laugh together, hug the child, and assure him that it will not happen after all.

Sometime during the fourth year the child makes a transition to the next stage, covering roughly ages four to six, when he is a *pottorello*. The child who had been led about, greeted, and fussed over now begins to lose his interest for older persons. Neighborhood girls look around for a younger child to borrow and ask less often for the privilege of taking this one with them. He now starts to spend time with children about his own age. At first the children play side-by-side with apparent mutual indifference, but they soon become real companions; such small children can be seen walking about in two's and three's, arms around each other's shoulders. Women refer to the child as being *sulla via* (on his way, i.e., able to move about without direct supervision), and they tell the mother she should now think about having another baby. The mothers themselves welcome their greater freedom but regret the passing of babyhood and miss the attention they enjoyed.

It is at this stage that boys and girls first separate into single-sex peer groups. However, since the number of children in this age group in any neighborhood is small, girls and boys often play together. Girls this age love to play games of etiquette: arranging dishes, receiving guests with appropriate formalities, serving coffee, reciting phrases of politeness. Boys may sometimes be recruited into such games, but their preference is for play that mimics the manual occupations of men.

The next period is that of childhood proper, *la fanciullezza*, which covers the span from roughly seven to fourteen, ending sooner for early-maturing girls. The local terms for this age are *potto* and *potta*, although the more formal *ragazzino* and *ragazzina* are also used. Today the age range corresponds to the legally required years of school attendance, but the period is not specifically linked to schooling. In the eyes of the church, this stage is initiated with the age of reason, marked by the ceremonials of Confirmation and First Communion, but for most children these events take place after they are well into the stage.[8]

In this period sexual segregation in play becomes very marked, and in school boys and girls are seated at opposite sides of the room. When out of the home, children of this age are almost constantly in the company of their peers, which in this small population may include quite a wide range of ages. Boys' groups tend to be large, often resembling roaming bands. Girls' groups generally are limited to three or four, and since girls have chores to do at home or younger siblings to look after, they wander about less often with their friends. Both sexes prefer active games, like tag, but their play also differs. Boys learn to play football and later bocce, while girls continue their doll-play, using real babies whenever possible. The religious authorities supervise much of their leisure activity. The priest holds after-school classes for the boys and tries to organize them in their games. The nuns of the asilo instruct the girls in handiwork and morality. While the nuns themselves are more objects of general amusement than models to be emulated, their messages about feminine virtues coincide with those of home, school, and street. For both sexes this period is treated as one of sexual innocence. The children do not openly express interests in sex, nor do adults acknowledge the possibility.

The lessons of this age emphasize the skills of social life and the need to curb one's own inclinations in relation both to real peer groups and to the more abstract expectations of society. Boys' play shows that they learn to direct aggression into verbal forms, and to contain hostility under an affable "face." Conflict erupts often enough in boys' games and the combatants make gestures of fighting, but actual fights rarely develop. Instead, insults are hurled or someone stomps off in rage, only to return to the group at the first excuse. The themes boys write describing their friendships reflect this pattern, often saying, in effect, "we quarrel a lot but we make it up quickly." Among girls, displays of physical aggression are almost nonexistent; even arguments seem rare, and their themes about their friendships contain few references to conflict.

These themes, written by children from eleven to thirteen, display a striking sex difference in the significance of "the skills of social life." This difference is evident in the themes on "My Dearest Friend," which suggest some of the qualities that the children value in others and, presumably, aspire to themselves. (These themes apparently do not indicate actual close friendships, for the choices are not usually mutual.) Boys seem to admire most the qualities that make for effective performances in the public arena. Most often mentioned are traits like "he is lively," "he talks a lot," or "he always makes me laugh." Other qualities described frequently have to do with the admired friend's successful impact on others—"he is intelligent," "he is good in school," or "he plays games well." Several boys are admired for being "generous," which usually means they treat others to snacks. The girls, on the other hand, inevitably emphasize the quality of being *buona*, meaning kind, helpful, nurturant, and obedient. Their descriptions almost always talk of the mutuality between the writer and her friend: "we talk together," "we love each other like sisters," "we laugh together." Thus, admired boys make others laugh, while girls laugh with each other; a boy who is *bravo* (good in school) impresses others, but a girl who is *brava* helps others; generosity among boys means a public display, while among girls it is private sharing, personal as well as material.

The different values emphasized for boys and girls are revealed also in the children's themes about "What I Would Like to Be." The reasons given for choosing certain professions are perhaps more informative than the choices themselves. The boys most often gave "to earn money" as their reason, which they wanted for a car, a big house, farms and peasants to work them, as well as to win an attractive wife, to enjoy entertainment and travel, and to be able to show generosity. Apart from earning money, boys hoped to have workers under their direction, to be admired by others, to live in the city, and to repay parents' sacrifices. Girls generally presented their goals in terms of the virtues associated with the work: gentleness, cultivation, the ability to create beautiful objects, the character to guide others.

The theme written by girls in answer to the question "Do you girls wish to be professionals or housewives?" is especially instructive. Regardless of the specific choice the responses were remarkably uniform: they refused to see a contrast. All discussed a common set of qualities, whether in the context of a profession or housewifery; the professions chosen were those that maximized feminine virtues; and most girls who talked about a profession added their intention to be a fine housewife at the same time. The themes depict an ideal woman as one who is responsible for the well-being, comfort, and above all the public presentation of the family. She arranges a beautiful home, guides the young to cultura and to good appearance and behavior, and with devotion and modesty assumes sacrifices on behalf of others. It is clear that boys and girls are learning different roles in relation to civiltà. Boys will enact civiltà on a public stage through the manipulation of outward symbols, while girls will provide the background for males' public performances and will be responsible for the display of a family's collective civiltà.

There is a curious style about all these children's themes, which suggests another aspect of the process of bending personal inclinations to the expectations of society. Almost invariably, a desire, ambition, plan, even fantasy, is hedged by a statement of cold reality: "I am still only a child and so I am not capable of understanding such a serious question"; "to accomplish this requires much study and I don't like to study, so it's not possible to do anything"; "I would be so happy if these things could happen but they won't"; "I will never be able to learn this trade and I am very sorry about that." In a similar way, boys speculating about a future football game imagine the Montecastellese team winning, express fervent hopes that they will win, and then conclude by saying "But we will lose." When they play games, boys—like adolescents and men at their games—usually stop trying or abandon the game as soon as they seem to be losing; sometimes an excellent player who suffers a rare loss refuses to play again for a long time. Success in games or in life is explained as dependent upon luck, fate, or God rather than individuals' plans, abilities or efforts; yet most people probably do not seriously think that the fates are actually involved in their personal affairs. What they are saying is that non-success is a consequence of the way things are, namely the way society is organized. This is a lesson well learned in childhood.

From Adolescence to Marriage

Adolescence begins for a girl with the signs of physical maturation; when she starts to menstruate, she is said to "become a woman." The time is not marked by any conspicuous change in role, but she is expected to be more "serious," in comparison with the presumably carefree childhood left behind. For a boy the transition to adolescence seems to be related less to physical development than to the beginning of his serious preparation for an occupation. Since schooling beyond the eighth grade is specialized and expensive, if a boy is to remain in school he must make decisions about his future occupation and must demonstrate specific abilities. Most boys in their early teens are either put to work with their fathers or are sent into apprenticeships with artisans. Peasant boys of this age in the past would have been working on the farm for several years, but today most peasants try to find their sons training in nonagricultural skills.

Although in childhood boys and girls have essentially similar, though separate, rhythms of activity, in adolescence these take different courses. The activity of boys is increasingly centrifugal, while the girls' becomes more centripetal. Boys are often sent away from home, to school or into apprenticeships, where their non-working hours are little supervised. Later in their teens they may even join groups of migrant laborers for temporary work in other regions of Italy or in the industries of northern Europe. Adolescent boys continue to spend much of their leisure time roaming about in groups of their peers, as they did in childhood, but their opportunities to move around now increase. Many belong to the football team, which plays half its games outside of Montecastello, providing an excuse for boisterous excursions to other towns. Apart from football, boys seem to spend their holidays looking for something lively to do or watch. The younger adolescents are restricted to the immediate vicinity for lack of transportation and cash, but as they get older and acquire pocket money for small treats and bus fares, they seek the nearby towns or anywhere that something might be happening. Those for whom such mobility is not possible try to liven things up within Montecastello, either by organizing some activity (for instance, in 1960 several boys formed a dance band) or by engaging in general antics.

In contrast, when a girl enters adolescence, her behavior becomes more circumspect; the active games of childhood are no longer appropriate. Her sphere of activity is close to home. If she is sent away to school or into an apprenticeship or domestic service, she is turned over to some other family that assumes responsibility for her supervision. All girls share in the woman's work of their households, which serves to keep them at home and to give them an aura of seriousness. Moreover, the adolescent girl begins to apply herself in earnest to the sewing and embroidery for her trousseau, and again the image she projects while absorbed in the work seems as important as what she accomplishes. While engaged in her normal tasks she moves freely around her neighborhood, but she does not go far beyond it unless it is for some specific purpose. Her leisure time is spent exchanging visits with the women and girls of other households (girls more often socialize with their elders than boys do) or strolling about the town in small groups of friends, sharing confidences. A girl goes to public social places, attends formal events, or goes outside the community only in the company of an older female relative or family friend.

The sexual division of labor in enacting civiltà becomes more marked in adolescence. Boys participate in street life, "perform" in public among their peers, and pursue urbanity—the life of the larger society. Girls, instead, practice the civile values of the domestic scene: they rehearse the etiquette of encounter and entertainment, and work on the elegant presentation of self and home. The divergence now is perhaps greater than at any other time; later, courtship will make the boys more concerned with manners, while girls, once they marry, will be more free to participate in public life.

When adolescent boys and girls meet, they do so mainly in groups, in public places, and within range of watchful relatives. The first steps of courtship are taken when a boy indicates his interest in a particular girl by paying her compliments and trying to talk to her or dance with her repeatedly. The girl may be noncommittal and passively receive such attentions for a while, but before long she must either accept the courtship or discourage it, or she will earn a reputation for frivolity. If she is amenable "they start to walk together" and begin to *fare l'amore* (court) in a kind of open secret. Within a few weeks or months, the boy "comes into the house" and asks the girl's parents for their permission. At this point, the family acknowledges the affair and the formal engagement, the *fidanzamento*, is initiated. The engagement typically lasts several years; two or three years is today's ideal, but even in recent times many engagements have gone on for five to ten.

The engagement years form a separate stage of life, defining an end to adolescence and a transition to the full adult status that comes with marriage. (Men who marry late or not at all are recognized as adults when everyone acknowledges that they *should* be married by now; unmarried women simply remain anomalies.) For girls (possibly for boys too) engagement is a highly stressful period; at the same time it is idealized and remembered as "the best time of life." It is a time of intense emotions, shifting between exhilaration and despair, when elaborate romanticizing is accompanied by perpetual anxiety.

Montecastellese folklore is full of references to the storm and strife of fidanzamento. For instance, the most common topic of stornelli is the hazards of courtship. There are insults directed to undesirable girls and arrogant boys, expressions of mourning and fury over being abandoned, and accounts of quarrels and crises. Surprisingly few of the stornelli I heard of were glorifications of love or tributes to the beloved. The following examples are taken from the considerable repertoires of some older men:

> E lo mi amore m'ha mannato 'n fojo
> L'ha sigillato co' no struccio d'ajo
> Ma drento ci sta scritto: nun ti vojo.

> (My love sent me a letter
> He sealed it with a clove of garlic [9]
> But inside it said: I don't want you.)

> Fior d'erba mora
> Tu credi che per te ce porto pena
> La città è granne e gente ce se trova.

> (Flower of blackberry
> You think that I'm suffering on account of you
> The city is big and there are plenty of others.)

Similarly, engaged boys and girls were the main victims in stories about *fatture*—hexes performed by someone with magical skills.[10] This case was discussed in Montecastello; it was reputed to have happened in a nearby community.

A certain boy had courted a girl for a few days, just for fun, and then he broke it off. Soon after, he went to do his military service. He returned in full health. After a short time he became engaged to another girl. All of a sudden he became ill and had to be taken to the hospital. Soon he became as thin as a cadaver; he lost water from his body, vomited continuously, and was unable to eat anything. His mother prepared every possible delicacy and brought it to him, but he could not eat. After a month of many different treatments, the doctors decided to operate. When they opened his abdomen, they found nothing else but a tuft of hair. From that moment he was cured; two days later he got out of bed by himself, walked out of the hospital and went home. The family then consulted a renowned magical specialist. She discovered that the boy had once left his footprint in a wet field, and that some girl (obviously the jilted *fidanzata*) had performed a fattura on it.

The elite of Montecastello have always sought their *fidanzati* from a fairly wide range of Central Italian towns, but among the lower classes the majority of matches are made within the community. Most are within the same social class, and usually the same occupational category, but the exceptions are important. Successful young entrepreneurs have occasionally been recruited into the elite through matches with women of the local upper class. On the other hand, women more easily cross the boundary between peasants and nonagriculturalists. Peasant men can only marry girls of their own status "who know the work," but country girls who are able to assume a veneer of civiltà may have broader prospects.

Traditionally, arranged marriages were common in families with substantial property, but in all classes today, the choice is theoretically free. This pattern is, in fact, most adaptive in the contemporary situation. The strategic assets of a marriage prospect are increasingly those that one carries as an individual: skills, education, social adeptness, and connections. The young people are shrewed judges of such qualities, though the language of courtship cloaks them in romantic euphemisms. Once the choice is made, the two families are asked for their consent. As the courtship proceeds, the couple and their families can more carefully match their value against each other, and if the imbalance proves to be great the engagement is broken off on whatever pretext is at hand. The romantic forms—falling in love, giving gifts to the beloved, lovers' quarrels, betrayal—provide the idiom for this quite rational action.

During the engagement, the *fidanzato* visits the girl in her home, strolls with her on holidays, and accompanies her to dances. Although her female relatives are usually close at hand, sexual relations are fairly common between engaged couples: it can be estimated that about a fourth of all married women in contemporary Montecastello had been pregnant at the time of marriage. While such lapses with the fidanzato do not break up an otherwise successful match, engaged girls are highly vulnerable to gossip, however unfounded, about their behavior with other men. (A favorite malicious practice is to send anonymous letters to a fidanzato, detailing the girl's past and present failings.) Engaged girls are thus extremely careful of their behavior, particularly when the fidanzato is absent. They are always accompanied; avoid places where boys and girls mix; do not talk lightly or unnecessarily to men; and in general try to create the impression of being modest and industrious. Still, some moral defect can always be found if a match proves unsuitable, and broken engagements are very common. This is a handicap for a girl, since people assume that "there must have been a reason." Eventually, however, it is followed by a new engagement, with its own round of scandal, breakup, reconciliation, and other crises.

As this drama goes on, the two families tend to the economic preparations of the engagement period. The girl's main obligation is the *corredo*, the trousseau of household and personal linen. A corredo is measured by the number of sheets it contains, other items being included in amounts proportional to the sheets. The minimum respectable corredo is twelve (although some women admitted to having only ten), while a middle-class girl is likely to have twenty-four, and a lavish corredo might be forty-eight or more.[11] The corredo seems a preparation less for practical housekeeping than for the enactment of civiltà, for at least half the items in a typical corredo are usable only for formal entertainment or display. The contents of a corredo are public information (although they are not listed in a formal contract, as in much of the South), and in the course of the engagement they are carefully examined by many women within both family networks.

In addition to the corredo, the girl brings a share of the bedroom furniture (*la camera*), including a mattress and a dresser and mirror; theoretically, her share is one-third the value of the *camera*. For most girls the corredo and furniture are the total dowry, but a well-to-do family might also give a daughter money or property at her marriage, as an advance against her share of the family patrimony. Such dower wealth is used and managed by her husband but it remains her property, to be passed on to her children or returned to her kin if she dies without heir. The dowry is, however, only one aspect of the bride's economic value. Just as important in the families' assessment of the match are her education, her job or marketable skills, the tools of her trade (such as a dressmaker's sewing machine), or her ability to be of use in her husband's economic activity. In fact, it seemed to me that several girls who possessed such assets had rather small trousseaux, and they, as well as their families and in-laws, appeared little concerned about the matter. Nevertheless, the corredo retains the symbolic value of being married off properly. (It may be significant that some girls who had unusually large *corredi* were of families that for various reasons were sensitive about their respectability or uncertain of their social status.)

The boy's main responsibility during engagement is to establish his livelihood. In addition, he must be able to contribute "two-thirds" of the bedroom furniture, including the bed, a large wardrobe, two end-tables, and sometimes a dressing table and chair. If the couple are going to live by themselves they will acquire furniture for the kitchen and sala later, on their own, but the bedroom is part of the marriage exchange itself. This pattern of preparing a *camera* for the new couple is an old one, but until recently it was mainly the elite who made major expenditures for the bedroom. In this class families exhibited a collective civiltà, which was displayed in furniture. Increasingly, however, the concern with an elegant *camera* has filtered down to all classes, along with the democratization of civiltà.[12]

Several gifts are exchanged during the fidanzamento. At the time of engagement, the boy offers a ring, usually a wide, engraved gold band. In recent years small diamond rings or watches have been substituted by some, evidence of the boy's good economic position and sophistication. The girl gives him a ring or gold chain in return. Throughout the engagement there is an exchange of clothing—dresses and outfits for the girl, shirts for the boy. The fidanzato also provides the wedding dress and "the gold" for the bride (traditionally, the bridal jewelry always included coral beads), while she buys the groom's wedding ring and minor articles of his outfit. If the engagement is broken, all gifts are supposed to be returned. (One girl, shameless or betrayed, depending upon one's point of view, cut up all the dresses her ex-fiancé had given her and returned them in pieces. He, ever civile, had his mother carefully wash and iron all his gift shirts before returning them.)

When both sides are ready with their contributions, the wedding is planned. A few weeks before the wedding date the marriage is announced by notices in the town hall and banns in the church. Some days before the wedding the couple appear at the local registry for the civil marriage, which involves little ceremony. The church wedding and the dinner that follows is the real event, and it is probably a family's most important public performance—its major opportunity to advertise its claims to civiltà, both in its own right and in the implicit comparison between the two families. As in weddings everywhere, the families' personal networks of kin, neighbors, and friends are activated for the event, but in Montecastello their main function seems to be to assist the families in making their performance before a wider audience.

Most weddings are held on a Sunday or holiday, "when more people are around to see the bride." At the bride's house there is a constant stream of people, who come to help with the preparations or merely to express their willingness to help. When it is time to go to the church, the bride's family (except for the mother, who usually remains at home to oversee the dinner) forms an orderly procession, and the groom's family may do the same. If the families live in town they walk through the streets; if they are from the country they drive up to the church in a procession of cars. The climax of the street appearance comes when the bridal party emerges from the church. People crowd into the piazza to watch the town photographer pose the party, to comment on the match and the day's event, and to count the upper-class and out-of-town guests, the cars, and other symbols of status.

The wedding dinner is held at the bride's house.[13] Formerly, when a couple were going into patrilocal residence this dinner would be followed by a procession of all the guests to the groom's house, where his family would offer a second dinner and where the guests would witness the couple's retreat to their bedroom. Today there is usually only one dinner, and the expenses are shared equally by the two families. The guests include not only the families' own relatives and friends but also representatives of the elite families of the community and other high-status acquaintances. As the guests wait for the dinner to begin, they file into a bedroom which contains a display of wedding gifts, bouquets of flowers, telegrams, and cards; there is some remembrance from every family in the town (among country people, the neighborhood) whether or not they have been invited to the dinner. The meal itself is a sumptuous affair, the object being to provide more courses than any guest can consume. Neighbors and friends handle the final preparations and the service (in some cases, dressed as waiters and maids); thus, even a lower-class family can achieve the standard of civile dinners. When the spumante appears toward the end of the meal, the most distinguished of the men present offer toasts, formal at first but soon lapsing into exchanges of stornelli and other hilarity. Then, the bridal couple move about the room and personally greet each guest, presenting each with a cluster of bridal *confetti* and receiving good wishes.

After the wedding, all those who helped out are given portions of the leftover food to take home. The next day, a member of the bride's family distributes mementos of the wedding to all the families who sent remembrances. Elite families and those who sent gifts are brought elaborate arrangements of *confetti* (for instance, a fancy ashtray holding five white candies, wrapped with ribbons and flowers and bearing a printed card with the couple's names); other families receive simpler versions. The two families and the community in general discuss how it all went, who was there, why this or that invited person was absent, who sent what gifts and tokens, and the good and bad omens of the day.

While this description applies to the civile way of getting married, departures from the norm underline the significance of the wedding. One form of irregular marriage involves the "stealing" of a bride. If a girl's parents are reluctant to give their consent, the couple may arrange to have the boy bring her quietly to the house of his parents or other sympathetic relatives, where they spend a few nights together. Since the girl's chances for a better match are substantially reduced by this episode, her family has no choice but to agree, and a marriage in church— with no festivity—follows quickly. Often, however, the stealing of a bride takes place when the match is approved by both families and the economic exchanges have already occurred. In such cases the stealing is a device to avoid the elaborate wedding. This also seems to be the motive of marriages that take place in secret. During the year of the fieldwork there were several of these secret weddings, and in each case the engagement itself had been completely regular and the families in full agreement. The couple would go quietly to the church, usually very early in the morning, and they would be married with dispatch. (One young man, evidently determined to marry in a thoroughly antisocial manner, chose not only the hour of 5 A.M. but also a Friday in May, a day and a month almost unheard-of for weddings. By midmorning he was back at his work as usual, his bride installed in his parents' house.)

Whatever reason is given for an irregular marriage, it is assumed by the community that the parties wished to avoid the expense and nuisance of a wedding, and they are ridiculed for their "uncivilized" behavior. People talk of the sacrifices they themselves undertook to marry off their children properly and how they were satisfied to have done things right.

When the festivities are over and the couple return from their wedding trip (if they can afford one), they assume adult status. The husband is expected to act like a man with responsibilities. The wife achieves the valued position of a signora (a permanent change of status, since until 1970 there was no divorce). However, her personal crisis of transition often continues through the early months of marriage and may not abate until she becomes pregnant. The new couple are thought to have an aura of romance about them for a few months, but they have already settled into the routines of adult life.

Adulthood: Private and Public

The transition to adulthood in Montecastello is marked by the highly public event of the wedding, but the main role changes are within the private sphere of the family. If the newly married couple establish neolocal residence, he becomes a capofamiglia, while she must learn to manage a household and a budget. If they go to live with the groom's family, the change is still greater for the bride, because she acquires a whole complex of new relationships. The groom's life, however, is little altered. The girl who was his fidanzata now shares his bed and assists his mother in looking after his needs, and with an end to the inconveniences of courtship he is free again to spend his leisure time with male companions. He continues to work under the direction of his father, the capo, who retains formal authority over the household and control over its resources, income, and expenditures. In peasant families the capo organizes the labor of the group, keeps the accounts, handles all dealings with the landlord, and in general makes the economic decisions. The son's move into adulthood means simply that he will be consulted more often and, particularly if he is literate, allowed to participate in the family's official business. In nonagricultural families where sons work with their fathers, the situation is much the same. Even if an adult son is an independent wage-earner, he is expected to turn over his income to the capo, perhaps keeping a small portion for his personal expenses. Such cases are increasingly common and almost inevitably lead to conflicts between father and son. The father who wishes to keep his son at home today finds that he must acknowledge the new consumption demands of the younger generation, making sure that the son has a little spending money and perhaps allowing him to purchase a motor scooter.

The main problem of an inmarrying bride is to adapt to the women of the household, especially her mother-in-law. Both work and leisure in the extended household are largely sex-segregated, and the wife of the capo is responsible for the female sphere. She directs the women's work and is accountable for their (and their young children's) manners and morals. She is in charge of the daily expenditures, within the limits allotted by the capo. She must also see to it that the female activities of the family are adequately but carefully financed. In part this is a matter of extracting extra money from the capo, but most families also have a small "women's budget"—income that the women obtain independently and use for clothing and various niceties. The sources are diverse: in agricultural families, the women carry on their own side business in poultry and eggs; women of all classes practice trades or earn wages, out of which they pocket some money; the more prosperous may have inheritances or gifts from their own relatives, which they keep separate from the household budget; and probably most women set aside small amounts conserved out of daily economies.

The relationship between mother-in-law (*suocera*) and daughter-in-law (*nuora*) is culturally defined as both important and difficult. Although a wife's mother is also suocera to her daughter's husband (*genero*), the term "suocera" when used in any context suggesting a problem is assumed to mean "husband's mother." It is the responsibility of the nuora to make the adjustment to her mother-in-law's ways, while the older woman must learn to accept this new wife-mother figure in her son's life. The qualities expected of a daughter-in-law are fertility, willingness to work, modesty and a peaceable temperament, while a good mother-in-law is kind and patient. Still, the suocera-nuora relationship is regarded as inherently conflictual. A proverb says: "*Suocera e nuora, tempesta e gragnola*" ("Mother-in-law and daughter-in-law, storm and hail"). Similarly, in a traditional wedding custom the suocera would await the bride at the threshold of her house and say to her as she entered:

Te benedico co' 'na frasca d'annoro
Si tu sei 'l diavolo io sono el demonio
Te benedico co' 'na frasca d'ulia
Porta la pace 'n ten casa mia.

(I bless you with a branch of the mulberry
If you are the devil I am the demon
I bless you with a branch of the olive
Bring peace into my house.)

The quality of the suocera-nuora relationship contrasts with that between mother and daughter. The first is a distant, respect relationship, while the second is one of affectionate intimacy. (Thus, the "voi" form of address is used toward parents-in-law, while "tu" is used toward mother and father.) The contrast can be painful for the inmarrying bride, who is expected to detach herself from her mother while witnessing the warmth between the suocera and her own daughter. However, once the initial period of the marriage is past, the bride's tie to her mother (and sisters, if she has any living in the community) is maintained through regular visiting, and these connections between female kin become major routes of interhousehold communication and reciprocity.

If the bride joins a houschold that includes another married son, she must also adjust to a *cognata* (sister-in-law). (The term "cognata" when unqualified is assumed to refer to the relationship between the wives of brothers.) This relationship is less charged and easier than that with the suocera, although it also has considerable potential for conflict. In the more successful extended families, the women enjoy the liveliness and companionship of the female group, and they find real advantages in coordinating their work. For example, in large mezzadria households one woman may stay at home and care for the house, while others assist with the work in the fields; one may go to work in the tobacco factory, and an unmarried girl may be sent to work for the padrone in town. The children are cared for alternately by all the women. Thus, persons who have grown up in extended families often think of the father's brother's wife as a second mother, in distinction from other aunts. A parallel distinction may be made between the coresident father's brother and other uncles. Similarly, cousins who grow up in the same household regard each other much like siblings. For instance, a child with a baby cousin at home is teased by adults in the same way that elder siblings are teased, with threats to take the baby away, and he reacts in the same way, with the anxiety or fury that is interpreted as "jealousy for (not jealousy *of*) his baby."

The newly married couple and everyone around them eagerly await the first pregnancy, for the act of marrying is regarded as truly completed only with the birth of a child. Throughout the early months of marriage the bride endures her suocera's keen observation for the first signs, but when they appear the "little mama" immediately achieves an honored position in the household. At this point her personal crisis comes to an end, and she often becomes visibly serene.

The idea of intentionally excluding children from a marriage is virtually unknown (it is said, "better not to marry at all than to have a marriage without fruit"), and the first child is never deliberately delayed. However, one child is sufficient to "establish a family." The ideal number of children is today one or two, and the only real difference of opinion is in the preference for one *or* two; the problem is summarized in the much-repeated saying, "*uno è poco, due è troppo*" or "one is too few, but two are too many." The trend to fewer children seems to have begun among the upper-class families of the town in the late nineteenth century, then spread to the nonagricultural lower class, and finally into the countryside. The ideal is now virtually universal in the community, and its real effectiveness is reflected in the low birth rate in all categories of the population.[14] The standard method of birth control (indeed the only method for most people as of 1960) is withdrawal, referred to colloquially as *stare attento* ("to be careful"). The extraordinary success of this practice suggests a very strong motivation to limit the number of children. The people themselves explain their family strategies in terms of aspirations for civiltà: children must be clothed and educated in accordance with today's standards, and the fewer the children the greater the hope of attaining a more civilized life for the family as a whole—a goal now defined as within the reach of all.

Family planning is an example of the way in which private and public domains intersect in the life of the Montecastellese adult. The family is an essentially private sphere, and behavior within its boundaries is not primarily a matter of civiltà, an ideology essentially about public life; but the values of civiltà intrude even into the most intimate activity. In general, the household serves as a place of preparation (both long-range and immediate) for public presentations. As has already been suggested, it is the task of women to train the young for their public performances, to maintan the proper appearance of all the family members, and to see to the public display of the household's collective identity. The men, however, leave the household as often as possible to spend their free time in the public arena. As one wife put it: "Every evening Giorgio eats supper, plays with the child for a few minutes, then changes his clothes and goes out. . . . The husbands of Montecastello are always *in giro* (gadding about)."

Between the private world of the household and the public life of the community stand various significant relationships. There is, first, the circle of kin around each individual. The closest kin beyond the household are the members of the family he grew up in. These relatives are supposed to be a person's first line of defense and aid, but since much is expected of them by cultural definition, disappointments and fallings-out are common.

The relationship of a man with parents who do not live in the same household is defined much the same as if they were coresident. The father has authority over the son, who should show him respect, and interaction between them tends to be rather formal. The mother-son relationship is also defined as hierarchical, but it is more intimate and more complicated emotionally. The son is responsible for supporting and looking after his parents if necessary, and this obligation takes precedence over his own wife and children—a situation which, as one might expect, often leads to trouble. A woman's relationship with her parents tends to be more openly affectionate and less ambivalent. She is supposed to be a source of comfort to her father and of companionship to her mother, but she is not ordinarily expected to provide material assistance, her primary obligations being to her husband and his kin.

Between adult siblings of the same sex there is ideally a comradeship that comes from having grown up together and having shared similar roles. Between brothers and sisters there is less intimacy, but a brother should be protective toward his sister, while she is expected to cater to his personal needs and be worshipful to an elder brother and nurturant to a younger. However, siblings are also competitors for the family patrimony. While their shares are supposed to be of equal value, there is often considerable uncertainty as to how a patrimony made up of various assets will actually be divided. Thus, disputes over inheritance are a frequent source of conflict between adult siblings or siblings' spouses. (As one male informant put it: the sisters-in-law sow discord among themselves and then recruit their husbands to the conflict.)

Beyond these primary relatives are a large number of kinsmen, who use the appropriate terms of address toward each other and show a degree of affection and concern. They are expected to help each other out in times of special need and to support each other's public performances. However, these are only potential obligations that are realized to very different degrees. Nonlineal kin (other than siblings) are assigned to terminological categories on the basis of sex and generation. Thus, the category *cugino/cugina* includes all nonlineal relatives of one's own generation and their spouses (a more restricted category than the American "cousin"). The very large category *zio/zia* applies to all nonlineal kin of a higher generation and their spouses; the terms are also extended to unrelated persons who are longtime familiars of one's parents and grandparents. The category *nipote* (*il nipote* or *la nipote*, diminutives *nipotino/nipotina*) is even more inclusive: it covers all nonlineals below one's own generation (descendants of cousins as well as siblings) and descendants of one's own children (thus merging into one category the American "grandchild", "niece" and "nephew", and all lower-generation "cousins"). The extension of these few kinship terms to so many people means, in effect, that the community, one's public audience, includes a large proportion of kinsmen. In fact, people are constantly shifting roles, being active supporters and critical audience of a kinsman in rapid succession.

The individual also takes part in various fictive kin relationships. Two godparents (*padrino* and *madrina*) are chosen at baptism and one (of the same sex as the child) at Confirmation. Godparents have few specific obligations to the child, apart from participating in the formal ceremony and presenting an appropriate gift, but they are supposed to be "interested" in the child's welfare—a concept that is conveniently vague. (Theoretically, they have full responsibility if the parents die and there are no "near" relatives; again, the ambiguity is functional.) The parents and godparents of a child call each other "compare" and "comare" and owe each other mutual respect and aid. However, it is recognized that where *comparaggio* is the only tie, this obligation generally produces only a surface show, a fact attested to by many proverbs. Because of this, godparents are usually chosen from among fairly close relatives, and the ritual tie becomes a way of increasing the likelihood that potential obligations between kinsmen will become real ones. Occasionally, however, good friends are chosen. Whether relatives or friends, persons of a slightly higher status than the parents seem to be preferred. In the past, landlords sometimes acted as godparents to the mezzadria family—again, fictive kinship being used to reinforce a pre-existing tie.

The terms of address of comparaggio are sometimes extended to two other relationships, which may take on much of the character of fictive kinship. The first is the important tie between *vicini* (neighbors). Neighbors—particularly in the country—exchange aid regularly, in more active reciprocity than obtains between kinsmen in different households. In addition, certain longstanding friends are admitted into a quasi-kin status, the *amici di casa* (friends of the house). Friendship in itself is a tenuous tie, carrying little expectation of loyalty or assistance. Only when friends are transformed into fictive kin is it assumed that the parties owe each other anything.

The fact that these several relationships straddle the private and public spheres makes them likely vehicles for gossip, a conspicuous feature of the civil life. Through such gossip, the community constantly brings private activity under public scrutiny, almost as if public life were threatened by whatever is kept outside its purview. Thus, the more intimate a detail, and the more an individual hopes to conceal it, the more avidly it is seized upon as a topic of gossip. (If satisfactory material for gossip is lacking, false information is simply substituted.) Gossip functions for civiltà in another way: it helps preserve ideals from the inroads of individual fallibility. The favorite targets of gossip are individuals who occupy statuses or claim values they don't quite live up to. Thus, the absentee landlord and the priest who neglect local obligations or deny a local identity are the subject of gossip, as are the local public official and would-be patron who have no connections or are inept in dealing with the outside world. As the gossip examines and criticizes the reality, it reaffirms the integrity of the ideal.

As the individual moves through adulthood, changes in role are for the most part gradual. A man approaching middle age tends to become a central participant in public life. Within the household he also comes into his prime. If he is the adult son in an extended family, he has increasingly assumed greater responsibility; by now he is likely to take effective leadership, though his position is still formally and ritually subordinate to his father. The actual status transition comes when he assumes the position of capo, either upon his father's death or, occasionally, when the old man relinquishes his position. This change in status usually goes along with the transfer of family property to the heirs. For a woman, the major change in role is becoming a suocera (which can either precede or follow her husband's taking on the status of capo). As a suocera she enjoys maximum authority within the domestic sphere, and though personal adjustments must be made when daughters-in-law come into the household and daughters (and sometimes sons) move out, they are less problematical than the changes at marriage. Grandparenthood—the status of *nonno* and *nonna*—follows naturally and with little fanfare soon after the marriage of one's children.

These years of middle adulthood, a time of dominance in both private and public roles, merge imperceptibly into old age. In the household, both men and women maintain their positions of formal authority and respect, while gradually retiring from active control. The old man continues to pass his leisure time in the discourse and games of public places—and now he has more time to spend this way—but he moves to a more peripheral position. The woman, free of her domestic responsibilities and some of the restraints on her behavior, may become more of a participant in the public scene. The old are allowed to cross boundaries of sexual and social propriety, and it is not unusual to observe old people engaging in rather obscene banter with the opposite sex or taking liberties with a social superior. The respect for the old is tinged with humor (as always, masking some hostility) and some fear, for old people have knowledge of the mysteries of "ancient times," including skills in magic.

Death brings the final, important public performance. When death is imminent, the priest is sent for and the close kin gather round; isolation at death—as at birth—is abhorred. Afterward, members of the family wash the body, dress it in the person's best clothing, adjust the face into a proper expression, and lay the body out on a bed, holding a flower or crucifix and surrounded by candles and plants. News of the death is announced by the tolling of the bells, briefly for a woman and longer for a man; in the past, a different tolling pattern would tell of a child's death, still another a pauper's. Soon after, death notices are posted on walls around the community. Throughout the day and evening relatives, neighbors and friends visit the house, the closer ones bringing food for the mourners and their guests. The usual formalities of visiting are not omitted but they are carried out in a more subdued manner. At night the close kin take turns sitting with the body. If the death occurs in a hospital, family members go there to stay with the body and care for it, until it is brought back to Montecastello for the funeral.

The funeral takes place on the day following death. In the morning there is official business: a representative of the family reports the death in the town hall and obtains the burial permit and other necessary papers. Soon the undertaker arrives from the next town (for "people do not die enough in Montecastello these days" to support a local business), bringing the elaborately decorated coffin and wreaths which have been ordered. The family, including small children, bid the dead one a formal farewell and place him in the coffin, adding a rosary or a holy image. The priest gives a benediction, and the coffin is nailed shut.

Meanwhile, a crowd has gathered outside for the procession, for all families with whom the mourners have any contact at all must be represented. The procession is the main public event at death, and later the family, as well as the community in general, will discuss how long it was, how many wreaths were carried, what notables were there, who was absent. Accompanied throughout by the tolling bells (and in times past by the town band marching behind), the procession moves from the house to the church, where the coffin is placed in the center aisle for a mass or benediction. The procession then reassembles and continues to the cemetery. As it moves through the streets, tradesmen hurriedly close their shops, and people stop to watch respectfully. A boy carrying a cross leads the procession. Behind him the people, dressed somberly and carrying tall white candles, walk in two widely-spaced and orderly single files, men and woman making up separate sections. Next come several pairs of men or women, each pair carrying a large wreath with a ribbon announcing the donor; most are from kin and the ribbon states the relationship, such as "the husband," "the daughters-in-law," or "the nipoti." The priest walks before the coffin, which is carried on the shoulders of four men, and the family walk behind, followed by the members of the confraternity of the deceased, carrying their banner. Finally, in some disorder, are the people who have caught up with the procession later, men and women separately.

At the cemetery the procession files into the little church, and the coffin is set down at the front. The people leave their candles, kneel briefly at the coffin, and then disperse around the cemetery to visit their own dead. The family lingers—it is here that they give full vent to their grief—until they are gently led away, and the coffin is left alone to await burial in the cemetery wall. The mood in the cemetery now takes on a rather festive air as people stop to chat and comment on their acquaintances among the dead, and everyone returns to the town in a sociable mood.

The next day the coffin is sealed into its place in the wall by a workman; some members of the family come to witness the burial, but there is no ceremony. For the following three evenings the nuns come to the house to say the rosary, and masses are said for the soul, the number depending upon its social status. Elite families later send out a card commemorating the deceased. The near relatives refrain from work for a day or two and for the first weeks will talk in subdued tones, weeping frequently. At least for several months of the official year-long mourning period, they avoid gay festivities, and until the end of the year they wear mourning—black clothing at first, then a black armband or lapel ribbon.

The cost of a funeral is considerable; it may amount to the family income for two months or more. Many people admit that the expenditure is primarily for a display in defense of reputation—in contrast to baptisms and weddings, which are rationalized as genuine expressions of the family's hospitality. As one mourner put it: "The dead are good. It is the living who are malicious . . . One must do things right to avoid their criticism."

The concern with public appearances does not end with death, and some people take the precaution of setting up their after-death arrangements exactly as they want them, even to the inscription and picture on their tombstone. The cemetery is witness to the immortality of the bella figura, and in it one sees a reflection of civiltà. Important public roles are in evidence there, in a special section set apart for major official figures of the commune.[15] Families of high status bury themselves in elaborate mausoleums, and one can follow the changing fortunes of families by their housing in the cemetery. As a family improves its place in the world, at the same time that it remodels its house or builds a new one in the modern section of town, it also sees to the construction of a proper tomb.

The cemetery itself is relatively new, the first burial dating only from 1877. Before that, the Montecastellesi were buried beneath the church, with even greater attention to the niceties of social distinctions than today. But the social changes of the time span during which the cemetery has existed are already reflected there. The year of the fieldwork saw two incidents that dramatized changes under way.

One rising family of professionals, relatively new to Montecastello, was seeking an especially desirable spot in which to construct their mausoleum. The place they managed to buy from the financially troubled commune was precisely that occupied by prominent community officials of the past. The famous turn-of-the-century sindaco, as well as two other officials of the era when civiltà was embodied in such public figures, were evicted from their resting places of honor, their bodies still partly intact due to the zinc lining of their coffins. Their remains were transferred to small boxes for reburial in a less valuable area. Some of their descendants, joined by curious townspeople, witnessed the event with philosophical dispassion. The local historian, who saw in the old sindaco a symbol of Montecastellese glory, spent the whole day painstakingly removing bits of loose flesh and extracting each tiny bone so that no part of him would be lost.

If these figures who personify traditional civiltà are losing out in the jockeying for position in the cemetery, other people who are now taking on civiltà in life are trying to find fitting places for their eternal repose. The wife of one of the wealthiest men in the community is an example. Her husband, who attained his success only since the war, has no intention of changing the ways of his past, but she has attempted to adopt a civile style of life and to act as a patroness toward their mezzadri and others. During 1960, she commissioned an elaborate and costly family mausoleum, confiding her plan only to her daughter-in-law and other female allies. When the community gathered in the cemetery on the Day of the Dead, the tomb was partly completed. Some people stopped a son of the family to remark on the extraordinary structure. "Beautiful," he said; "whose is it?" "Yours, of course," was the response. The son rushed to report this news to his father, who took off after his wife in a rage. The woman took refuge with their peasants, and the crisis continued for several days. In the end, the husband was remorseful and consented to have the mausoleum finished. Whatever comes of the signora's aspirations for life, she would have her place for eternity.

CHAPTER 8

———◆———

Ten Years Later

WHEN I RETURNED to Montecastello in 1971, it was by way of a new four-lane superhighway through the Tiber Valley, which shortened the trip from Perugia to little over half an hour by automobile. The Montecastellese plain was verdant, and newly planted vineyards were visible on the hillsides. On a number of farms, combines—unknown in this area in 1961—harvested the wheat. At the crossroads, the hamlet of Madonna del Piano had grown into a lively village of new houses and workshops; one of its carpentry shops had developed into a busy plant employing half a dozen workers. The road climbing up to the hilltop had finally been paved, after twenty years of bitter complaints by Montecastellesi about its condition and about the government that had left them "abandoned." The town now extended farther down the slope, for the San Giovanni section had burgeoned, and several houses were still under construction. The area also boasted a gasoline station, a new bar and food shop, and a proper sports field—the work of Montecastello's still-active priest.

Inside the walls there were many signs of a new and more widely distributed prosperity. Many houses had been remodeled or spruced up, and masons moved about between jobs. The piazzas had become small parking lots. The shops had all expanded their wares, and a new general store offered an elaborate selection of luxury foods, as well as toys and other merchandise not sold in Montecastello in the past. The variety of

items and fresh foods suggested that goods were now trucked in
frequently. The town had acquired several new shops, including one
that displayed fashionable ladies' clothing, and a restaurant-pension,
whose proprietress (the wife of an unskilled laborer) spoke of plans to expand it into a real hotel. This appearance of prosperity was matched by a
generally higher standard of living. It had become usual for families to
eat a second complete dinner, instead of the light evening meal that had
formerly sufficed for all but the elite. Almost half the houses in the commune had bathrooms, as compared to only a tenth in 1961 (ISTAT
1973, 1965). Automobiles were now as common as motorcycles and
scooters had been ten years before, and many of the autos were owned
by peasants. In the evenings the sounds of television sets could be heard
from many houses, instead of only a few.

There was also an unmistakable change in the social face of the town.
New people, most of whom were once contadini, now outnumbered the
"old" townsmen. Aged members of the old landowning families walked
about together, as if in retreat before new forces; they no longer dominated merely by their presence. People from the country managed the
new shops, lived in many of the new "villas" in San Giovanni, and filled
the afternoon "mass of the signori." A family of ex-mezzadri, now agricultural laborers, owned the palazzo displaying the crest of the Pettinelli
family, whose last descendant had recently died.

Modifications in the local economy only partly account for these
changes. Advances in mechanization had enabled a depleted agricultural
labor force to keep the better land under cultivation and realize greater
per capita returns. However, the amount of land in arable had decreased
(over a third of the total area was now woods or unproductive land),
while wheat, forage, and minor crops were grown in about the same
proportions as previously (ISTAT 1972). Except for a few fairly large estates raising cattle, smallholdings continued to be the rule and the polyculture pattern had yielded only to a limited degree. The most significant innovation was a shift to specialized arboriculture—vineyards and,
to a lesser extent, olive groves—that now covered about 10 percent of the
land area.[1] With the stimulation of government subsidies, over half of all
holdings had acquired vineyards by 1971, and the area in vines increased
steadily over the next years.

It soon became evident that the main sources of Montecastello's afflu-
ence were external. Throughout the 1960s the community had exported

labor for the factories of the Common Market countries, the tourist industry of Rome, and the construction boom of the region. Some of this labor migration was temporary: groups of men went north to work on short-term contracts; couples were recruited for periods of hotel or domestic service in Rome; families split up to take advantage of different opportunities. By 1971 the pattern of long-distance temporary migration had diminished, but small-scale industrialization in the Perugia-Todi basin had opened job opportunities near enough for Montecastellesi to commute on a daily basis. One reason for this was that the region of Umbria, which finally became an administrative reality in 1970, was attempting to plan its development on a more systematic basis (see CRU 1965). An industrial center was being created in the plain near Pantalla, some ten kilometers from Montecastello, and in 1971 consisted of five manufacturing plants for plastic products, household fixtures, and building materials. Clerical workers and professionals living in Montecastello could also hold jobs in Perugia and other towns, brought closer by the automobile and improved roads. In addition, government pensions had become a substantial source of income for Montecastello. Finally, the community had entered the national real-estate market. Deserted farms where being bought up by Romans seeking weekend rusticity, and three or four had even been acquired by foreigners. This income from outside gave impetus to the local building industry and the ever-expanding sector of commerce and services.

The community had suffered a 20 percent decline in population in ten years. It had also seen a redistribution of population, mirroring a phenomenon that at the national level had achieved massive proportions: the movement of people from the countryside into the urban centers. As Table 15 shows, the population loss in Montecastello holds only for the country; the town, instead, grew. The loss, moreover, affected mostly the higher altitudes, for the plain now had a larger proportion of the community population than it did in 1960. Steady emigration during this period accounts for the overall decline: there was a net migratory loss each year, ranging from a high of 117 (in 1961) to a low of 36 (in 1968). After a net loss of 105 individuals in 1970, the next three years saw more balanced rates of in- and out-migration, and the population remained fairly stable. During the entire 1960–73 period, the community maintained a slight but steady rate of natural increase (an excess of births over deaths averaging about five per year).

Table 15   Population of Montecastello, 1971

	Montecastello Town	Plain	Hills	Total Community [a]
Population,				
1971	366	540	602	1,508
Absolute change				
1960–71	+21	−41	−357	−377
Percentage change				
1960–71	+6%	−7%	−37%	−20%
Distribution of				
population,				
1971	24%	36%	40%	(100%)
Distribution of				
population,				
1960	18%	31%	51%	(100%)
Relative change				
1960–71	+6%	+5%	−11%	—

[a] This unit is comparable to the "community" as defined in 1960, which excludes Doglio (see discussion in chapter 2, and Table 1). In 1971 the population of Doglio village was under 140 (a decline of about 23 percent since 1960), and the population of the Doglio countryside, the "high-hill zone," was less than 250 (a decline of at least 45 percent since 1960).

The population had grown older. According to the census of 1971 (ISTAT 1973), people over 45 comprised 43 percent of the commune population, compared with 35 percent in 1961, while the 16–45 age range took in only 39 percent (46 percent in 1961). The relative number of children (both under 15 and under 5) remained the same. At the same time, the average size of households decreased to 3.6 (from 4.1), reflecting the exodus of young adults and the large number of households left only with aged individuals. Observation suggests, however, that this departure of the young has slowed since 1971. What is more, a number of people who have official residence elsewhere return to Montecastello frequently and plan to move back eventually.

The population in Montecastello today is clearly less committed to agriculture than in 1961. Table 16 shows the drastic decrease of the agricultural labor force and the growth in industrial occupations (including independent artisans). The number of workers in construction, commerce, and services has also increased. Even more striking is the number of pensioners, which exceeds every occupational category and constitutes almost a fourth of the population over age 10 (24 percent, compared to 4

Table 16   Labor Force of the Commune According to Branch of
Economic Activity, 1971

Branch of Economic Activity	Active Population			
	No.	%	% active pop., 1961	% change from 1961
Agriculture	282	43.4	70.3	−27.
Industries and manufacture	141	21.7	7.5	+14.
Construction	97	14.9	10.1	+5.
Transport and communications	21	3.2	3.0	—
Commerce	41	6.3	3.2	+3.
Services	46	7.1	3.5	+4.
Public administration	16	2.4	2.3	—
Public utilities	3	.5	—	—
Credit and insurance	3	.5	.2	—
Total active population	650 [a]	100.0	100.1	

Inactive Population	No.
Seeking first occupation	29
Housewives	423
Pensioners	346
Students [b]	83
Other	34
Total inactive population	915
Total resident population over age 14	1,565

SOURCE: ISTAT 1973

[a] The active population comprises 42 percent of the total population over 14 (the lower age limit included in the 1971 census of the labor force). This corresponds to 38 percent of the population over age 10, as compared with 44 percent over age 10 in 1961 (see Table 2).

[b] Since this figure does not include students between 10 and 14, it cannot be compared with the 1961 data on students in Table 2.

percent in 1961). A breakdown of the labor force by age emphasizes the move out of agriculture (see ISTAT 1973). Only 17 percent of working men under 30 are in agriculture, as compared with 46 percent of those in the 30–54 age range and 76 percent of those over 55. Industrial and artisan occupations, in contrast, account for 60 percent of the male labor force under 30, 32 percent of the men aged 30–54, and only 17 percent of active men over 55.

This occupational structure reflects the decade's most significant transformation: the decline of the mezzadria system. In 1961, 63 percent of the agricultural land included in the census of the commune had been in mezzadria farms, 18 percent was worked by owner-cultivators, and 19 percent was in wage-labor enterprises (ISTAT 1962). By 1970 only 33 percent of that area was in mezzadria tenure, while 38 percent was owner-cultivated, 25 percent was in wage-labor concerns, and 4 percent was abandoned (ISTAT 1972).[2] The mezzadria area continued to diminish, evidently at an accelerating rate, in the following three years. Legal and economic changes (discussed in chapter 3) have condemned the system to almost-certain death, though in Montecastello the process has been more gradual than in Central Italy as a whole. Wage labor, government credit, and the regulations governing the sale of property in mezzadria have made it easier for peasants to buy farms. Landlords, for their part, have been increasingly inclined to get out of the mezzadria, but their alternatives are limited by the fact that they are not free to sell farms on the open market or to convert to more profitable forms of production so long as the peasant family remains on the farm. Owners who are unable to remain active in the enterprise (because they are too old or live too far away or are too far removed from agriculture) are likely to sell out, usually to their own mezzadri. Landlords who are still active may simply continue in mezzadria until the peasant family leaves, and then concentrate on wine-growing or livestock-keeping with the use of hired labor. In some instances, landowners pay off the mezzadri to leave, and the payment may finance the family's move to town or the purchase of some land of their own.

The move out of the mezzadria has led in two directions. The greater part of the land no longer in mezzadria has been converted into owner-operated holdings. These holdings are larger, on the average, than the peasant-owned units of 1961; well over half, however, are under 3.5 hectares, generally too small an area to support a family (see Table 17). The other direction is toward "capitalistic" enterprises that employ a small force of permanent laborers; these, for the most part, are devoted to livestock—cattle and swine. There is one estate of 250 hectares and half a dozen ranging in size from about 30 to 150 hectares. Some of these were

Table 17   Mezzadria Farms and Owner-Cultivated
Holdings by Size and Location, 1970

Size (hectares)	Mezzadria Farms				Owner-Cultivated Holdings			
	Plain	Low & mid. hills	High hills [a]	Total	Plain	Low & mid. hills	High hills [a]	Total
Under .5	0	0	0	0	7	6	0	13
.5– 1.9	4	1	0	5	29	29	4	62
2.0– 3.4	2	2	0	4	16	16	2	34
3.5– 4.9	2	6	0	8	1	7	1	9
5.0–7.4	6	9	6	21	6	12	4	22
7.5–9.9	7	11	0	18	2	3	9	14
10.0–12.4	4	4	0	8	2	2	16	20
12.5–14.9	0	3	4	7	2	2	0	4
15.0–17.4	2	1	1	4	0	1	0	1
17.5–19.9	1	1	2	4	1	1	0	2
20.0–24.9	0	2	0	2	0	0	5	5
25.0–34.9	0	3	1	4	0	2	3	5
Over 35.	0	0	2	2	0	0	0	0
Total	28	43	16	87	66	81	44	191

SOURCE: Data sheets for the agricultural census of October, 1970.
[a] *Frazione* of Doglio.

created out of fattorie, while others grew out of the consolidation of land
formerly worked by hired labor into fewer and larger units. Most are
held by new proprietors from outside of Montecastello.

The mezzadria farms that still remain tend to be located on better
land, are somewhat better equipped, and are, on the average, a little
larger than those of 1961.[3] The 1970 distribution of mezzadria farms in
Montecastello is summarized in Table 17. The remaining mezzadria families are smaller than those of 1961, since the younger members have
often left the farms, but the economic position of these families has undoubtedly improved. The contractual terms are more favorable to the
mezzadri, now giving them 60 percent—under certain conditions, even
two-thirds—of the returns. Equally important, most families now have
access to other sources of income.

The agricultural census data do not adequately reflect the extent to
which nonpermanent wage labor is now employed in Montecastellese agriculture, both on farms still in mezzadria and on those run directly by
the landowner. Despite the overall decrease in the agricultural labor
force, more hired labor is available now than in the past, since most fam-

ilies who work their own land lack enough land to fully absorb their labor. Thus, in contrast to the relatively discrete categories of agricultural workers that existed in Montecastello in 1960, today's agricultural families generally depend upon a variety of income sources: land of their own (or worked under an old mezzadria contract), wage labor on other people's land, nonagricultural jobs, and pensions.

In the community as a whole, the distinctions that formerly marked out fairly clearcut socioeconomic categories have eroded. The major landowners of today are not part of the local social system, and even relations with their own employees have become impersonal. The remaining mezzadria landlords generally have reduced holdings, and they no longer command automatic status. Differences among families of cultivators are based upon their individual circumstances, while agricultural and nonagricultural pursuits are merged within families. The blurring of categorical distinctions is due to increased occupational mobility as well as to changes in local agriculture. Thus, many of the children of town artisans and laborers (who were schoolchildren at the time of the field study) are today government clerks and teachers, or are marrying quasi-professionals. Perhaps the most conspicuous difference from 1961 is that town and country no longer correspond to a definitive social contrast. This is not to say that class differences have been eliminated, but rather that they are more accurately described as a continuum of ranks; moreover, the differences are no longer underlined by obvious markers of categorical identity.

Since few local families derive substantial income from land ownership, the major determinant of socioeconomic status within the community is now occupation. The local elite of today consists largely of professionals; the term "local" must be qualified, however, for this group includes both Montecastellesi who work outside or spend much of their career span living elsewhere, and newcomers to Montecastello. Though access to elite status is more open than it was in 1961, the degree of change should not be exaggerated. Advanced schooling, the basis of mobility, is still highly restricted: by 1971, only 14 percent of the population held a diploma beyond the elementary level (as compared with 5 percent in 1961), and only 5 percent had completed an upper-level high school (2 percent in 1961) (ISTAT 1973). Even for those with a diploma, finding an appropriate position is just as uncertain as ever.

As the local landowning elite has disappeared, so also have some of the traditional patterns of interclass relations. Patron-client ties certainly continue within formal institutions and political parties, but in personal and work interaction within the local context class differences are played down. Little regret is voiced over the passing of the padrone; most people know patronage as the reverse side of exploitation. (One young man, who manages a family business employing several laborers, told me that he persuaded his father to retire because his old-style manner of dealing with workers was causing friction.)

This depolarization at the local level has apparently defused the class conflict that had been expressed in communal politics. In the election of 1970 the Center-Right gained control of the local administration by a narrow majority (winning 52 percent of the vote, as compared to their 45 percent return in the local election of 1960). Their victory does not, however, reflect a general shift in the political affiliations of Montecastellesi. In the provincial and regional elections also held in 1970, 55 percent of the community's vote went to the Left—the same proportion that had voted Left in 1960. In fact, election results from 1953 to 1970 show great stability in the balance between Left and Center-Right. The major changes took place within each faction: the Communist party vote increased steadily at the expense of the Socialist parties (from a 22 percent vote for the PCI in 1953 to about 40 percent in 1970), while the DC gained at the expense of the parties of the far Right (the DC vote going from 25 percent to 38 percent). This consolidation around the two major parties continued in 1972 (when each won about 44 percent of the total vote), but in 1972 the overall balance also changed slightly, to a 50–50 split between Left and Center-Right. In that year the Left lost 2–4 percent in each section of Montecastello proper, but its major loss was in Doglio, a consequence of the continuing depopulation of the high hills. Nevertheless, these political shifts are minute in comparison with the economic and demographic changes of the past twenty years. Ex-peasants who move into town evidently do not change their politics, while the most prosperous area of the countryside continues to give 70 percent of its vote to the Left.

The Montecastellesi themselves tend to explain the local election upset of 1970 in terms of specific circumstances. Under the previous administration the commune had been deeply in debt, and there had been accusations of mismanagement and graft. The Center-Right capitalized on the troubles while running a slate of candidates who could not be associated with the class abuses of the past. Perhaps their most fortunate choice was the candidate for sindaco: a man at once "local" and an outsider (an elderly physician from Doglio, who had recently returned from many years abroad), civile and gentle in manner, and with no apparent personal interests at stake in local politics. However its election may be explained, the new administration has been treated well by DC powers in the national government. The party, of course, publicizes these favors to Montescastello, and DC notables sing the praises of the new sindaco. By 1973 the community had a long-needed aqueduct, plans were under way to pave the road to Doglio, and the local schools had some improved facilities.

The new aqueduct was inaugurated with an elaborate public festival, which was generously financed by local contributions. Shortly before this, there had been a celebration to mark both the restoration of an ancient abandoned church and the 100th birthday of the matriarch of a local landowning family. Though public events based on local initiative evidently continue, they are now limited to such infrequent special occasions and tend to involve a great deal of planning. The town no longer forms a bounded arena of social life. Most people move in and out of the community frequently, and the town population is more diverse than it was a decade ago. Thus, public and private occasions are now clearly distinguished, and public sociability is less woven into the course of daily life. Montecastellesi draw on personal networks of kin and friends to exchange visits, to watch television together, to participate in family celebrations, and to form cliques at dances. While such networks are of course not new in themselves, they no longer automatically include families by virtue of their neighborly or general social status, and they are as apt to take in outsiders as Montecastellesi.

The major festivals of the church calendar are still celebrated, but many of the local elaborations have been modified. For instance, the series of processions and other community events that underlined the Holy Week reenactment has been abbreviated. In those that remain there have been some modern adaptations. Because the number of participants in the Easter Monday procession dwindled over the years, in 1973 the procession was officially motorized, and a long line of cars carried priest, banners, and the Montecastellese faithful to the monastery. The processes of individualization and universalization observed ten years before had continued. Little appears to have remained of the specifically

local ceremonial patterns, and the loss of local traditions no longer provokes conflict. The priest is still involved in controversy at times, but it
is more subdued. Even the dances that now take place quite openly during Lent create little stir. The issues that arouse controversy, moreover,
such as the 1974 national referendum on divorce, have little to do with
the community as such.

Yet local identity and civic spirit are by no means extinct; indeed they
are being rediscovered, if not re-created. In 1961 the young people
deprecated Montecastello for its obscurity and boredom and thought of
ways to get away to more urban places, for an evening, or even permanently. Throughout the 1960s letters from Montescastellesi reported that
"everyone" was leaving, that the old ways were dying out with the old
people, and that little was left of the community's special quality. This
mood still prevailed in 1971, but by 1973 it was clear that something had
changed. The flow of outmigration had lessened. Some families were
moving back, and many others were investing in permanent residences
in Montecastello. Young people were talking about the "good air" and
the charm of "our *piccolo paesino.*" A few were even reclaiming their families' country houses for year-round homes of their own. Montecastellesi
had come, rather late, to awareness of the problems of city life; besides,
now that it was possible to come and go at will, the community no
longer seemed so confining.

In 1973 a new elite (the adolescents and young adults of the fieldwork
year) organized a Pro Loco, modeled on the chambers of commerce of
larger towns. Its explicit purpose is to encourage tourism in Montecastello. The organizers see this as a way of reviving social and "cultural"
life in the town, and in fact they themselves do not stand to gain economically by tourism. Their continuing inspiration is the hope of restoring the theater, and they have devised various plans to raise money
locally, obtain government backing, and arrange productions. Meanwhile, the Pro Loco sponsors occasional festivals, acts as a link with
Montecastellesi who have moved away, and above all, promotes community identity. The innovators of the Pro Loco have re-created something
of the public role of the traditional elite. The president, daughter of a
local landowner, is the town pharmacist; in acquiring the pharmacy she
also took on the wider social role of her predecessor, the pharmacist of
the field study. Another young professional initiated the project to restore the abandoned church and collected contributions for it. A third in-

dividual donated statues for the public gardens. Once again the rhetoric of civic pride has become fashionable.

The styles of life in Montecastello today reflect the broader prosperity, the superficial egalitarianism, and the influence of national and international models, but the changes have not been sweeping. Signorile dress, urban-style houses, automobiles, and tangible symbols of the world outside have spread widely among the population. Since these acquisitions no longer serve as simple indicators of class status, Montecastellesi are learning new and more subtle ways of demonstrating and judging social distinctions. In general, patterns closely tied to material goods have been more susceptible to change than the nuances of behavior. For example, female clothing styles now allow more latitude of choice and are no longer taken as clear-cut signs of a woman's sexual morality. Similarly, modes of entertaining guests at home have taken on a rather self-conscious informality; in many houses the sala has been rearranged to create a sitting area, with newly purchased sofa and easy chairs arranged for conversation. However, the forms of public interaction, the patterns of talk, the etiquette, the guarding of bella figura, the behavior toward children—all are little changed.

My brief revisits to Montecastello permit no more than speculation about change in the idea of civiltà. It would appear that the reference points of value and status no longer reside in the community; the "civilized" is now defined in terms of national models rather than the attributes of a local elite. It may also be significant that several contexts in which I encountered the term "civiltà" had to do with national issues. At the same time, it continues to be a slogan of local distinctiveness. In the Pro Loco headquarters, where symbols of local glory are displayed, one exhibit asks why so small a paese had need of a theater and then answers its question: "Civiltà is not measured by the cubic meter!"

Both persistence and change in the social context of civiltà are manifest. The town is still a centripetal force within its territory, attracting population and forming the setting in which bids for social mobility are made. However, the town no longer controls the resources or economic life of the community, nor does it represent a local concentration of power. The values and symbols of urbanity still dominate, but they can now survive in the country, and even residence in town or country no longer marks a basic line of social differentiation. The forms of civile behavior remain, but the economic and social order that used them is gone.

The piazza continues to be a forum for debate and intrigue, but the issues and alignments articulated there crosscut localities. While the social boundaries of community have blurred, community identity—focused on the town, as always—has been reasserted. The civil life has always meant a vigorous localism combined with a receptiveness to urban influences. National integration and modern communications have produced another version of this combination.

CHAPTER 9

————————◆·◆————————

The Heritage of the Town

DISCUSSIONS of Italian society or culture inevitably begin, or end, with the city. Justifiably so; this is a society that is, and has long been, organized around urban centers. Italy's urban quality resides not only in its great capitals but also in the multiplicity of its cities and towns, each a center in its own right and each encompassing a rural territory. The centers of long-distance trade and manufacturing that played so crucial a role in the formation of modern Europe represent only the most conspicuous part of the urban history of Italy. In fact, most Italian cities and towns, from medieval times until very recently, have lived off agriculture, serving above all as distributive centers for the produce of their rural areas (Hyde 1973:12, 157). Yet the urban phenomenon extends also to small nuclei of the hinterlands; in a real sense, it has fashioned the countryside.

Montecastello is not typical of small towns in Central Italy; no single community could represent a region "writ small." For instance, Montecastello has had greater political importance than most Umbrian towns of similar size, a fact still reflected in its modern status as a communal seat. Furthermore, the local landowning class might have had an unusually important role in Montecastello. At least since the sixteenth century, much of its land was held by medium-scale, local proprietors; in contrast, many communities in the mezzadria area were dominated by large holdings, while in most communities in the higher altitudes small peasant properties prevailed. In looking outward from Montecastello it is necessary to take account of its particular circumstances. Nevertheless, the processes observed there can illuminate the ways in which the urban influence reaches into the countryside, and indeed what "urban" and "rural" might mean in Central Italy.

In Montecastello several institutions intersect to form the background of the civil life. In many ways this structure resembles that of much larger towns of Central Italy. If one looks at towns of this region for similarities rather than variations, and for continuities over a broad sweep of time, some basic patterns emerge. The town is a corporate entity, comprising political institutions once related to citizen-government and local autonomy, which survive in form or spirit within the administrative machinery of the state. The town claims an identity distinguishing it from others, pivoted upon a church and underlined in public ritual and in a folklore of local terms, names, proverbs, and traditions. A landowning, professional, commercial class in town capitalizes, manages, and is supported by agriculture in the surrounding area. This class constitutes a locally based elite. Its members not only control resources and positions of power within the community but also play a civic role in local government, sponsor community activities, and promote the town's glory. These functions, however, are not limited to the elite. Many of the town's citizenry own land, act as entrepreneurs, engage in political activity (official and unofficial), and participate in civic affairs. Within the town a routine of intense public sociability is enacted, accented with urban styles of dress, language, and forms of interaction. I have tried to explore connections among these several dimensions of town life by tracing their manifestations, over time, within the limited universe of a single community.

The importance of scale for the social structure of a town should not be underestimated. Nor do I intend to ignore the many small settlements that, in structure and functions, are more properly "villages" than "towns." However, Montecastello illustrates what seems to me a fundamental characteristic of this region (and to some extent, of Italy as a whole): the replication of an "urban" structure, including certain political, social, and cultural patterns, and bearing a particular relationship to its surrounding territory. We find this structure repeated in cities, towns, and even hamlet-sized *piccoli paesi* like Montecastello. In part, this replication is related to the Italian administrative system that assigns uniform status to all communes, each identified with the town that is its seat. Still, far more than administrative functions are reproduced; moreover, small towns that are not administrative centers may in other ways resemble those that are. "Rural" Central Italy—an area of peasant farms and relatively small town-populations—must first and foremost be understood as a constellation of numerous small centers that repeat certain patterns of urban life, and that bring cultivators settled on the land directly into the orbit of a town.

This replication emerged out of the complex of processes that constitutes the urban history of the region. About the eleventh century, urban communes evolved out of settlements that had been Roman cities and episcopal seats. While the medieval cities of northern Europe also created an alternative to the rural social order, they never submerged the countryside. In Italy the urban communes went further, incorporating the aristocracy and bringing the rural area into their domains. Central Italy saw a proliferation of independent cities and towns, whose commercial (and, in some cases, manufacturing) activities went hand in hand with sponsorship of agriculture in the contado. While the major towns dominated lesser ones nearby, the region as a whole at any given time contained several equipotential centers. The absence of a centralized state and the frequent intrusion of foreign powers furthered the competition among cities. Smaller centers could enhance their effective autonomy by playing off the larger ones against each other; Montecastello's own history exemplifies how small towns could exploit the situation.

While it was still within the contado of Todi, Montecastello developed a version of the governmental institutions, informal public life, community ritual, and other patterns that characterized Todi itself.[1] Larger towns of the contado, especially those near its borders, approximated even more closely than Montecastello the structure of the dominating city; these towns repeatedly broke off from Todi and had to be repeatedly submitted. Thus, within the domain of larger centers there were smaller ones that reproduced some of the urban forms and could become the nuclei of their own spheres. In fact, when changes in the larger political field increased Montecastello's leverage against Todi, it declared itself an independent commune. Though always subject to outside powers and always economically tied to Todi, Montecastello formed a separate sociopolitical entity with its own "urban" center; as cultivators were settled on the land, that center became increasingly identified with direc-

tive, commercial, and service functions. As part of Montecastello's claim
to a degree of autonomy, it emphasized symbols of local identity. Within
this multicentric society, the basic similarity among towns extended also
to a common insistence upon uniqueness: minute differences between
one town and another were—and still are—exaggerated, while "local
traditions" were nurtured.

If one can speak of structural replication in this region, the unit is not
the town as such but the town with a dependent territory. The town
controls its contado and its contadini, while linked with them in many
ways. The town created a landscape for urban purposes and in an urban
image. The town idealizes the country even as it sets itself apart. This
pattern is rooted in the Roman civitas, in which town and country were
part of a political unity and an integral tradition. It contrasts, for example, with northwestern continental Europe, where the town developed as "a foreign body" within a countryside that was politically separate, culturally distinct, and oriented to a different economic system (see
Ennen 1967). But Central Italy developed its own version of the Mediterranean town-country unity. This variant is a function of specific kinds
of urban investment in land, as exemplified by the classical mezzadria
system. However, it is not the mezzadria itself but the social and cultural
forms built upon it that account for the town-country relationship described in this book.

This relationship presents a contrast with accounts of town and
country in Southern Italy. The contrast must be seen against the background of general differences between the two regions in settlement pattern, land tenure, and agricultural organization.[2] The Southern town is
typically an island in an uninhabited countryside. The major landowners
tend to be absentee, while local middle-class proprietors are generally
inactive rentiers; the managerial role of landlords, institutionalized in the
mezzadria, is rare. Cultivators go out to work scattered plots—both their
own and those worked under diverse, often short-term arrangements. At
least since the early nineteenth century, there has been greater flux in
land ownership and far more variability in land-tenure forms and contracts than in the Center. These factors militate against stable relationships between landowners and their land and between landowners
and cultivators, while creating marginal differences of status within the
population. Central Italian landowners, and townsmen in general, are
more clearly differentiated from the cultivators, yet tied to them by con-

tractual and personal relationships. To the Southern agrotownsman the country represents hardship, livelihood at best, and above all, asocial existence; the town spells human contact, security, and civilization (see Davis 1973:9–11). The Central Italian town, in contrast, knows the country mainly through the benefits it provides. Thus, townsmen talk of the beauties and bounties of their countryside, the virtues of the peasantry (in the abstract), and the attachment town landlords feel to their "own" land and peasants. These sentiments are, of course, in the realm of myth, but they underscore the fact that in Central Italy the country represents an essential, though subordinate, element of social structure and values.

The material from Montecastello suggests that the structural replication is paralleled by cultural replication; certain understandings and modes of behavior appear at each level of town organization. Montecastello, primarily through its elite, repeats ideas and assumptions about urban life, urban qualities, and urban tradition: elements I have summarized as the ideology of civiltà. This ideology is neither fixed nor well-ordered but consists of a fluid set of themes, evolving over time and constantly subject to manipulation. Nevertheless, civiltà is not all-inclusive; for instance, it has little to do with inner motivation, personal character, individual freedom, friendship, equality, fair play, or several other possible dimensions of value. The catchword "civiltà" is highly elastic, but it also sets limits to the terms of discourse. This is as true when a revolutionary leader like Gramsci calls for a new hegemony of the working classes through a process of "incivilimento" or "a work of civiltà," as when a landowner uses the same words to justify the traditional social order.[3]

More than through political slogans, the assumptions of civiltà are communicated informally, as when people talk about isolation from town as "the life of a beast." But cultural communication is behavioral as well as verbal. I have used "style" to refer to behavior in the aspect of form rather than content, manner rather than instrumentality; it describes behavioral variations that have a purely social meaning.[4] Styles are not only expressive; as means of social identification, they have important effects upon action. The styles described in this book—the patterns of interaction and etiquette, ways of speaking, and emblems of self-presentation—tell who people are, or who they claim to be, within the framework of "civilized" society. The styles themselves derive largely from urban sources; indeed, visible markers of identity are always more essential among city people and strangers than among *compaesani* in a small community. I have suggested that these styles became important in the local context because of the community's involvements in a wider political field, and that the specific styles reflect the nature of those involvements.

In Montecastello ideas related to civiltà are urban in the Central Italian sense: they refer not only to the city in general or to the cities that concentrate state power, but also to citizenship in a particular "city"—one's own paese. The civile person, descendant of the gentleman-citizen, has urban attributes and connections, but he also participates in the social and political life and identity of his town. That the ideology of the traditional Montecastellese elite brings together values of urbanity with those of locality is intrinsic to their strategies for survival. From the time that a local landowning class appeared in Montecastello, its interests depended not only on connections with outside powers but also on freedom to maneuver among the markets and polities of the region; hence the concern with autonomy, alongside an eagerness to identify with overlord or pope. Within the nation-state, the ideological emphasis changed somewhat; autonomy became community identity, while at the same time wider identifications became increasingly important. "Montecastello" was, in fact, the elite: in the name of "community" they could promote their local interests within the nation and forestall pressures to change. It is in this light that one must look at public patronage, localism in ceremonial, and the process whereby Montecastellese tradition was regularly invented.

Through these cultural patterns—explicit ideology, implicit understandings, and behavioral styles—the urban influence is incorporated into the details of everyday life in Montecastello. A "civilized" way of life is thus re-created in the small town. This "civilization" is not just a matter of aesthetics or an expression of values: in this case study it emerges as an instrument of external politics and internal domination.

This book was written from the standpoint of the town rather than the country. It has emphasized the town elite because of the pivotal position they occupied in community and region and because their strategies help to explain prevalent patterns of behavior and ideology. How the culture of the dominant class affected the peasants is a complex matter, about which I know too little. The peasantry, however, are part of the civil life and in many ways they too adopt the terms of discourse of civiltà. They participate in public life and ritual and promote the symbols of community. To some extent they enact the same behavioral styles as townsmen. They use some of the same criteria and values in making social distinctions, in claiming status vis-à-vis those with lesser claims, and in aspiring to a better life. Many examples come to mind: the ex-peasant boasting, albeit ironically, about local signori; the mezzadro's schoolboy son hoping for a lucrative occupation so that he can one day have mezzadri of his own; the countrymen putting on signorile dress and manners for a Sunday in town, or to escape peasant status permanently.

The influence of civiltà, however, does not prevent peasants from acting in pursuit of their own interests. Such action must be understood in terms of real possibilities and constraints. In the contemporary situation, Communism and emigration are the major forms of peasant action, but they are not without antecedents. Labor movements were gaining momentum among mezzadri in this area before Fascism, and peasant emigration to the cities is as old as the cities themselves. Peasant strategies within the civil life could draw on neighborly relations among peasant families, which extended across the countryside and across community boundaries. In the past as at present, these ties created networks of communication as well as of reciprocity. Tactics of subterfuge were always important. The peasant response to their subjection is reflected in ideology; thus, the elite's concern with signorilità is matched by the peasant's emphasis upon *furbizia* (cunning). Peasant humor abounds with mockery of townsmen and often carries subversive overtones. The personification of the doctor in peasant versions of the Segavecchia conveys messages clear to everyone, but the humor renders it harmless; it is, in fact, co-opted by the town and sponsored by signori.

These indirect modes of protest point up the fact that alternatives open to the peasant were limited by the town-centered organization of rural society. The domination of landlords operated at close range; it penetrated into work, family, social, and ritual life; and it was exercised "benevolently," through ties of dependence. It was, moreover, a cultural domination. Elite ideology—ideas about patronage, public spirit, community, and civilization—not only validated the social order, but also set out terms of meaning and value for peasants as well as townsmen.

After World War II this structure of domination began to give way, and the past ten years have witnessed its dissolution. As part of broader political and economic transformations within the region and nation, the Montecastellese landlords lost their positions of legitimate authority and informal control, and eventually relinquished their hold over the local economy. The professionals who replaced them at the top of the status-hierarchy inherited neither their interests nor their preponderant role within the community. More generally, the loci of power shifted from the town to national-level institutions and interest groups, while communications and the market brought the population increasingly into the life of the larger society. These changes have greatly undermined the social and cultural dominance of the town over its countryside, and of the town elite over the lower classes. On the one hand, social distinctions are no longer bounded by the categories of the community but are based on national-level determinants of status. On the other hand, political parties and labor organizations offer new routes of mobility and social action that bypass the town. They also offer new idioms. In fact, the appeal of the Communist party may lie partly in the fact that it provides terms of evaluation different from those of the town.

Yet for Montecastello, as for Italy, the cultural consequences of an urban past remain. From the time they reemerged in medieval Italy, the towns have been the major source of cultural creativity, absorbing or subordinating many of the social forces that might have generated alternative modes of action and thought. The towns drew together nobles, landowners, clerics, merchants, artists, literati, soldiers, artisans, mobile peasants, and entrepreneurs of all kinds, blurring the boundaries between such categories and giving rise to new social alignments. Within the walls different institutions developed in conjunction with each other; the commercial and political life of the town influenced church and university and in turn were influenced by them. The town always contained diverse and contending interests, but struggles for power were played out in a common arena and their outcomes validated by town government.

Thus the town—each town—was the nerve center of its region and the repository of cultural elaborations. There were, of course, other institutional forms in the countryside, such as monasteries, fattorie, and peasant villages; but these were linked to powers in town. New ideas were therefore continually reinterpreted through an urban view of the world. Though the significance of the individual town—especially a small town like Montecastello—has changed, national life is still embedded in its urban history. The urban view pervades contemporary institutions, from Italian Catholicism to Italian Communism. In the present as in the past, the urban tradition shapes Montecastello's encounter with the modern world.

Notes

CHAPTER 1: THE QUALITY OF CIVILTÀ

1. "Civiltà" is pronounced "chee-veel-TA." "Civile" is pronounced "chee-VEE-lay."

2. In the Sicilian village described by Blok, the term "civile" is used as a noun, synonymously with "signore," and the local elite is referred to collectively as *civili*. The term "civile" contrasts with the epithet *viddanu*, which is applied to peasants. The definition reported by Blok is *uomo dalla campagna e lontano da ogni civiltà*, "a man from the countryside lacking any civility" (1974:49).

3. The ideal summarized by Hyde was set forth in the book *Della Vita Civile* written by Matteo Palmieri about 1430.

CHAPTER 2: THE COMMUNITY

1. The saying continues: ". . . *l'omini becchi e le donne putane*" (the men are cuckolds and the women whores).

2. In the census of 1961 the commune had 566 occupied dwellings with a total of 2,131 rooms, an average of 3.8 rooms per dwelling. This amounts to somewhat less than one room per inhabitant; the average number of persons living in a dwelling was 4.2. Of the 566 dwellings, 348 had electricity; 176 had indoor lavatories; 46 had baths; 149 had water inside the house; 487 had stoves using bottled gas; only 3 had central heating (ISTAT 1965).

3. National law requires that every commune be serviced by a resident physician, midwife, pharmacist, and veterinarian. All of these individuals live in the town of Montecastello, although shortly after I left, the midwife married a man from Doglio and moved there.

4. These population figures, which refer to the situation at the end of 1960, are based on the local population register. This register lists the composition of each household and vital statistics on every member, and it indicates all additions and subtractions to each household

by birth, death, or change of residence. The register is quite complete and accurate, for the law requires that all changes in family status be reported. Moreover, the official in charge not only is meticulous, but he also personally knows the situation in almost every household.

5. Equivalent data were not available for the commune. However, the pattern of land use in Montecastello appears to be substantially the same as in this larger area comprised of several neighboring communes of similar agricultural character.

6. Yields vary a great deal—by altitude, by specific farm, and by year. In general, they range from 30 to 35 quintals (one quintal equals 100 kilograms) per hectare in the plain in a good year, to 20 to 30 in the middle altitudes, to 15 or less in the higher hills.

7. The available machinery served more farms than their numbers would suggest, since many were owned by fattorie including several farms. Moreover, some machines were available for rental; for instance, a tractor could be hired for about L.10–12,000 per day.

8. This notion of good manners might be contrasted with the rationalizations contained in modern etiquette books in American culture, where manners are viewed as expressions of kindness and consideration for others. The Montecastellesi do not find it necessary to introduce ideology of this kind: for them, etiquette is form.

CHAPTER 3: THE MEZZADRIA SYSTEM

1. Sharecropping of the first kind is common in Southern Italy; the landowners and agents are mainly inactive share-collectors, while individual cultivators must provide most of the working capital and have control of actual operations. The second kind occurs mainly in the capitalistic enterprises, in which the cultivators have only a tenuous relationship to the enterprise. Sharecroppers of this type in Italy, the *compartecipanti*, attend either to certain tasks connected with specialized tree cultivation or to all the work connected with a single field crop, in return for which they receive a share of the crop concerned. The duration of the contract is normally less than a year (Lutz 1962:157).

2. The quantitative data on the mezzadria were collected in the late 1950s by the Istituto di Economia e Politica Agraria dell' Università degli Studi di Perugia, who made available the portions pertaining to Montecastello. These data may be considered quite accurate, for the government records they are based on draw information from both landlords and peasants; and since the interests of the two parties are different, sources of error tend to be canceled out.

3. The increased income that a mezzadria landlord could realize by dividing large farms has been demonstrated quantitatively in studies from various areas of Central Italy, referred to by Milletti (1949:20–23). These studies also suggest that there has been a continual process of breakup of farms since the beginning of the century.

4. The rental of the threshing machine may be paid in grain, at about 3 percent of the amount of grain harvested, or in cash, at L. 180–250 per quintal (depending upon the total quantity threshed). In Montecastello the landlord pays three-fourths of the rental cost and the mezzadro one-fourth.

5. The most important sources for this section were Desplanques (1969), Jones (1966; 1968) and Sereni (1962). Other sources dealing in detail with the mezzadria system include Albertario (1939), Bellini (1955; 1958), Bologna (1924), Einaudi (1946), Gennari (1949), Imberciadori (1951; 1953), INEA (1930; 1931–33), Luzzatto (1948), Medici (1956), Radi

(1962), and RAG (1934). The agricultural situation in central Umbria during the early 1960s is dealt with by Cassano (1965) and Guerrieri (1964).

General sources for the agrarian and economic history of Italy, which were also useful in providing background for the history of land ownership (chapter 4) and political history (chapter 5), include the following: Acerbo (1961), Bandini (1957), Bloch (1970), Braudel (1972–73), Cipolla (1952; 1959; 1972), Clough (1964), Dal Pane (1944), Delumeau (1957–59), Leicht (1946), Luzzatto (1949; 1955–58; 1961; 1967), Mancini (1914), Niccoli (1902), Pugliese (1908), Romano and Vivanti (1973), Serpieri (1947), and Smith (1967).

6. See Bologna (1924:74), Solmi (1923:21), and Medici (1956:48).

7. The landowner's share consisted of between one-tenth and one-fifth of the produce; in addition, the cultivator owed a certain number of days each month of labor to the landowner (Solmi 1923:22–23).

8. This paragraph and other discussions of the Tuscan mezzadria draw primarily on Jones (1968).

9. The statutes of Bologna in 1376 even made the mezzadria the obligatory form for leasing agricultural land (Bloch 1970:147).

10. The regalie, however, were maintained. A household budget study of a mezzadria family on a farm near Montecastello, carried out in 1906, gives some idea of the scope of these payments. This family (a large one, consisting of 21 members and occupying a 35-hectare farm) owed the following items: at Carnival, eight hens; at mid-August, eight pullets; at Christmas, ten capons and eighty eggs; at Easter, one hundred eggs; as well as fourteen baskets of grapes (ten kilos each), four bushels (*scope*) of millet, eight quintals of hay, and one quintal of maize husks (Priori 1906:629).

11. According to Schmidt, this increase in the number of mezzadri drew not only from the ranks of wage-laborers but also included many peasant proprietors who during and after World War I had acquired land which they were subsequently unable to maintain (1938:133).

12. The magnitude of the 1950–1959 decline in numbers of mezzadri in Montecastello is somewhat less than that for Umbria as a whole (cf.Bellini 1959: 44–47). In Montecastello the decline is accounted for equally by the total number of contracts and the average number of workers per farm—a decrease of about 10 percent in each. Precise data on the destination and occupational changes of ex-mezzadri is not available at the local level, partly because the initial change is often only the first of a series of residential and occupational changes. The figures on peasant proprietors are subject to error; they are likely to be overstatements, since there are government benefits to be derived from reporting oneself as a peasant proprietor. For Umbria as a whole, it has been estimated that 80 percent or more of the ex-mezzadri move out of agriculture (MLP 1959; Bellini 1959:49).

CHAPTER 4: THE CARRIERS OF CIVILTÀ

1. The discussion of the history of property in Umbria is based primarily on data reported by Desplanques (1969:115–70).

2. In most communes outside the mountain areas, church lands occupied 25 to 40 percent of the total area, and in Todi the figure was 43 percent in 1842 (Desplanques 1969: 126–29).

3. Primogeniture does not, of course, mean that younger sons and daughters are excluded from any share in the patrimony. Though they do not inherit directly they are generally provided for in some way, and obligations to do so often devolve upon the heir. The forms of primogeniture (or other unigeniture) should be thought of in terms of a continuum, with strictly equal partibility at the other end and many variations between.

4. Colclough (1971) shows how such stories are used as popular rationalizations to explain social mobility in a Southern Italian village.

5. According to Schmidt (1938:27–28), some 700,000 to 800,000 hectares were purchased by about a million peasant families in the postwar period. In addition, a great deal of land changed hands at this time as urban speculators attempted to profit from the difficulties of hard-pressed landowners and from the rise in farmland values.

6. At the same time, the total amount of land under cultivation has increased. According to cadastral survey data summarized by Desplanques (1969:252–53), the cultivable area in Montecastello increased from roughly 50 percent to 75 percent of the total area during the past hundred years. This would have increased the amount of cultivated land in mezzadria tenure through the first decades of the twentieth century, but by 1960 the mezzadria area was probably not much different than it had been in 1868; the additional land under cultivation is accounted for by other forms of tenure.

7. The discreteness of social-economic categories contrasts with many areas of Southern Italy, where clearcut, stable categories (other than the distinction between upper and lower classes) are not readily identified. Typically in the South, the distribution of land ownership is broad and continuous; there is a great variety of short-term arrangements for cultivating land; most families combine several different economic activities; and both property and occupations are in constant flux. Under these circumstances, sharp boundaries between economic categories are difficult to define (MacDonald and MacDonald 1964; Silverman 1968). In such cases, it seems more accurate to conceptualize the lower class as nuclear families ranked along a continuous range, with a family's position determined by its particular combination of economic attributes at any given time.

8. Some of these programs are carry-overs from earlier governments, such as the charity organization (Congregazione di Carità) established after the unification. However, until the Fascist period, the functions of government (both local and national) tended to be confounded with the elite individuals who executed them. Indeed, only with the overt conflict of the postwar years did the distinction become very clear.

9. Further detail on the method, as well as its theoretical underpinnings, is given in Silverman (1966). It is important to note that its purpose was to uncover some of the subtleties of social distinction rather than to determine an order of general social position, for which an occupational or other economic scale might suffice. Moreover, the object was to arrive at the principles underlying prestige, rather than to assign all persons to pigeonholes. The method is superficially similar to those used in some subjective studies of social stratification, such as Warner (1949), Hollingshead (1949), and Lopreato (1961; 1967). However, my approach was different in several ways. My main purpose in asking informants to differentiate specific persons was to learn how they applied the rules of the code. They built up their picture of prestige ranks through separate comparisons, instead of describing their views of local stratification. My overall model was based on the criteria used by informants, rather than their achieved sortings.

Four informants were used, themselves ranging from Categories A-2 to C-1. Following an informal interview, each was given a stack of cards representing all families of the town and a selected sample of the country households. The informant was asked how "the people here" would rank a particular pair of families—"higher" or "lower." After many paired comparisons, each informant began to form them into groupings that he judged to be roughly uniform in rank. The task was continued until he felt satisfied with his sorting. Then he was asked to characterize each group and to compare the gaps between groups. Finally, he was questioned about the judgments he found difficult to make, about how he would place certain hypothetical persons, and about how people's positions could change. The interviews and sortings provided data for an initial model, which was then elaborated and modified on the basis of observation of actual behavior, volunteered statements, and informal questioning of other Montecastellesi.

10. The concept of "order of action" is based on Chapple and Coon (1942:439).

CHAPTER 5: THE CONTEXT OF POWER

1. Sources for this section include both published accounts and original documents in local, state, and church archives in Montecastello, Todi, and Perugia. Fragmentary histories of Montecastello were written by Ceci (1888) and Rossi (1889), and there are references to Montecastello in Alvi (1910) and Mancini (1960).

The most important source for the early and communal-period history of Todi is Ceci (1897). Other works pertinent to the history of Todi include Ceci and Pensi (1897), Scalvanti (1897), Leonii (1856; 1889), and Mancini (n.d.). Background on the communal period was provided by Hyde (1973), Waley (1961; 1969), Salvatorelli (1940b), Volpe (1961), Fiumi (1956), Barraclough (1968), Lopez (1971), Sella (1952), and various works on particular communes, especially Bonazzi (1959–60), Angelini (1965), Waley (1952), Fiumi (1961), Volpe (1902), and Herlihy (1968). Useful perspectives on the Renaissance period were provided by Burckhardt (1960), Laven (1966), Partner (1972), and Hay (1961).

For the period of the Papal States, the more ample archival sources were supplemented by DeMaddalena (1964), Dal Pane (1954), Galli (1840), DeMarco (1949), Hobsbawm (1962), and King (1967). The post-unification period is documented by a variety of materials on local population, government, formal associations, and festivals; I also had access to some diaries and notes in the possession of certain individuals, and of course the reminiscences of older people. General sources for this more recent history include Mack Smith (1959), Albrecht-Carrié (1950), Vaussard (1972), Thayer (1964), and Neufeld (1961). Other general histories of Italy that were consulted include (in addition to items already noted in the text and in note 4 to chapter 3): Trevelyan (1956), Salvatorelli (1940a), Seton-Watson (1967), and Valeri (1959–60).

2. There is an earlier reference of dubious validity. Calindri, who produced a compendium of information on cities and towns in the Papal States, says that Montecastello was built by the Atti family in the year 980 (1829:318). The basis for this claim is unclear.

3. The estimate of Beloch is that the population of the Papal States increased from 1.7 million to 2 million between 1550 and 1600 (cited in Braudel 1972:408).

4. The Foligno sugar refinery was opened in 1900, and a match factory opened in Perugia in 1902. Between 1906 and 1908 several other manufacturing plants came into existence in the province, producing bricks, cotton, leather goods, candy (the Perugina company), chemical products, and carriage fittings (Bellini 1964:5–7).

5. The Thursday market is attested since 1662, though it may be older. It died out in the late nineteenth century. Many local people frequently went to the Saturday market in Todi as well, as they still do. The Montecastello fair of May 2, held in conjunction with the of-

ficial patron-saint festival, is documented since 1516; the festivities used to last as long as two weeks, though today they are limited to one or two days. Other fairs of some antiquity, all still in existence, include the Benediction of St. Antony, held on the Wednesday following January 17, and two fairs established at least by 1693, one held on April 25 and the other on August 29. Two more recent fairs, instituted during the nineteenth century, are held during July. In addition, Montecastellesi regularly attended fairs in other communities within a radius of some 20 or 30 kilometers.

6. This naming also illustrates the ease with which local identity could be acquired, for some figures who were clearly outsiders—like the fourteenth-century Michelotta—were also defined as Montecastellesi.

7. An example of how conflicts are publicized and resolved is provided by a case in which my husband and I were the accused. While we were out of town one day, a woman (whose general grievance toward us appeared to be rooted in an ancient conflict with our house-keeper's family) denounced us before the maresciallo, claiming that our dog had invaded her attic and eaten two of her pigeons. Each development in the conflict was quickly circulated throughout the community, and discussion produced a series of public judgments; these opinions were based not only on the actual incidents but also on the reputation, history, and status of the persons involved. (Our accuser was at a disadvantage because of her lower-class status and her much-discussed personal misbehavior; furthermore, it was considered inhospitable of her to provoke trouble with guests of the paese.) When we offered what public opinion considered an overly generous settlement, her demands for compensation progressively increased. Finally we refused to negotiate further, whereupon all her former allies (including her brothers) approved our action and withdrew their support of her, and she had to accept a settlement lower than our original offer. The carabinieri played little part in the resolution, serving primarily as a place for the complaint to be registered. More serious accusations would not, of course, be so informally settled, and extended lawsuits do occur in the community.

8. An incident that occurred shortly before the fieldwork began illustrates the close connection between party politics and local divisions. The participants in a circle of reciprocal work exchange refused to thresh the wheat of a mezzadro who was outspoken in his criticism of the Communist party. The landlord eventually hired laborers to do the work and charged the cost to his other mezzadri, who were among the boycotters.

9. Davis reports that the main political parties and labor organizations in Italy have formal powers to act as bureaucratic intermediaries for their members and are paid by the state for doing so—a set fee for each document or bureaucratic procedure successfully negotiated (1973:19). This would, of course, be additional reason for them to take on intermediary functions, but the political incentive seems more fundamental.

CHAPTER 6: FESTIVALS

1. One peasant calls to another: "O! Domani, che è?" ("What day is tomorrow?")
The response: "È l'Ascensione." ("It is the Ascension.")
Returned by:

"Sia ringraziato Dio nostro Signore,
  Dove arriva la voce mia,
  Non possa arrivà l'acqua cattiva."

("Thanks be to God our Lord,
  Where my voice reaches,
  May the bad water be unable to reach.")

2. Curiously, May is also called the "month of the asses," i.e., the time when asses mate. Furthermore, the name of the month is used in human sexual allusions: *mettere il maggio* means to put horns on someone, and throughout the month people joke with each other by saying "Attenta, è maggio" ("Beware, it is May"). People generally avoid marrying during May, and when a marriage occasionally does occur it evokes considerable criticism.

3. A proverb says:

"A San Giovanni pija la falce e tajeme le gamme,
  A San Pietro pija la falce e 'n te volta di dietro."

("On San Giovanni take the sickle and cut off my legs [says the grain],
  On San Pietro take the sickle and don't turn back.")

4. The landowning families are most conspicuous in the documents describing the festa, contributing the more elaborate items and assuming leadership roles, but the expenses were shared by the whole population. The priest collected pledges at every home during the Easter benediction of the houses, and thirteen pairs of priors (primarily peasants and artisans) collected donations of grain from the threshing floors.

5. Such an interpretation does not imply that all Montecastellesi who participate in these events do so to express opposition to the church. Some emphasize local identity without reference to the church; others express anticlerical attitudes without reference to localism; still others see these events as occasions for hilarity and sociability.

6. In 1961, at about 8:30 on the morning of Ash Wednesday, there was a total eclipse of the sun. People returning from their revelry did not bother to go to sleep but joined the crowd watching the eclipse from the Piazza of the Church, and then went on to their usual day's work.

7. Toschi gives several variants of this verse which have been collected throughout Central Italy. He sees it as a parody of a traditional funeral lament (1955:318 ff.).

8. One example:

Fiore de menta
L'insalata 'n se magna se 'n se pianta
L'amore nun se fa se nun se monta.

(Flower of mint
You can't eat salad unless you plant it
You can't make love unless you mount.)
For other examples, see chapter 7.

9. Though always referred to as *la Passione* in Montecastello, the songs are Marian laments. (For a discussion of the origins and transformations of the laments, see DeMartino 1958.) The Umbrian laments are partly creations of an important medieval development of popular theater. They were produced by intellectuals and poets, both ecclesiastics and laymen, but they were "popular" in the materials they drew on and the actors and audience for whom they were written (see Toschi 1955:684 ff.). In the Montecastello area, the influence of the great thirteenth-century Franciscan poet, Jacopone of Todi, is especially important.

10. The following version was sung in Montecastello during the youth of the 90-year-old peasant man who dictated it:

Piangi piangi Maria povera donna
Lo vostro fijo è annato a la condanna (repeat)
Mi lo piangete più chè n'aritorna (repeat)
È entrato 'n casa de Pilà e de Donna.
Sentì lo pianto che fa la Madonna
Vieni Giovanni a consolà Maria.
Dimme Giovanni che nova me porti
Siccaro 'l mio fijolo è vivo o morto.
O vivo o morto lo ritroveremo
La strada del Calvario noi faremo.
Quanno saremo alle prime cittàne
La butteremo 'na strillente boce (repeat)
Lo fijo de Maria nun arispose
Nun arispose ch'era abbeverato
E morto e condannto su la croce.
Passò lo lancio e la cavalleria
Passò Gesù che disse: —Madre mia!
Di chiodi e de martelli ò preparato
Questi nun so' li piedi che lavavo.
In casa de Simone e Maddalena.
Dove se scurerà 'l sole e la luna
Quilla boccuccia tanto ben troata
Jel'hanno chiusa che nun parla più.
O cara gente ch'avete ascoltato
La pena e la passione che 'Ddio ha patuto
L'ha patuta con pena e con dolore
E 'Ddio ce la concede in salvazione.
In salvazione dove stanno i santi
E dove un giorno andremo tutti quanti
In salvazione dove sta' il Signore
Un giorno ce conceda in salvazione.

Cry cry, Mary poor woman
Your son has gone to the condemning (repeat)
You cry all the more because he's not coming back (repeat)
He has gone into the house of Pilar and Donna.
Hear the sob of the Madonna
Come John to console Mary.
Tell me John what news you bring me
If my dear little son is alive or dead.
Whether alive or dead we will find him
We will go to the street of the Calvary.
When we are at the beginning of the city
We will shout out in a loud voice.
The son of Mary doesn't answer
He doesn't answer because he was drunken
And dead and condemned on the cross.

The lancer and the cavalry passed
Jesus passed and said: —Mother mine!
With nails and hammers I was prepared.
These aren't the feet that I washed,
In the house of Simon and Magdalen.
Where the sun will darken and the moon
That dear mouth that was so fine
They have closed so that it no longer speaks.
O dear people what you have heard
The pain and the passion that God has contracted
He has contracted it with pain and suffering
And God gives it to us in salvation.
In salvation where the saints are
And where one day we will go, all of us
In salvation where the Lord is
One day he will give it to us in salvation.

11. At first there was no entrance fee for women, in order to assure partners for the young men, until it developed that many of the women who attended were elderly and were coming as chaperones or simply to watch. The lottery was a popular innovation. The winner gets the privilege of choosing the queen of the dance, and also the prize of a chicken or cake, which he and his queen eat together. The queen chosen in the first lottery was the middle-aged patroness referred to earlier.

12. The Communist festa actually featured only a minimum of overt propaganda. The day's events included a bocce competition, a foot-race, and a contest for "a prize of two pigeons to the first one to finish a plate of pasta'sciutta with both hands tied." A brief rally followed these events, and in the evening there was a dance.

CHAPTER 7: THE LIFE CYCLE

1. The equivalence of famiglia to "household" is suggested by the fact that a bride or groom who joins the household of the spouse is said to "enter into the famiglia" of the spouse, while if the couple establish separate residence they are said to "make a famiglia of their own."

2. In 1960 the size range of mezzadria families was from 2 to 14, with an average of 5.6, as compared to an average family size of 4.4 for the community as a whole.

3. Several town families were omitted from this classification by occupation, namely those without an active occupation (including landowners without other occupation) and those whose occupations could not be assigned unambiguously to major categories.

4. Social class as such does not seem to be highly significant for family structure. However, class differences within the town appear to be correlated with the initial residence decision of a newly married couple. The higher the social class, the more likely it is that a couple has lived in the parental household for a time after their marriage; among the lower class of the town, the nuclear family is generally the initial and continuing form.

5. This reduction has been accompanied by the elimination of extremely large households. In 1900 the largest family had 21 members and there were thirteen that had more than 14 members (the maximum size in 1960).

6. The discussion of the life cycle is organized by the culturally defined phases that structure the life span in Montecastello.

7. A generation or two ago the whole body was swaddled, including arms and legs, but the area wrapped has been progressively reduced. Today, the abdominal wrapping is followed by folding a long cloth snugly over the infant's body and legs.

8. The ceremonies of Confirmation and First Communion are held simultaneously, once a year, for all children who are eligible at that time.

9. Garlic is a symbol of the agonies of love and courtship, as in the expression "to eat the garlic of love."

10. A *fattura* is a deliberate act performed by someone with the necessary skill, which can be learned, in contrast to the *malocchio* (evil eye), the unintentional power that some people have to cause harm, usually when they feel envy. Despite the difference in etiology, both are diagnosed and treated in the same way. Certain persons (both men and women) practice such magical curing as a part-time specialty. I heard of at least three practitioners in the Montecastello area in recent years, though for a really serious problem well-known specialists in other parts of Umbria may be consulted. The most common diagnostic test is the "proof of the oil": the *mago* slowly drops three drops of oil into a dish of water; if the drops dissolve it means there is a "caused evil." A simple treatment is for the curer to repeat the oil-in-water ritual while reciting a formula, until the drops remain whole. Another routine measure is to tear open the victim's bed-pillows. If the stuffing is knotted there has been a fattura, and the pillows are ritually burned.

11. The observed corredo of one town bride, the daughter of a minor bureaucrat, included the following items of household linen:
    24 sheets: 12 embroidered linen, 12 simple cotton or hemp
    48 pillowcases: 24 embroidered, 24 simple
     8 bedcovers: 2 heavy blankets, 6 light blankets and bedspreads
    36 bath towels
    24 hand towels
    24 kitchen towels
     9 sets of tablecloths and napkins
     2 bedroom footrugs
In addition, the trousseau contained personal linen, with most items included in quantities of twelve. The overall cost of this corredo, apart from the labor, might be estimated at 300,000 to 400,000 lire, or about half a year's income for a family of this category.

12. The total cost of bedroom furniture purchased by Montecastellesi marrying in 1960–61 ranges from 100,000 to 300,000 lire. The figure would be higher in a few well-to-do families.

13. Recently it has become prestigious to have the wedding dinner in a restaurant in Assisi, which has good facilities and lends something of the air of a religious pilgrimage. This choice also implies that the families have access to enough cars to transport all the guests.

14. The following table gives two rough comparative measures of fertility in different categories of the population.

Measures of Fertility According to Population Category

Category	Fertility Ratio [a] 1960	Average No. Children, Women over 45 [b]
Town	.234	1.81
Country, total	.370	2.96
Plain	.280	2.68
Hill	.416	2.90
Occupational category		
Mezzadri	.365	3.29
Peasant proprietor	.429	2.62
Nonagricultural		
low status	.306	2.12
middle and high status	.250	1.73
Commune total	.348	2.77 (N = 490)
Commune total (1881–1907) [c]		3.78 (N = 549)

[a] Ratio of children under age 5 to women between 16 and 45.

[b] The category includes all women of completed reproduction (over age 45) listed in the 1933–1960 population register, whose history could be traced since age 16, and who had ever married or given birth to a known illegitimate child. The figure reflects the total number of children inscribed in the population register (includes all children born alive).

[c] All women whose completed reproductive history (as defined above) could be reconstructed from the population registers of 1881–1907.

15. The change in expectations as to the local obligations of bureaucrats can be read from tombstones. Several officials who died before the mid-twentieth century are eulogized as having been dedicated to the public welfare and the glory of Montecastello, as if their posts were a calling. In contrast, the inscription for a contemporary bureaucrat, who died recently after forty years of service, describes him primarily in terms of his devotion to his family, adding that he was "a tireless worker."

CHAPTER 8: TEN YEARS LATER

1. Specialized arboriculture means that tree cultivation is not combined with other cultigens on the same plot. The new "vineyard" thus contrasts with the existing pattern of vine cultivation in Montecastello, in which the vine was trained over supporting trees planted in and around fields.

2. The 4 percent of "abandoned" land refers to land not included in any property covered by the agricultural census of 1970. Much of the land reported as "woods and unproductive" but included within properties is effectively "abandoned" in terms of agricultural use.

3. The average size of mezzadria farms in the commune in 1970 was 10.1 hectares, compared to 8.7 in 1961. However, the 1970 farms were concentrated more in the lower altitudes.

CHAPTER 9: THE HERITAGE OF THE TOWN

1. These patterns appeared, of course, in modified form in the smaller town. In Montecastello, local autonomy was obviously limited; the functions of the communal government must have been largely concerned with matters of land and agriculture; artisans were too few to permit the guild organization so important in Todi; and there may have been other consequences of its size. I believe, however, that the differences between Montecastello and Todi were of the same order as those between the *comuni di castrum* and the *comuni di città* discussed by Volpe, which he regards as *qualitatively* similar (1961:163–65). Jones too sees the differences between the castella and the urban communes as matters of degree rather than kind, and he states that in medieval Italy "no line divides urban from rural" (1966:348–49). In the case of rural communes that were essentially associations of cultivators, however, the "communal" organization would have been very different from that of the larger towns.

2. Some of these differences, and their implications for social structure and values, are discussed at greater length in Silverman (1968), which also contains relevant bibliographical references on the South.

3. I am indebted to Williams (1960) for his discussion of Gramsci's concept of *egemonia* and for particular citations from Gramsci's *Il Materialismo Storico*.

4. This view of style draws, in part, on Duncan (1962:273–75, *passim.*). As I use the term, "style" may be thought of as a choice (though often an unconscious choice, especially when it pertains to behavior inculcated in early socialization) among alternative ways in which an instrumental act can be carried out. For example, the act of offering food to someone can be accomplished through various modes of behavior, different styles. Verbal behavior may also be described as style—aspects of speech that are not semantic in terms of the ostensible message, but that convey meaning about the speaker and about the situation.

Bibliography

Documents

Note: Titles given in Italian are the actual titles of the documents. Titles given in English are supplied.

A.C.M. ARCHIVIO COMUNALE DI MONTECASTELLO DI VIBIO
1. Tasse sui Beni, 1557.
2. Survey of land owned in Montecastello and Fratta by the Abbey of San Lorenzo, 1751.
3. Libbro osia Registro del Comune di Montecastello, 1778–81.
4. Attestati Notarili sui Privilegi, Facoltà, Esenzioni Concessi alla Comunità di Montecastello, 1797–1816 [including quotations from documents of the fifteenth to eighteenth centuries].
5. Notizie sulle Chiese Esistenti nel Territorio del Comune di Montecastello [from a manuscript by G. B. Alvi recording a pastoral visit, late eighteenth century].
6. Visita della Comunità di Montecastello, 1804.
7. I Privilegi di Montecastello, c.1814.
8. Riparto Censuario per le Stime, 1826.
9. Brogliardo di N. 89 Censi Spettanti alla Comunità di Montecastello nell'Umbria, 1854.
10. Census, parish of Montecastello, 1855.
11. Atti Consigliari e della Giunta dal Ottobre 1860 a Maggio 1873.
12. Deliberations of the communal council of Montecastello, January 12, 1896.

A.C.T. ARCHIVIO COMUNALE DI TODI
1. Book of hearths of the contado of Todi, 1292. Fondo Archivio Segreto di San Fortunato.
2. Confini di Montecastello [20 documents, 1517–96]. Fondo Archivio Segreto di San Fortunato, Armadio II, Casella II.
3. Carte Diverse di Luc'Alberto Petti. N. 1, parte 40 (Fratta e Montecastello), [pp.] 4–10 (c.1600). Armadio VI, Casella X.

A.C.V.   ARCHIVIO DELLA CURIA VESCOVILE DI TODI
Visita Gazzoli dal 1806 al 1809, [pp.] 127–29.

A.S.P.   ARCHIVIO DI STATO, PERUGIA
Archivio Storico del Comune di Perugia
  1. Act of submission of Montecastello to Perugia, 1563, and letter revoking submission.
     Scritture Diverse Alfabetica 23, n. 12.
  2. Lettere dirette all'Amministrazione Dipartimentale del Trasimeno dalla Municipalità
     del Cantone di Montecastello, 1798–99. Periodo 1797–1816, serie 45.
  3. Lettere dell'Anno XII spedite all'Amministrazione Dipartimentale del Trasimeno dal
     Prefetto Consolare del Cantone di Montecastello, 1798. Periodo 1797–1816, serie 51.

Archivio della Prefettura dell'Umbria (1860–1870)
  4. Ruolo della Tassa sulle Bestie da Tiro da Sella e da Soma, Montecastello di Vibio,
     1868. Seconda serie, n. 124.

Archivio della Prefettura di Perugia
  5. Deliberations of the communal council of Montecastello di Vibio, 1901–30. Seconda
     serie, n. 416.
  6. Correspondence pertaining to the priest of Montecastello parish, 1901. Terza serie, n.
     290.
  7. Inventory of property of the parish of Montecastello, 1921. Terza serie, n. 290.
  8. Miscellaneous administrative documents of the commune of Montecastello di Vibio,
     1938–40. Seconda serie, n. 419.

Italy: Government Publications

CRU, see under CRU in main alphabet.
INEA. Istituto Nazionale di Economia Agraria. 1930. *Rapporti fra Proprietà, Impresa, e Mano
    d'Opera nell'Agricoltura Italiana.* Vol. V: *Umbria,* by Zino Vignati. Rome: Fratelli Treves
    dell'Ali.
—— 1931–33. *Monografie di Famiglie Agricole.* Vol. I: *Mezzadri di Val di Pesa e del Chianti
    (Toscana),* 1931; Vol. II: *Mezzadri della Media Valle del Tevere (Umbria),* by C. Papi, 1931;
    Vol. V: *Mezzadri e Piccoli Proprietari Coltivatori in Umbria,* by G. Proni, 1933. Studi e
    Monografie No. 14. Rome: Fratelli Treves dell'Ali.
—— 1947. *La Distribuzione della Proprietà Fondiaria in Italia.* Unnumbered volume, "Mar-
    che, Umbria." Rome: Failli.
ISTAT. Istituto Centrale di Statistica. 1958. *Sommario di Statistiche Storiche Italiane:
    1861–1955.* Rome: Isituto Poligrafico dello Stato.
—— 1960. *Comuni e Loro Popolazioni ai Censimenti dal 1861 al 1951.* Rome.
—— 1961a. RAI (Radiotelevisione Italiana). *Gli Abbonamenti alle Radiodiffusioni nel 1960.*
    Rome.
—— 1961b. *La Grande Conta delle Nostre Campagne.* Rome: A.B.E.T.E.
—— 1962. *1° Censimento Generale dell'Agricoltura, 15 Aprile 1961.* Vol. II, Fasc. 54. Rome:
    A.B.E.T.E.
—— 1964. *4° Censimento Generale dell'Industrie e del Commercio, 16 Ottobre 1961.* Vol. II,
    Fasc. 54. Rome: Failli.
—— 1965. *10° Censimento Generale della Popolazione, 15 Ottobre 1961.* Vol. III, Fasc. 54.
    Rome: A.B.E.T.E.
—— 1972. *2° Censimento Generale dell'Agricoltura, 25 Ottobre 1970.* Vol. II, Fasc. 51. Rome:
    A.B.E.T.E

—— 1973. *11° Censimento Generale della Popolazione, 24 Ottobre 1971.* Vol. II, Fasc. 51. Rome: A.B.E.T.E.

MAIC. Ministero di Agricoltura, Industria e Commercio. 1883. *Statistica Elettorale Politica: Elezioni Generali Politiche* (1882). Rome: Tipografia Elzeviriana.

—— 1885. *Statistica degli Elettori Amministrativi e degli Elettori Politici* (1883). Rome: Tipografia della Camera dei Deputati.

MC. Ministero per la Costituente. 1947. *Rapporto della Commissione Economica.* Vol. I: *Agricoltura.* Rome: Istituto Poligrafico dello Stato.

MLP. Ministero dei Lavori Pubblici. 1959. *Piano Territoriale di Coordinamento della Regione Umbra: Studi Preliminari.* Città di Castello: Società Poligrafica Editoriale.

Secondary Sources

Acerbo, Giacomo. 1961. "L'Agricoltura Italiana dal 1861 ad Oggi." In *L'Economia Italiana dal 1861 al 1961.* Biblioteca della Rivista "Economia e Storia," n. 6. Milan: Giuffrè.

Albertario, Paolo. 1939. "Le Fattorie dell'Italia Centrale." In *Annali di Statistica,* Series VII, Vol. 3, pp. 99–191. Rome: Istituto Centrale di Statistica.

Albrecht-Carrié, René. 1950. *Italy: From Napoleon to Mussolini.* New York: Columbia University Press.

Alvi, Pirro. 1910. *Todi, Città Illustra dell'Umbria, Cenni Storici.* Todi: Tipografia Tuderte.

Angelini, Sergio. 1965. *La Diplomazia Comunale a Perugia nei Secoli XIII e XIV.* Florence: Olschki.

Bandini, Mario. 1945. *Politica Agraria.* Bologna: Edizioni Agricole.

—— 1957. *Cento Anni di Storia Agraria Italiana.* Rome: Edizioni Cinque Lune.

Banfield, Edward C. 1958. *The Moral Basis of a Backward Society.* Glencoe, Ill.: Free Press.

Barbano, F. and M. Viterbi. 1959. *Bibliografia della Sociologia Italiana (1948–1958).* Turin: Ramella.

Barraclough, Geoffrey. 1968. *The Medieval Papacy.* London: Thames and Hudson.

Battaglia, Salvatore. 1961. *Grande Dizionario della Lingua Italiana.* Turin: Unione Tipografico.

Bellini, Luigi. 1955. "La Mezzadria in Umbria dall'Unità alla Fine del Secolo XIX," *Movimento Operaio* 7(n.s.):561–72.

—— 1958–59. "L'Agricoltura Umbra negli Ultimi Cento Anni: Appunti per uno Studio," *Cronache Umbre* 1:23–33 and 2:28–34.

—— 1959. "Aspetti e Problemi Economici dell'Umbria," *Cronache Umbre* 2:41–66.

—— 1964. "Appunti per una Storia dell'Economia Umbra: 1840–1910," *Bollettino della Deputazione di Storia Patria per l'Umbria* 61:167–80.

Beloch, G. 1959. "La Popolazione d'Italia nei Secoli Sedicesimo, Diciassettesimo e Diciottesimo." In Carlo M. Cipolla, ed., *Storia dell'Economia Italiana.* Saggi di Storia Economica, Vol. I. Turin: Edizioni Scientifiche Einaudi.

Bloch, Marc. 1970. *French Rural History: An Essay on its Basic Characteristics.* Berkeley and Los Angeles: University of California Press. (First published in 1931.)

Blok, Anton. 1974. *The Mafia of a Sicilian Village, 1860–1960: A Study of Violent Peasant Entrepreneurs.* Oxford: Basil Blackwell.

Bologna, M. Luigi. 1924. "Origini e Sviluppi della Mezzeria Toscana sino all'Editto Leopoldino," *Rivista di Diritto Agrario* 3:73–84.

Bonasera, F., H. Desplanques, M. Fondi, and A. Poeta. 1955. *La Casa Rurale nell'Umbria.* Ricerche sulle Dimore Rurali in Italia, Vol. 14. Consiglio Nazionale delle Ricerche. Florence: Olschki.

Bonazzi, Luigi. 1959–60. *Storia di Perugia dalle Origini al 1860*. Guiliano Innamorati, ed. 2 vols. Città di Castello: Unione Arti Grafiche. (First published in 1875–79.)

Bowring, John. 1837. "Report on the Statistics of Tuscany, Lucca, the Pontifical, and the Lombardo-Venetian States." *Parliamentary Papers 1839*, Vol. 16. London: W. Clowes.

Braudel, Fernand. 1972–73. *The Mediterranean and the Mediterranean World in the Age of Philip II*. Translated by Siân Reynolds. 2 vols. New York: Harper and Row. (Second French edition published in Paris in 1966.)

Burckhardt, Jacob. 1960. *The Civilization of the Renaissance in Italy*. London: Phaidon Press. (First published in 1860.)

Calindri, Gabriele. 1829. *Saggio Statistico Storico del Pontificio Stato*. Perugia: Garbinesi e Santucci.

Caro Baroja, Julio. 1965. *El Carnaval (Analisis Historico-Cultural)*. Madrid: Taurus.

Cassano, Cosimo. 1965. *Il Recente Adattamento delle Strutture Agricole nella Media Valle del Tevere (1961–1964)*. Istituto Nazionale di Economia Agraria, Osservatorio Economico per l'Umbria e le Marche, Quaderno n. 8. Foligno: Salvati.

Ceci, Getulio. 1888. *Cenni Storici di Monte Castello di Todi*. Todi: Foglietti.

—— 1897. *Todi nel Medio Evo*. Todi: Trombetti.

Ceci, Getulio, and G. Pensi. 1897. *Statuto di Todi del 1275*. Todi: Trombetti.

Centro Regionale per il Piano di Sviluppo Economico dell'Umbria, *see* CRU.

Chapple, Eliot D., and Carleton S. Coon. 1942. *Principles of Anthropology*. New York: Holt.

Ciaurro, Italo. 1963. *L'Umbria e il Risorgimento: Contributo dagli Umbri all'Unità d'Italia*. Rocca San Casciano: Cappelli.

Cipolla, Carlo M. 1952. "The Decline of Italy: The Case of a Fully Matured Economy," *The Economic History Review* 5:177–88.

Cipolla, Carlo M., ed. 1959. *Storia dell'Economia Italiana*. Saggi di Storia Economica, Vol. I. Turin: Edizioni Scientifiche Einaudi.

—— 1972. *The Fontana Economic History of Europe: The Middle Ages*. London and Glasgow: Collins/Fontana Books.

Clough, Shepard B. 1964. *The Economic History of Modern Italy*. New York: Columbia University Press.

Colclough, N. T. 1971. "Social Mobility and Social Control in a Southern Italian Village." In F. G. Bailey, ed., *Gifts and Poison*. Oxford: Basil Blackwell.

Corridore, Francesco. 1906. *La Popolazione dello Stato Romano, 1656–1901*. Rome: Ermanno Loescher.

Corvisieri, Adalberto. 1972. *Lo Sviluppo della Proprietà Coltivatrice: Nuove Disposizioni e Provvidenze*. Rome: Ramo Editoriale degli Agricoltori.

CRU. Centro Regionale per il Piano di Sviluppo Economico dell'Umbria. 1965. *Il Piano di Sviluppo Economico dell'Umbria*. Vol. I: *Relazione Generale Del Piano*. Foligno: Salvati.

D'Agata, Rosario. 1956. *La Tregua Mezzadrile e l'Equo Canone*. Milan: Studio Editoriale Ambrosiano.

Dal Pane, Luigi. 1944. *Storia del Lavoro in Italia dagli Inizi del Secolo XVIII al 1815*. Milan: Giuffrè.

—— 1959. *Lo Stato Pontificio e il Movimento Riformatore del Settecento*. Milan: Giuffrè.

Davis, J. 1973. *Land and Family in Pisticci*. London School of Economics Monographs on Social Anthropology, No. 48. London: Athlone Press.

Delumeau, Jean. 1957–59. *Vie Économique et Sociale de Rome dans la Seconde Moitié du XVIᵉ Siècle*. 2 vols. Paris: E. de Boccard.

De Maddalena, Aldo. 1964. "Il Mondo Rurale Italiano nel Cinque e nel Seicento." *Rivista Storica Italiana* 76(2):349–426.

De Marco, Domenico. 1949. *Il Tramonto dello Stato Pontificio. Il Pontificato di Gregorio XVI*. Turin: Einaudi.

De Martino, Ernesto. 1958. *Morte e Pianto Rituale nel Mondo Antico: Dal Lamento Pagano al Pianto di Maria*. Turin: Edizioni Scientifiche Einaudi.

Desplanques, Henri. 1969. *Campagnes Ombriennes: Contribution à l'Étude des Paysages Ruraux en Italie Centrale*. Paris: Librairie Armand Colin.

Duncan, Hugh Dalziel. 1962. *Communication and Social Order*. London: Oxford University Press.

Einaudi, Luigi. 1946. "Problemi della Mezzadria," *Rivista di Economia Agraria* 1:3–34.

Ennen, Edith. 1967. "The Different Types of Formation of European Towns." In Sylvia L. Thrupp, ed., *Early Medieval Society*. New York: Appleton-Century-Crofts.

Fei, Hsaio-Tung. 1939. *Peasant Life in China*. New York: Dutton.

Ferrantini, A. 1948. "Un Censimento Inedito dello Stato Pontificio, 26 Marzo 1769," *Statistica* 8(3):280–341.

Fiumi, Enrico. 1956. "Sui Rapporti Economici tra Città e Contado nell'Età Comunale," *Archivio Storico Italiano* 114:18–68.

—— 1961. *Storia Economica e Sociale di San Gimignano*. Florence: Olschki.

Francesconi, Francesco. 1872. *Alcuni Elementi di Statistica della Provincia dell'Umbria*. 2 vols. Perugia: G. Boncompagnie.

Franchi, L., V. Feroci, and S. Ferrari. 1973. *Codice Civile*. Editio Minor. Milan: Ulrico Hoepli.

Fried, Robert C. 1963. *The Italian Prefects: A Study in Administrative Politics*. Yale University Studies in Political Science, No. 6. New Haven: Yale University Press.

Friedl, Ernestine. 1961. "A Greek Village as a Micropolis." Paper presented at the 60th annual meeting of the American Anthropological Association, Philadelphia.

Friedmann, Fredrick G. 1953. "The World of *La Miseria*," *Partisan Review* 20:218–31.

Galli, Angelo. 1840. *Cenni Economico-Statistici sullo Stato Pontificio*. Rome: Tipografia Camerale.

Gennari, Giulio. 1949. "Presente Situazione Contrattuale nei Rapporti di Mezzadria, Colonia Parziaria e Compartecipazione," *Rivista di Economia Agraria* 4(2):245–90.

Goodenough, Ward H. 1956. "Residence Rules," *Southwestern Journal of Anthropology* 12:22–37.

Grohmann, Alberto. 1968. "La Società di Mutuo Soccorso fra gli Artisti ed Operai di Perugia (1861–1900)," *Bollettino della Deputazione di Storia Patria per l'Umbria* 65:69–190.

Guerrieri, Giuseppe. 1964. *Struttura, Dinamica e Problemi dell'Agricoltura in Umbria. Collana degli Studi per la Elaborazione del Piano Regionale di Sviluppo Economico per l'Umbria*. Vol. V: *Agricoltura, Parte Prima*. Foligno: Salvati.

Harris, Marvin. 1956. *Town and Country in Brazil*. New York: Columbia University Press.

Harris, W. V. 1971. *Rome in Etruria and Umbria*. Oxford: Clarendon Press.

Hay, Denys. 1961. *The Italian Renaissance in Its Historical Background*. Cambridge: Cambridge University Press.

Herlihy, David. 1968. "Santa Maria Impruneta: A Rural Commune in the Late Middle Ages." In Nicolai Rubinstein, ed., *Florentine Studies: Politics and Society in Renaissance Florence*. London: Faber and Faber.

Hobsbawm, Eric J. 1962. *The Age of Revolution*. London: Weidenfeld and Nicolson.

Hollingshead, August de B. 1949. *Elmtown's Youth*. New York: Wiley.

Hyde, J. K. 1973. *Society and Politics in Medieval Italy: The Evolution of the Civil Life, 1000–1350*. London and Basingstoke: Macmillan.

Imberciadori, Ildebrando. 1951. *Mezzadria Classica Toscana con Documentazione Inedita dal IX al XIV Secolo.* Florence: Vallecchi.

—— 1953. *Campagna Toscana nel '700.* Florence: Accademia Economico-Agraria dei Georgofili.

Jones, Philip. 1966. "Medieval Agrarian Society in Its Prime: Italy." In M. M. Postan, ed., *The Agrarian Life of the Middle Ages,* Vol. I of The Cambridge Economic History of Europe. Cambridge: Cambridge University Press.

—— 1968. "From Manor to Mezzadria: A Tuscan Case-Study in the Medieval Origins of Modern Agrarian Society." In Nicolai Rubinstein, ed., *Florentine Studies: Politics and Society in Renaissance Florence.* London: Faber and Faber.

King, Bolton. 1967. *A History of Italian Unity.* 2 vols. New York: Russell and Russell. (Reprinted from the revised edition of 1924.)

La Palombara, Joseph. 1964. *Interest Groups in Italian Politics.* Princeton: Princeton University Press.

Laven, Peter. 1966. *Renaissance Italy: 1464–1534.* London: Methuen.

Leicht, P. S. 1946. *Operai, Artigiani, Agricoltori in Italia dal Secolo VI al XVI.* Milan: Giuffrè.

Leonii, Lorenzo. 1856. *Memorie Storiche di Todi.* Todi: Raffaello Scalabrini.

—— 1889. *Cronaca dei Vescovi di Todi.* Todi: F. Franchi.

Limpens, Jean. 1956. "Territorial Expansion of the Code." In Bernard Schwartz, ed., *The Code Napoleon and the Common-Law World.* New York: New York University Press.

Lopez, Robert S. 1971. *The Commercial Revolution of the Middle Ages, 950–1350.* Englewood Cliffs, N.J.: Prentice-Hall.

Lopreato, Joseph. 1961. "Social Stratification in an Italian Town," *American Sociological Review* 26:585–96.

—— 1967. *Peasants No More: Social Class and Social Change in an Underdeveloped Society.* San Francisco: Chandler.

Lorenzoni, Giovanni. 1938. *Inchiesta sulla Piccola Proprietà Coltivatrice Formatasi nel Dopoguerra.* Vol. XV: *Relazione Finale.* Istituto Nazionale di Economia Agraria, Studi e Monografie N. 12. Rome: Fratelli Treves dell'Ali.

Lutz, Vera C. 1962. *Italy: A Study in Economic Development.* London: Oxford University Press.

Luzzatto, Gino. 1949. *Storia Economica d'Italia.* Vol. I: *L'Antichità e il Medioevo.* Rome: Edizioni Leonardo.

—— 1955–58. *Storia Economica dell'Età Moderna e Contemporanea.* 2 vols. Padua: Milani.

—— 1961. *An Economic History of Italy from the Fall of the Roman Empire to the Beginning of the Sixteenth Century.* Translated by Philip Jones. London: Routledge and Kegan Paul.

—— 1967. "Changes in Italian Agrarian Economy (from the Fall of the Carolingians to the Beginning of the 11th Century)." In Sylvia L. Thrupp, ed., *Early Medieval Society.* New York: Appleton-Century-Crofts.

Luzzatto, Mario. 1948. "Contributo alla Storia della Mezzadria nel Medio Evo," *Nuova Rivista Storica* 32:69–84.

MacDonald, John S., and Leatrice MacDonald. 1964. "Institutional Economics and Rural Development: Two Italian Types," *Human Organization* 23:113–18.

Mack Smith, Denis. 1959. *Italy, A Modern History.* Ann Arbor: University of Michigan Press.

Mancini, Ferdinando. 1914. *L'Umbria Agricola, Industriale, Commerciale.* Foligno.

Mancini, Franco. 1960. *Todi e i Suoi Castelli.* Città di Castello: Unione Arti Grafiche.

—— n.d. *La Cronaca Todina di Gian Fabrizio degli Atti.* (Copy in the Biblioteca Comunale di Todi.)

Medici, Giuseppe, ed. 1956. *La Distribuzione della Proprietà Fondiaria in Italia.* Vol. I: *Relazione Generale.* Istituto Nazionale di Economia Agraria. Rome: Failli.

Milletti, Roberto. 1949. *La Casa Rurale nell'Azienda Mezzadrile.* Perugia: Simonelli.

Neufeld, Maurice F. 1961. *Italy: School for Awakening Countries.* Ithaca: New York State School of Industrial and Labor Relations, Cornell University.

Niccoli, V. 1902. *Saggio Storico e Bibliografico dell'Agricoltura Italiana dalle Origini al 1900.* Turin: Unione Tipografico.

Partner, Peter. 1972. *The Lands of St. Peter: The Papal State in the Middle Ages and the Early Renaissance.* Berkeley and Los Angeles: University of California Press.

Pitkin, Donald S. 1954. *Land Tenure and Family Organization in an Italian Village.* Ph.D. dissertation, Harvard University.

Priore, Gennaro O. 1906. "Una Famiglia di Mezzadri nella Media Valle del Tevere," *La Riforma Sociale* 13(8):602–35. (See also a discussion of this study by Emanuele Sella, pp. 581–601, in the same issue.)

Procacci, Giuliano. 1972. *La Lotta di Classe in Italia agli Inizi del Secolo XX.* Rome: Editori Riuniti.

Pugliese, Salvatore. 1908. *Due Secoli di Vita Agricola: Produzioni e Valore dei Terreni, Contratti Agrari, Salari e Prezzi nel Vercellese (Sec. XVIII e XIX).* Turin: Fratelli Bocca.

Radi, Luciano. 1962. *I Mezzadri: Le Lotte Contadine nell'Italia Centrale.* Rome: Edizioni Cinque Lune.

RAG. Reale Accademia dei Georgofili. 1934. *La Mezzadria negli Scritti dei Georgofili (1833–1872).* Vol. I of Biblioteca di Coltura per i Rurali. Florence: G. Barbèra.

Rapport, Victor A., Stephen C. Cappannari, and Leonard W. Moss. 1957. "Sociology in Italy," *American Sociological Review* 22:441 47.

Redfield, Robert. 1956. *Peasant Society and Culture.* Chicago: University of Chicago Press.

Romano, Ruggiero and Corrado Vivanti, eds. 1973. *Storia d'Italia.* Vols. II, III, V. Turin: Einaudi.

Rossi, Silvio. 1889. *Il Ponte nello Stretto di Montemolino.* Todi: Foglietti.

Rossi-Doria, Manlio, et al. 1959. *Aspetti e Problemi Sociali dello Sviluppo Economico in Italia.* Atti del IV Congresso Mondiale di Sociologia. Bari: Laterza.

Salvatorelli, Luigi. 1940a. *A Concise History of Italy from Prehistoric Times to Our Own Day.* Translated by B. Miall. London: Allen and Unwin.

—— 1940b. *L'Italia Comunale dal Secolo XI alla Metà del Secolo XIV.* Vol. IV of *Storia d'Italia.* Milan: Mondadori.

Scalvanti, Oscar. 1897. "Lo Statuto di Todi del 1275," *Bollettino della Regia Deputazione di Storia Patria per l'Umbria* 3:325–72.

Schmidt, Carl T. 1938. *The Plough and the Sword.* New York: Columbia University Press.

Sella, Pietro, ed. 1952. *Rationes Decimarum Italiae nei Secoli XIII e XIV: Umbria.* 2 vols. Vatican City: Biblioteca Apostolica Vaticana.

Seppilli, Tullio. 1960. *I Ruoli Maschili e Femminili e l'Istituto Familiare in un Comune Rurale in Transizione nell'Italia Centrale.* Relazione al Congresso Internazionale di Studio sul Progresso Tecnologico e la Società Italiana. Milan.

Sereni, Emilio. 1968. *Il Capitalismo nelle Campagne (1860–1900).* Turin: Piccola Biblioteca Einaudi.

—— 1972. *Storia del Paesaggio Agrario Italiano.* Bari: Laterza.

Serpieri, A. 1947. *La Struttura Sociale dell'Agricoltura Italiana.* Rome: Edizioni Italiane.

Seton-Watson, Christopher. 1967. *Italy from Liberalism to Fascism, 1870–1925.* London: Methuen; New York: Barnes and Noble.

Silverman, Sydel F. 1966. "An Ethnographic Approach to Social Stratification: Prestige in a Central Italian Community," *American Anthropologist* 68:899–921.

Silverman, Sydel F. 1968. "Agricultural Organization, Social Structure, and Values in Italy: Amoral Familism Reconsidered," *American Anthropologist* 70:1–20.

Silvi, Nazzareno. 1911. *Relazione ai Soci della Fratellanza e Mutuo Soccorso, Società Cooperativa di Montecastello di Vibio*. Todi: Tipografia Tuderte.

Smith, C. T. 1967. *An Historical Geography of Western Europe Before 1800*. New York: Praeger.

Snowden, Frank M. 1972. "On the Social Origins of Agrarian Fascism in Italy," *Archives Européennes de Sociologie* 12(2):268–95.

Solmi, Arrigo. 1923. "Sullo Sviluppo Storico dei Contratti Agrari nel Medio Evo," *Rivista di Diritto Agrario* 2:15–28.

Thayer, John A. 1964. *Italy and the Great War: Politics and Culture, 1870–1915*. Madison: University of Wisconsin Press.

Toschi, Paolo. 1955. *Le Origini del Teatro Italiano*. Turin: Edizioni Scientifiche Einaudi.

Trevelyan, Janet P. 1956. *A Short History of the Italian People*. London: Allen and Unwin.

Valeri, Nino, ed. 1959–60. *Storia d'Italia*. 5 vols. Turin: Unione Tipografico.

Vaussard, Maurice. 1972. *Histoire de l'Italie Moderne, 1870–1970*. Paris: Librairie Hachette.

Volpe, Gioacchino. 1902. *Studi sulle Istituzioni Comunali a Pisa (Città e Contado, Consoli e Podestà) Sec. XII–XIII*. Annali della R. Scuola Normale Superiore di Pisa, Filosofia e Filologia, Vol. XV. Pisa: Fratelli Nistri.

—— 1961. *Medio Evo Italiano*. Florence: G. C. Sansoni. (First published in 1922.)

Waley, Daniel. 1952. *Medieval Orvieto*. Cambridge: Cambridge University Press.

—— 1961. *The Papal State in the Thirteenth Century*. London: Macmillan.

—— 1969. *The Italian City-Republics*. New York: McGraw-Hill.

Warner, W. Lloyd, M. Meeker, and Kenneth Eells. 1949. *Social Class in America*. Chicago: Science Research Associates.

Williams, Gwyn A. 1960. "The Concept of 'Egemonia' in the Thought of Antonio Gramsci: Some Notes on Interpretation," *Journal of the History of Ideas* 21(4):586–99.

Wylie, Laurence. 1957. *Village in the Vaucluse*. Cambridge: Harvard University Press.

Index